Contents

THE JESUS PAPERS

Exposing the Greatest Cover-Up in History

— ◆ —

MICHAEL BAIGENT

HarperElement
An Imprint of HarperCollins*Publishers*
77–85 Fulham Palace Road,
Hammersmith, London W6 8JB

The website address is: www.thorsonselement.com

and *HarperElement* are trademarks of
HarperCollins*Publishers* Ltd

First published in the US by HarperSanFrancisco 2006
This edition HarperElement 2006

1 3 5 7 9 10 8 6 4 2

All scriptural quotations are taken from either The Jerusalem Bible
or The Authorized King James Version

© Michael Baigent 2006

Michael Baigent asserts the moral right to be
identified as the author of this work

A catalogue record of this book is
available from the British Library

ISBN-13 978-0-00-724233-7
ISBN-10 0-00-724233-6

Printed and bound in Great Britain by
Clays Ltd, St Ives plc

This book is proudly printed on paper which contains wood
from well managed forests, certified in accordance with
the rules of the Forest Stewardship Council.
For more information about FSC,
please visit www.fsc.org

Mixed Sources
Product group from well-managed
forests and other controlled sources
www.fsc.org Cert no. SW-COC-1806
© 1996 Forest Stewardship Council
FSC

Acknowledgments

I finally emerged from the night, red-eyed and pale-skinned, clutching a manuscript, wondering what day it was. I could not have done it without help:

Above all, I should like to thank my wife, Jane, for her support and her ability to lead a normal life while mine tumbled into the west with increasing velocity. The day star finally rose; I was hanging on to its tail.

And I should like to thank my family who put up with a laptop apparently becoming an item of addiction; they never once suggested that I should seek professional help.

Of course, that was already there in the figure of my wonderful agent, Ann Evans, of Jonathan Clowes Ltd., London. *Thanks, Ann.*

Further help arrived from the best editor I have known, Hope Innelli, executive editor at HarperCollins, New York. *Thanks, Hope.*

I should also like to thank Claudia Riemer Boutote,

associate publisher, HarperSanFrancisco, an initiate into the Great Mysteries of publicity and promotion. *Thanks, Claudia.*

Finally, as will become apparent to all who read this book, I have long been driven by wonder at the potential of humanity, yet tempered by caution (though not much) in the face of the power of those who constantly try to limit our freedom to approach things Divine as we see fit.

For the truth is that there are many paths to the top of the mountain. Who is to say which one is best?

Introduction

May 28, 1291, The Holy Land: Acre, the Crusader Kingdom's last city port, lay in ruins. Only the great sea tower of the Knights Templar remained standing.

For seven weeks the Arab armies of Khalil al-Ashraf, the young sultan of Egypt, had first besieged and then attacked the city. The last capital of the Christian kingdom was finished. Its streets, once crowded with warriors and nobles, merchants and beggars, were now filled with tumbled buildings and bodies. There was no sense of embarrassment over "collateral damage" in those violent days; when a city fell, slaughter and theft were freely indulged.

The Arabs were determined to force every last vestige of the Crusaders into the sea; the Crusaders were equally determined to survive with the hope, however forlorn, that they might be able to resurrect their kingdom. But this hope faded once Acre had fallen. Beyond the smoking, bleeding ruins of the city only the great tower of the Templars stood undamaged. Crammed inside were those who had so far survived, together with fifty or sixty knights – the last remnants of what was once a great fighting force, a standing army, in the Christian kingdom of Jerusalem. They waited. There was nothing else they could do. No one was coming to save them. A few ships returned, a few more knights and civilians fled. The others waited for the end to come and for the next week fought off continual assaults.

Such had been the intensity of the fighting that even the Templars despaired. When the Sultan offered to let all the knights and civilians depart unharmed if they abandoned the castle, the Marshal of the Templars, who was directing the resistance, agreed. He allowed a group of Arab warriors led by an emir to enter the castle and raise the Sultan's standard above it. But the ill-disciplined Arab troops soon began to molest the women and boys. In fury, the Templars killed them all and hauled down the Sultan's standard.

The Sultan saw this as treachery and set about his own brutal retaliation: the next day he repeated his offer of safe passage. Again it was accepted. The Marshal of the Templars, together with several knights, visited him under a truce to discuss the terms. But before they reached the Sultan, in full sight of the defenders manning the walls of the Templar castle, they were arrested and executed. There were no further offers of an orderly surrender from the Sultan, and none would have been considered by the Templars: it was to be a fight to the end.

On that fateful day, the walls of the Templar castle, undermined by Arab miners, started to crumble: the Arabs began their assault. Two thousand white-robed mameluk warriors crashed their way into the breach made in the Templars' tower. Its structure, compromised by weeks of assault, gave way. With a sudden roar the stones fell, tumbled down upon themselves, crushing and burying both attackers and defenders. When the stones stopped moving and the dust settled, the silence proclaimed that it was all over. After almost two hundred years, the dream of a Christian kingdom in the Holy Land had been quashed.

Even the Templars now abandoned their few remaining castles and withdrew from the land that had claimed some twenty thousand of their brethren over 173 years of often bitter fighting.

The Templars had long fascinated me. Not just their role as a professional army and their great but much ignored contribution to the beginnings of our modern world — they introduced the power of money over the sword by means of checks and safe financial transfers from city to city and country to country; they drove a wedge between the dominant aristocracy and the exploited peasantry that helped open a space for a middle class — but the aura of mystery there had always been about them. In particular, at least some of them seemed to hold to a type of religion that ran counter to that of Rome. Bluntly, they seemed to harbor heresy within their ranks, but little was known about this.

I was curious, and I was determined to seek out some answers. I began to research the mysterious side of the Knights Templar.

One day while I was sitting in a bookshop in London, a friend of mine who happened to own the store came up to me and said that there was someone I should meet, someone who had information about the Templars that might interest me. And that is how I met my colleague, Richard Leigh. We ended up writing seven books together over the next twenty years.

Richard was certainly sitting on some interesting information – data that had been passed on to him by Henry Lincoln. Richard and I quickly realized that we should combine forces. A few months later Henry came to the same conclusion. We formed a team, and as they say, we went for it. The result, six years later, was the best-selling book *Holy Blood, Holy Grail*.

Our major hypothesis involved an insight into both the Crusades and the Grail legends – two subjects rarely linked by historians. Behind both subjects, we discovered, lay an important bloodline, a dynasty: that of the Jewish royal lineage, the Line of David.

The Grail legends combined elements from ancient pagan Celtic tradition with elements of Christian mysticism. The symbol of a bowl or cup of plenty that ensures the continued fertility of the land derived from the former, while from the latter came the descriptions of the Grail in terms of mystical experience. But significantly for us, the legends stressed that the Grail Knight, Perceval or Parsival, was "of the most holy lineage," a lineage stretching back through history to Jerusalem and the foot of the cross. Clearly, this was referring to the Line of David. This point had been missed by all commentators on the Grail before us.

We argued that the term for the Grail, the *Sangraal* or *Sangreal,* which was rendered as *San Graal* or *San Greal* – Holy Grail – had been a play on words: splitting them slightly differently, as *Sang Real,* gave the game away: *Sang Real* translates as "Blood Royal," meaning, we argued, the royal blood of the Line of David. Truly, for medieval times, this was a "most holy lineage."

That the Line of David existed in southern France in the early medieval period is not in doubt. It is a fact of history.

When Charlemagne was establishing his kingdom, he named one of his close companions, Guillem (William), Count of Toulouse, Barcelona, and Narbonne, as ruler of a buffer princedom between the Christian kingdom of Charlemagne and the Islamic emirate of Al Andalus – Islamic Spain, in other words. Guillem, the new prince, was Jewish.[1] He was also of the Line of David.[2]

The twelfth-century Jewish traveler Benjamin of Tudela, in his chronicle of his journey from Spain to the Middle East, revealed that the prince at the head of the Narbonne ruling nobility was "a descendant of the House of David as stated in his family tree."[3] Even the *Encyclopedia Judaica* mentions these "Jewish kings" of Narbonne – but ignores their bloodline.[4] Of course, no one liked to ask where this bloodline, mentioned by Benjamin of Tudela, might have come from. In fact, as we were to find out, the situation was quite complicated.

When looking at the genealogies of these princes of the Line of David in the south of France, we discovered that they were the same figures as the ancestors of one of the leaders of the First Crusade, Godfrey de Bouillon, who became the king of Jerusalem.[5] There had been four great noble leaders of this crusade. Why was Godfrey de Bouillon alone offered the throne, and offered it by a mysterious and still unknown conclave of electors that assembled in Jerusalem to rule over the matter?[6] To whom would these proud lords have submitted, and for what reason? We argued that blood took precedence over title – that Godfrey was reclaiming his rightful heritage as a member of the Line of David.

And what was the source of this bloodline? Well, from Jerusalem, from Jesus, the result of – we argued in *Holy Blood, Holy Grail* – a marriage between Jesus and Mary Magdalene.[7] In fact, we wondered, was not the marriage at Cana that of Jesus and Mary? At the very least, that would explain why he was "called" to the wedding and subsequently had the responsibility over the wine! Naturally, with the publication of our book, worldwide controversy erupted.

"Mr. and Mrs. Christ," wrote one commentator, searching for a smart sound bite. And as sound bites go, it was rather a good one.

That was in 1982. In 2002, Dan Brown published his

novel *The Da Vinci Code*, which draws in part from our books' theories. A media circus erupted once more. "Mr. and Mrs. Christ" were back in the news. It was clear that people still had a hunger for the truth behind the gospel legends. Who was Jesus really? What was expected of him? The world still clamors today for clarity about Jesus, Judaism, Christianity, and the events that took place two thousand years ago.

Since the publication of *Holy Blood, Holy Grail*, I have had twenty-two more years to reflect on these very questions, to do more research, and to reassess the history and implications of those events. In other words, two decades of research over and above what is explored in *The Da Vinci Code*. Here I endeavor to reconstruct my twenty-two-year-long journey of discovery, taking readers down each path with me – some paths leading to dead ends, others to great realms of possibility. All paths lead to a broader understanding of the life of the man we call Jesus, as history proves he lived it, not how religion says he did.

The data I present herein need to be read at your own speed. Each of the building blocks of my explanation should be considered in your own time. This is extremely important, for when long-held beliefs are being challenged, as they are here, we need to be able to justify each step taken along the way so as to be clear about why we have taken them. For that way, we can be confident in where we stand on the issues in the end. A questioning, contemplative read will allow you to wade through the new findings in such a way that you will ultimately make your own choices and hold firm your own beliefs. If you're ready for that journey, let's start now.

I

Hidden Documents

My telephone rang. It was about 10:00 a.m. I remember the sun dappling the wall before me. It sparkled. It was the perfect day to be in an English country village.

"Can you get the next train to London? Don't ask why."

I groaned silently: wall-to-wall cars. Scarce taxis. Noise, pollution, crowded subways. A day spent either inside rooms or traveling between them, the sun a distant memory.

"Sure," I replied, knowing that my friend would never have made such a request unless it was important.

"And can you bring a camera with you?"

"Sure," I replied again, vaguely bemused.

"And can you hide the camera?"

Suddenly he had my attention. What was up? My friend was a member of a small and discreet group of international

dealers, middlemen, and purchasers of high-value antiquities – not all of which carried the required paperwork permitting them to be traded on the open market.

I put a camera and some lenses in a standard-looking
briefcase, threw in plenty of film, and jumped in my car for
the drive to the station.

I met my friend outside a restaurant in a famous London
street. He was an American, and with him were two Palestinians, a Jordanian, a Saudi, and an English expert from a
major auction house.

They were all expecting me, and after brief introductions
the expert from the auction house departed, apparently not
wishing to be involved in what was to happen. The rest of
us walked to a nearby bank, where we were quickly led
through the banking hall, along a short corridor, and into a
small private room with frosted windows.

As we all stood around a table placed in the middle of the
room, making desultory small talk, the bank officials carried
in two wooden trunks and laid them down before us. Each
trunk bore three padlocks. As the second was carried in, one
of the officials said pointedly, as if "for the record": "We
don't know what is in these trunks. We don't want to know
what is in them."

They then brought a telephone into the room and departed, locking the door behind them.

The Jordanian made a telephone call to Amman. From
the little conversation that ensued (which was in Arabic),
I gathered that permission had been requested and

obtained. The Jordanian then produced a set of keys and unlocked the trunks.

They were stuffed full of exact-fitting sheets of cardboard. And on each sheet, I was horrified to note, there were hundreds of pieces of papyrus text roughly fixed to the cardboard by small strips of clear adhesive tape. The texts were written in Aramaic or Hebrew. Accompanying them were Egyptian mummy wrappings inscribed in demotic – the written form of Egyptian hieroglyphics.

I knew that it was common for such wrappings to bear sacred texts, and so the owners of this hoard must have unwrapped at least a mummy or two. The Aramaic or Hebrew texts looked, at first sight, like the Dead Sea Scrolls, which I had seen before, although they were mostly written on parchment. This collection was a treasure trove of ancient documents. I was very intrigued and increasingly desperate to let some scholars know about their existence, perhaps to secure access for them.

As the cardboard sheets were removed from the trunks, I was told that the owners were trying to sell the documents to an unspecified European government. The price asked was £3 million (approximately $5.6 million). Those present wanted me to take a representative selection of photographs that could be shown to the prospective buyer in order to move the sale one stage further toward a successful conclusion. I then realized which government was the most likely to be interested. But I kept my thoughts to myself.

Over the next hour or so, as the trunks were emptied,

certain pages were pointed out to me, and standing on a chair, by the soft light filtering through the frosted windows, I took black-and-white photographs. In all, I shot six rolls of thirty-five-millimeter film – over two hundred photographs.

But I was becoming increasingly anxious that these documents might simply vanish into the limbo from which they had emerged. That they might be bought by some purchaser who would sit on them for many years, as had happened with the Nag Hammadi texts and the Dead Sea Scrolls. Or worse, I feared that without a purchaser, they might simply disappear back into the deepest, darkest recesses of the bank, joining the many other valuable documents known to be locked away in safe-deposit boxes and trunks around the world.

It seemed likely that since I had taken a lot of photographs, and since no one would be counting, I would be able to hide at least one of the rolls of film so that there might be at least some proof that this collection even existed. I successfully slipped one into a pocket.

When the photography was finished and the cardboard sheets were being placed back into the trunks, I gave a handful of exposed film rolls to one of the owners. He looked down at them.

"Where is the other film?" he said immediately. He had been counting.

"Other film?" I said lamely, trying to present an image of abstracted innocence while ostentatiously patting my pockets.

"Oh. You're right. Here it is." I produced the film I was

hoping to keep. I was irritated and rather depressed. I really wanted to have some proof of what I had seen.

At that point my friend realized what I was up to and, in an inspired move, came to the rescue.

"Where are you getting these films developed?" he asked innocently.

"At a photographic shop," replied the man holding my film.

"That's not very secure," said my friend. "Look, Michael was a professional photographer, and he could do all the developing and print you off as many sets as you need. That way there is no risk."

"Good idea," the man said and handed back the films.

Naturally I printed a full set of photographs for myself. Later I arranged to meet the Jordanian – who seemed to be in charge – for lunch, where I was to give him the prints and negatives. During lunch I argued that if some scholars could look at the texts and identify what they saw, then perhaps their insight would be helpful in raising the value of the collection. I asked the Jordanian if he would give me permission to speak to a few experts on the matter – very discreetly, of course. After some thought, he agreed that this was probably a good idea, but he made it very clear that neither I nor the experts could talk about this collection to anyone else.

Several days later I went to the Western Asiatic Department of the British Museum with a full set of prints. I had dealt with the department before during the course of researching one of my books, *From the Omens of Babylon*, and

I trusted the scholars there not only to give me an honest opinion but to maintain confidentiality as well.

The expert I had dealt with before was not there, and one of his colleagues came into the small anteroom and spoke with me instead. I briefly told him the story about the trunks of documents and about my photographs. I stressed that this was a commercial exercise for the owners and that I would be very grateful for his discretion, since large sums of money sometimes cause equally large problems. I requested that he find someone competent in the field to take a look at these photos to see if they were of any importance. If so, I would do my best to get the interested scholar access to the entire collection. I then passed over my set of prints.

Weeks passed. I heard nothing from the British Museum. I became concerned. Finally, after a month, I returned to the museum and made my way up to the Western Asiatic Department. I met with another expert there.

"I brought a set of photographs in a month ago, which I had taken of a large number of papyrus texts. I have not heard anything back from you. I wonder if anyone has had a chance to take a look at them?"

The expert stared at me blankly.

"What photographs?"

I went through the story again for his benefit. He seemed distracted, unconcerned. He had not heard of any such photographs being brought into the department; in any case, it wasn't his field. They were most likely given to another specialist who was working there for a time and who had now left.

"Where has he gone?" I asked.

"I don't know" was the reply. "I think to Paris. I am sorry about your photographs."

I never heard any more about them. Without a written receipt for them, there was nothing I could do. Luckily I had a few reject prints still at home so I could prove that the collection did in fact exist, but not nearly enough to give anyone an idea of the range of subjects that might have been in it. An expert, looking at my few remaining prints, identified most of the texts as records of commercial transactions.

Ten or twelve years later I was walking down a street lined with expensive shops in a large Western city when I saw one of the Palestinians who had been present in the bank that day. I went up to him and asked if he remembered me.

"Of course," he replied. "You were the colleague of ..." and he gave the name of my friend.

"You know," I began, "I have always wondered what happened to those ancient texts I photographed that day in the bank. Were they ever sold?"

"I haven't heard anything about them," he quickly replied, unconvincingly, and then, giving a good impression of being rather busy, he elegantly and politely excused himself and walked off.

I cannot say that I was surprised, for I have spent many years living in a world where potentially crucial keys to the mysteries of our past are simultaneously available and elusive. As we will see, these trunks of documents are not the only such examples of important evidence remaining, tantalizingly, just out of reach.

2

The Priest's Treasure

Throughout my career I've enjoyed correspondence with other historians and researchers into the truth behind accepted history, but some letters demand more attention than others. This letter certainly did.

"May I advise you that the 'treasure' is not one of gold and precious stones, but a document containing incontrovertible evidence that Jesus was alive in the year A.D. 45. The clues left behind by the good curé have never been understood, but it is clear from the script that a substitution was carried out by the extreme zealots on the journey to the place of execution. The document was exchanged for a very large sum and concealed or destroyed."

Richard Leigh, Henry Lincoln, and I simply didn't know what to do with this note. It came from a respected and highly educated Church of England vicar, the Rev. Dr. Douglas William Guest Bartlett. By "the good curé" Bartlett was referring to the Abbé Béranger Saunière, the priest of the small hilltop village of Rennes le Château, nestled in the foothills of the Pyrenees.

Abbé Saunière was appointed priest at the village in 1885. His annual income was approximately ten dollars. He gained a notoriety that has lasted to the present day by obtaining, in the early 1890s, from mysterious sources, for equally mysterious reasons, considerable wealth.[1] The key to his wealth was a discovery he made while restoring the church in 1891. But the "treasure" he found, according to Bartlett, was not the glittering deposit we had at first supposed (perhaps the lost treasure of the Temple in Jerusalem), but something far more extraordinary – some documents concerning Jesus and therefore the very basis of Christianity. At the time this seemed too wild for us to even consider and so we left it "on file."

We had certainly suspected that something odd was going on in the dark corridors of history, but while working on *Holy Blood, Holy Grail* we were discovering all manner of unexpected and highly controversial data that would take us far away from the concerns of this letter, so we tabled it for future scrutiny. Jesus's survival was simply not an important issue for us at that time, as our focus had become fixed on the possibility that prior to the crucifixion he had at least one child – or had left his wife pregnant. So whether Jesus's life ended on the cross or not seemed irrelevant to our developing story of his marriage, the survival of his bloodline down through European history, and its symbolic expression in the stories of the Holy Grail, stories that formed the backbone of our best-selling book *Holy Blood, Holy Grail*, first published in 1982.

Yet, intrigued by this bland, outrageous, but confident letter, we kept returning to it. "What," we asked ourselves, "would constitute 'incontrovertible evidence' that Jesus survived and was living long afterwards?" "What, in fact," we thought, racking our brains, "would constitute incontrovertible evidence of anything in history?" Documents, we supposed, but what sort of documents would be beyond doubt?

The most believable documents, we thought, would be the most apparently mundane, those with no agenda to serve, no argument to support – an inventory perhaps, a historical equivalent of a shopping list. Something like a Roman legal document stating in a matter-of-fact manner: "Item: Alexandria, Fourth year of Claudius (A.D. 45), report of Jesus ben Joseph, an immigrant from Galilee, formerly tried and acquitted in Jerusalem by Pontius Pilate, today confirmed as the owner of a plot of land beyond the city walls."

But it all seemed a bit far-fetched.

After *Holy Blood, Holy Grail* appeared and the dust had settled, out of personal curiosity more than anything else, we decided to visit the author of the letter and see what we could make of him. We needed to know whether he was believable or not. He lived in Leafield, Oxfordshire, a rural county of England comprising idyllic villages with stone houses centered upon the ancient university town of Oxford. The Rev. Bartlett lived in one of the small villages set in the higher country to the northwest of the county. We talked to him one afternoon in his garden, sitting on a wooden bench. It was the normality of the setting that made the topic of our conversation all the more remarkable.

"In the 1930s, I was living in Oxford," reported the Rev. Bartlett. "In the same street was a 'high-powered' figure in the Church of England, Canon Alfred Lilley. I saw him every day." Canon Alfred Leslie Lilley (1860 – 1948) had been, until his retirement in 1936, Canon and Chancellor of Hereford Cathedral. He was an expert in medieval French and for that reason was often consulted on difficult translation work.

During their daily talks, Lilley and Bartlett became closer, and Lilley eventually trusted Bartlett sufficiently to tell him an extraordinary story. In the early 1890s, Lilley reported, he had been asked by a young man, a former student of his, to travel to Paris to the Seminary of Saint Sulpice to advise on the translation of a strange document (or perhaps documents – Bartlett could no longer remember exactly) that had appeared from a source that was never divulged. At Saint Sulpice there was a group of scholars whose task it was to comb through all the documents that came in – a task performed, Lilley suspected, at the request of a Vatican cardinal. The scholars asked for help on the translation because they couldn't really make out the text. Perhaps it seemed so outrageous to them that they thought they were misunderstanding it in some manner.

"They didn't know that it was so close to the bone," Bartlett recalled Lilley explaining. "Lilley said that they wouldn't have a long and happy life if certain people knew about it. It was a very delicate matter. Lilley laughed over what was going to happen when the French priests told anyone about it. He didn't know what happened to them [the documents], but he thought that they had changed hands for a large sum of money and had ended up in Rome." In fact, Lilley thought that the Church would ultimately destroy these documents.

Lilley was quite certain that these documents were authentic. They were extraordinary and upset many of our ideas about the Church. Contact with the material, he said, led to an unorthodoxy. Lilley did not know for certain where the documents had come from but believed that they had once been in the possession of the heretical Cathars in the south of France during the twelfth and thirteenth centuries, even though they were much older. He was also sure that following the demise of the Cathars the documents had been held in Switzerland until the wars of the fourteenth century, when they were taken to France.

"By the end of his life," Bartlett explained, "Lilley had come to the conclusion that there was nothing in the Gospels that one could be certain about. He had lost all conviction of truth."

Henry and I were stunned. Bartlett was no fool. Not only was he a church minister with a master's degree from one of the Oxford colleges, but he also held a science degree in physics and chemistry from the University of Wales, as well as a medical degree, also from Oxford. He was a member of the Royal College of Surgeons and the Royal College of Physicians. To call him highly educated was something of an understatement. He clearly admired Canon Lilley and greatly respected his learning and had no doubt whatsoever that Lilley had been accurately describing the document, or documents, he had seen during that trip to Paris. We needed to study Lilley and see if we could glean any further information about the material concerning Jesus and determine who at the Seminary of Saint Sulpice and the Vatican might have had an interest in it.

The key to understanding Canon Lilley was that he considered himself a "Modernist"; he was the author of a book on the movement that was extremely influential at the beginning of the twentieth century. The Modernists wished to revise the dogmatic assertions of church teachings in the light of the discoveries made by science, archaeology, and critical scholarship. Many theologians were realizing that their confidence in the historical validity of New Testament stories was misplaced. For example, William Inge, Dean of St. Paul's Cathedral, was once asked to write on the life of Jesus. He declined, saying that there was not nearly enough solid evidence to write anything at all about him.

During the nineteenth century the Vatican was becoming increasingly anachronistic. The Papal States stretching from Rome across to Ancona and up to Bologna and Ferrara still existed, and the pope ruled like a medieval potentate. Torture was regularly practiced by the anonymous minions of the Inquisition in their secret jails. Those convicted in papal courts were sent as oarsmen to the galleys or were exiled, imprisoned, or executed. A well-used gallows stood in the town square of every community. Spies lurked everywhere, and repression was the rule; modernity was being kept at arm's length – even railways were banned by the pope for fear that travel and communication between people would harm religion. And all this was occurring against a backdrop of a Europe where pressure for social change in the form of liberation movements opposing despotic power and encouraging parliamentary rule had become the norm.

Despite willful ignorance, the outside world was spilling over the crumbling borders of the papal domains. Change was beginning to seem inevitable. Democratic political philosophy, a growing social awareness, and the mounting criticism of biblical texts and their inconsistencies were causing religious certainties to buckle under the strain. And to the horror of Catholic conservatives, papal political power too was under direct threat. This was a real problem: in 1859, following a war between Austria and France that saw the defeat of the Catholic Hapsburg forces, the great majority of the papal lands joined the newly created kingdom of Italy.

The pope, Pius IX, summarily demoted by events, now ruled over only Rome and a fragment of the surrounding countryside. And it grew worse: on 21 September 1870, even this small patrimony was taken away by Italian troops. The pope found himself left with just the walled enclave of Vatican City, where his successors continue to rule today.

Just before the loss of Rome, the pope, in what seems to have been considerable desperation, had called a General Council of Bishops to shore up his power. Yet by calling this council, the pope was implicitly recognizing the limitations of that power. The question of who held the reins had long been a festering sore at the Vatican. The uncomfortable truth was that the pope derived his legitimacy, not from the apostle Saint Peter, two thousand years earlier as he claimed, but from a much more mundane and worldly source: a Council of Bishops that had met at Constance in the early fifteenth century. At that time there had been three popes – a trinity of pontiffs united only in mutual loathing – all claiming, simultaneously, to have supreme authority over the Church. This ludicrous situation had been resolved by the bishops, who claimed – and were recognized in this claim – to hold legitimate authority. From that point on, the popes held their authority by virtue of the bishops. Accordingly, every pope was bound, when wishing to make a major change, to seek their approval.

It was Pope Pius IX, though, who wanted to make the most major of changes: he was determined to be declared infallible, thus receiving unprecedented power over all the faithful. But he knew that he would have to use guile to achieve this goal. Hence, the First Vatican Council was convened in late 1869. Its real aims were kept secret by a small group of powerful men that included three cardinals, all of whom were members of the Inquisition. No mention was made of papal infallibility in any of the documents circulated about the objectives and direction of the council. Meanwhile, the bishops gathered and found themselves subjected to strong-arm tactics. There were no secret votes, and the cost of criticism was immediately apparent: the loss of Vatican stipends was the least that a dissenting bishop could expect.

After two months the issue of papal infallibility was introduced to the council. Most of the bishops present were surprised, shocked, even outraged. Certain church leaders who stood and spoke against the move were "dealt with" by house arrest, while others fled. One leader was physically assaulted by the pope himself. Despite the intimidation, only 49 percent of the bishops cast their vote for papal infallibility. And yet, a majority vote in favor of the move was declared, and on 18 July 1870, the pope was pronounced infallible. Just over two months later Italian troops entered Rome and consigned the freshly "infallible" pope to the limits of Vatican City – a divine response, perhaps, to his lack of humility.

The desire of the pope and his supporters, of course, was that the doctrine of infallibility would buttress the Vatican against the challenges it was facing – in particular from biblical criticism and the discoveries of archaeology.

The aim of the Modernists, on the other hand, was quite the opposite. They sought to revise church dogma in light of their scholarly findings. The historical evidence their research produced was helping to unravel the myths the Church had created and perpetuated, especially the myth about Jesus Christ. The Modernists were also greatly opposed to the centralization of the Vatican. The Modernist movement at this time was especially strong in Paris, where the director of the Seminary of Saint Sulpice, from 1852 to 1884, was a liberal Irish theologian named John Hogan. Hogan welcomed and openly encouraged Modernist studies at the seminary. Indeed, Canon Lilley saw him as the "greatest single influence" on what became Modernism.[2] Many of Hogan's students also attended lectures by the Assyriologist and Hebrew expert, Father Alfred Loisy, who was director of the Institute Catholique in Paris and another prominent Modernist.

At first the Vatican seemed not to mind. The new pope, Leo XIII (who was elected in 1878 and served until 1903), was sufficiently confident in the strength of Rome's position to allow scholars access to the Vatican archives. But he had not realized what scholarship would subsequently discover and the church doctrines these findings would call into question. It soon became apparent to him that this scholarship posed a serious threat to the very foundations of the Church. Just before his death in 1903, Pope Leo XIII moved to repair the damage. In 1902 he created the Pontifical Biblical Commission to oversee the work of all theological scholars and to ensure that they did not stray from the teachings of the Church. The Commission had close connections with the Inquisition, having been ruled by the same cardinal.

The danger, apparent to all, was expressed succinctly by Father Loisy: "Jesus proclaimed the coming of the Kingdom, but what came was the Church."[3] Loisy, among other Modernists, believed that the historical scholarship conducted during that time had made many church dogmas impossible to maintain, dogmas such as the founding of the Church by Jesus, his virgin birth, and his divine sonship — in essence, Jesus's very divinity.[4]

The leading British Modernist George Tyrell opposed the unrelentingly autocratic authority of the Vatican. "The Church, he thought, had no business being an official Institute of Truth."[5] Of course, the Church considered that to be exactly its role.

The Modernists asked an uncomfortable and impertinent question: what should be done when history or science point to a conclusion that contradicts the Church's tenets? The response of the Church in the face of these direct challenges was to withdraw further behind its walls of dogma: it resolved all uncertainty by ruling that the Church was always right, under all circumstances, about everything.

In 1892 Hogan's successor at Saint Sulpice ordered students to stop attending lectures by the Modernist Alfred Loisy. The next year Loisy was dismissed from his teaching post at the Institute Catholique, and he was eventually excommunicated. In fact, the Vatican suspended or excommunicated many Modernists and placed their books on the "Index." In 1907 Pope Pius X issued a formal ban against the entire movement, and on 1 September 1910, all priests and Catholic teachers were required to swear an oath against Modernism. Just to be sure that the ever-changing world outside would not intrude upon their delicate theological sensibilities, students at seminaries and theological colleges were forbidden to read newspapers.

But before the veil came down in 1892, the atmosphere at the Seminary of Saint Sulpice had been very heady. The center was a place of learning, stimulated by curiosity and discovery. Adding continuously to a great sense of excitement was a steady stream of new translations and archaeological discoveries. It was in this milieu that Canon Lilley was called to Paris to look at the document or documents that provided incontrovertible evidence that Jesus was alive in A.D. 45. Upon witnessing this level of analytical study, Lilley must have wondered how much longer the Vatican could maintain its rigidly dogmatic position. He must have guessed that it would soon react against these discoveries and shut the door on free scholarship. As he relayed to Bartlett, he believed that the documents he was working on ended up in the Vatican, either locked away forever or destroyed.

When we first heard this story about Jesus being alive in A.D. 45, we were reminded of a curious statement in the work of the Roman historian Suetonius. In his history of the Roman emperor Claudius (A.D. 41 – 54), he reports that, "because the Jews at Rome caused continuous disturbances at the instigation of Chrestus, he expelled them from the city."[6]

The events he writes about took place around A.D. 45. This "Chrestus" was evidently an individual present in Rome at the time. We wondered: could this individual have been "Christ"? We should remember that "Christos" was the Greek translation, and "Messiah" the Greek transliteration, of the Aramaic *meshiha*, which itself derives from the Hebrew *ha-mashiah*, "the anointed (king)." The Greek "Messiah" thus comes from the Aramaic word, which was the commonly spoken language at the time, rather than from the Hebrew.

Was there a messianic individual active in Rome? And if so, why would the Jews have been rioting? Would they have been attacking the Romans under this agitator's encouragement, or would they have been attacking the agitator? Or, even more strangely, could this agitator have set one man against another in the Jewish community to provoke rioting among them? Suetonius does not give us any information on the aims of the rioters or who they might have opposed. But we wondered nevertheless, could Jesus, like Paul, have ended up in Rome?

Suetonius wrote his histories in the early second century A.D. and for some years was chief secretary to the Roman emperor Hadrian (117 – 38). He was official keeper of the

Roman archives and controller of the libraries. He would obviously have had full access to all imperial documentation, and so his report can be considered accurate. Who truly was "Chrestus"? No one knows.

There was another visitor to Saint Sulpice in those provocative days of the early 1890s: the Abbé Saunière, the priest of Rennes le Château. The story – which has proved implacably resistant to verification – relates Saunière's discovery of documents during the renovations of his church. After showing these documents to his bishop, he was ordered to travel to Paris, where a meeting with experts at the Seminary of Saint Sulpice was arranged. This occurred in or around 1891. Reportedly, Saunière stayed in Paris for three weeks. When he returned, he had access to considerable wealth, sufficient to construct a new road up the hill to the village, to renovate and repaint the church, and to build a comfortable and fashionable villa, an ornate garden, and a tower that served as his study.

Could Saunière's documents have been those seen and translated by Canon Lilley? Could Saunière's sudden wealth be due to his finding them? The Rev. Bartlett certainly thought so. And if this were true, then it would certainly explain a very curious image still on the wall of the church at Rennes le Château – an image that reveals something very heretical indeed about the beliefs of the Abbé Saunière.

Although the church at Rennes le Château is small, it is

decorated inside like a Gothic fantasy, something more at home in a Bavarian castle for King Ludwig II than a Pyrenean hilltop village. It is bulging with images and color. Investigators have spent years trying to decipher the many clues Saunière embedded in the symbolism. But there is one image that is very clear – one image that does not take any great occult or symbolic knowledge to understand.

Like all Catholic churches, this one has, around its walls, plaster reliefs of the Stations of the Cross. They are a set sequence of images depicting the stages of Jesus's walk along the road to Golgotha after his trial. They are used for contemplation and prayer, serving as a kind of map to the resurrection for the faithful. Those about the walls of the church at Rennes le Château are from a standard pattern of casts supplied by a company in Toulouse that can be found in a number of other churches. At least, the plaster-cast images are identical. They differ in one important respect, however: those at Rennes le Château are painted, and in a very curious manner indeed. One image, for example, shows a woman with a child standing beside Jesus; the child is wearing a Scottish tartan robe. Others are equally curious. But the most curious of all is Station 14. This is traditionally the last of the series illustrating Jesus being placed in the tomb prior to the resurrection. At Rennes le Château the image shows the tomb and, immediately in front of it, three figures carrying the body of Christ. But the painted background reveals the time as night. In the sky beyond the figures, the full moon has risen.

If the full moon has risen, it would mean that the Passover has begun. This is significant because no Jew would have handled a dead body after the beginning of the Passover, as this would have rendered him ritually unclean. This variation of the fourteenth station suggests two important points: that the body the figures are carrying is still alive, and that Jesus – or his substitute on the cross – has survived the crucifixion. Moreover, it suggests that the body is not being placed *in* the tomb, but rather, that it is being carried *out*, secretly, under the cover of night.

It is important to note that the Stations of the Cross at Rennes le Château were painted under the direct supervision of Abbé Saunière. He appears to be telling us that he knows – or at least believes – that Jesus survived the crucifixion. Could he have learned this on his visit to Saint Sulpice, we wondered? Did he meet there the same group of scholars who called Canon Lilley to Paris? If we accept the story as it has been relayed to us, then on the face of things the answer to both of these questions seems likely to be yes.

Whatever the answers – and we are hardly in a position to come to any definite conclusions just yet – Station 14 as it is depicted on the wall of this church serves as an eloquent testimony to a secret heretical knowledge that once lay in the hands of a priest in deepest rural France.

It seemed unreasonable for us to suppose that Saunière was alone in his belief. We thought surely there must be other clues in other churches, in documents, and in the writings of those who held the same convictions. Would finding them prove any validity to this story? We needed to know how the crucifixion could have been managed such that Jesus, or his substitute, might have survived. And we needed to know what this might mean. We thought it was time to look at the biblical accounts of the event from this fresh perspective.

3

Jesus the King

The idea of a rigged crucifixion has been around a long time; even the Koran mentions it.[1] But just how could a fraudulent crucifixion have been arranged? According to the gospel accounts, everyone except Jesus's disciples seemed to want him dead, or at the very least, well out of the way. The Jewish authorities and the vociferous mobs gathered in the street wanted to be rid of him, as did the Romans, albeit by default. According to the common interpretation of the gospel reports – which we have seen in countless films – Jesus was tried in public before "the Jews," the crowds cried out that he should be crucified, Pilate washed his hands of the matter, Jesus then had to carry his own cross to the place of execution through crowds of bystanders who wished him ill, and finally, he was nailed to a cross between two thieves in a public place of execution called Golgotha – the "Place of the Skull."

Had he tried to escape, either from the trial or the trek to Golgotha, it would have immediately been noticed. There would have been plenty of volunteers who'd have quickly pushed him back onto his road of execution. The Gospels inform us that the Romans had abdicated all responsibility for him; they no longer cared what happened.

JUDAEA, JESUS, AND CHRISTIANITY

Before 4 B.C.	Birth of Jesus, according to Matthew's Gospel (2:1).
4 B.C.	Death of Herod the Great.
A.D. 6	Birth of Jesus, according to Luke's Gospel (2:1–7). Census of Quirinius, Governor of Syria.
A.D. 27–28	Baptism of Jesus (traditional date) in the fifteenth year of the reign of Emperor Tiberius (Luke 3:1–23).
A.D. 30	Crucifixion of Jesus, according to Catholic scholarship.
C. A.D. 35	Following the marriage of Herod Antipas and Herodias in c. A.D. 34, John the Baptist is executed, following the evidence in Josephus.
A.D. 36	Passover – crucifixion of Jesus, according to Matthew's timetable.
A.D. 36–37	Conversion of Paul on the road to Damascus.

c. A.D. 44	Execution of James, the brother of Jesus.
A.D. 50–52	Paul in Corinth. Writes his first letter (to the Thessalonians).
A.D. 61	Paul in Rome under house arrest.
c. A.D. 65	Paul supposedly executed.
A.D. 66–73	War in Judaea. The Roman army under Vespasian invades Judaea.
c. A.D. 55–120	Life of Tacitus, Roman historian and senator, who mentions Christ.
c. A.D. 61–114	Life of Pliny the Younger, who mentions Christ.
c. A.D. 115	Ignatius, Bishop of Antioch, quotes from letters of Paul.
c. A.D. 117–138	Suetonius, Roman historian, mentions "Chrestus."
c. A.D. 125	Earliest known example of a Christian gospel, John 18: 31–33, Rylands Papyrus, found in Egypt.
c. A.D. 200	Oldest known fragment of Paul's letters, Chester Beatty Papyrus, found in Egypt.
c. A.D. 200	Oldest virtually complete gospel (John's), Bodmer Papyrus, found in Egypt.
A.D. 325	Council of Nicaea is convened by the Roman emperor Constantine. The divinity of Jesus is made official dogma by a vote of 217 to 3.
A.D. 393–397	Council of Hippo, formalizing the New Testament, is finalized at Council of Carthage.

THE MACCABEES AND HEROD

401 B.C.   Rebuilding of the Jewish temple on Elephantine Island, Aswan, southern Egypt, is completed.

332 B.C.   Alexander the Great invades Israel and Egypt.

323 B.C.   Death of Alexander. His generals split his empire: after years of struggle, Ptolemy takes Egypt, and Seleucis takes Syria, Mesopotamia, and Persia. Israel at first is ruled by Ptolemy.

170 B.C.   The Seleucid ruler of Syria, Antiochus Epiphanes, invades Judaea and Egypt. Onias III, high priest of the temple, flees to Egypt with many priests. Establishes a Jewish temple in Egypt.

169 B.C.   Syrians invade Judaea a second time. Temple is looted.

167 B.C.   Syrians again invade, massacre populace of Jerusalem, and rededicate the Temple to Zeus. The Temple priest, Mattathias (of the Hasmonean dynasty), and his sons begin a revolt against the Syrians.

166 B.C.   Mattathias dies. His son, Judas Maccabee, takes over command.

160 B.C.   Judas Maccabee is defeated and killed. His brother Jonathan takes command.

152 B.C.   Jonathan is appointed high priest of the Temple in Jerusalem.

143 B.C.   Jonathan is imprisoned. His brother Simon becomes high priest and ruler of Judaea.

142 B.C.   Judaea becomes independent under Simon, who forms an alliance with the Romans.

134 B.C.	Simon is killed. His son John Hyrcanus succeeds him as high priest and ruler of Judaea.
104 B.C.	Aristobulus rules and takes the title of King of Judaea (of the Hasmonean dynasty).
103–76 B.C.	Alexander Jannaeus is king and high priest of Judaea.
67–63 B.C.	Aristobulus II is king and high priest of Judaea.
63 B.C.	The Roman general Pompey takes Jerusalem.
37 B.C.	Herod marries Mariamne, granddaughter of Judaean King Aristobulus II. Herod takes Jerusalem and becomes king.
4 B.C.	Death of King Herod.

But the Jewish authorities, representatives of the priestly Sadducees, did care; they wanted him dead. Those in Jesus's small community of disciples were powerless to protect him and could only watch helplessly as the tragedy unfolded. So if his escape did not serve some purpose of either the Roman or Jewish authorities, who did have cause and power enough to make it happen, one would think that such an escape would have been impossible. And yet, there are enough hints in the gospel accounts to give one pause for thought. The situation is not as clear-cut as it is presented.

First, and importantly, crucifixion was historically the punishment for a political crime. According to the Gospels, however, Pilate gave Jesus over to the mobs, who then brayed for his execution on the basis of religious dissent. The Jewish execution for this particular transgression was death by stoning. Crucifixion was a Roman punishment reserved for sedition, not religious eccentricity. This contradiction alone illustrates that the Gospels are not reporting the matter truthfully. Could they be trying to hide some vital aspects of the events from us? Trying to blame the wrong people perhaps?

Jesus was, we can be certain, sentenced for execution on the basis of political crimes. We can also be certain that it was the Romans, not the Jewish authorities, who called the shots, whatever spin the Gospels might try to put on it. And the Gospels certainly spun the message to the point that modern Christians still find the suggestion of any political action on the part of Jesus to be outrageously, even dangerously, "off-message." Yet it has been over fifty years since Professor Samuel Brandon of Manchester University in England drew attention to this critical theological distortion: "The crucial fact remains uncontested that the fatal sentence was pronounced by the Roman governor and its execution carried out by Roman officials."[2] Brandon continued:

> It is certain that the movement connected with [Jesus] had at least sufficient semblance of sedition to cause the Roman authorities both to regard him as a possible revolutionary and, after trial, to execute him as guilty on such a charge.[3]

In fact, in later years Brandon became blunter, perhaps exasperated with those who continued to ignore this important fact: "All enquiry," he wrote forcefully, allowing little room for doubt on the matter, "concerning the historical Jesus must start from the fact of his execution by the Romans for sedition."[4]

We will find that we are dealing not only with the intricacies of religion but with the machinations of politics. Even today not all the mines have been cleared.

Apart from the brutal mode of execution, we are left to wonder whether there is any other suggestion in the Gospels that the Romans were ultimately in charge and that the crime involved was sedition rather than contravention of Jewish teachings.

The answer: indeed there is. Jesus was crucified between two other men, described as thieves in the English translations of the Bible. However, if we go back to the original Greek text, we find that they are not called thieves at all there but are described as *lestai*, which, strictly speaking, translates as "brigands" but which was, in Greek, the official name for the "Zealots," the Judaean freedom fighters who were dedicated to ridding Judaea of its Roman occupation (Matthew 27:38).[5] The Romans considered them to be terrorists.

The Zealots were not just seeking some kind of political land grab but had a less venal motive: they were concerned, above all else, with the legitimacy of the priests serving in the Temple of Solomon and, in particular, with the legitimacy of the high priest – who was, at the time, appointed by the Herodian rulers.[6] They wanted priests who were "sons of Aaron," priests of the bloodline of Aaron, the brother of Moses, of the Tribe of Levi, who founded the Israelite priesthood and was the first high priest of Israel. "The sons of Aaron" had become the term used to describe the sole legitimate line of priests in ancient Israel.

The undeniable implication of Jesus's placement between two condemned Zealots at Golgotha is that, to the Roman authorities, Jesus was also a Zealot. As was Barabbas, the prisoner released under what is described as a feast-day amnesty by Pilate. The prisoner was described in Greek as a *lestes* (John 18:40).[7] There really seem to have been a lot of Zealots around Jesus.

This observation also extends to Jesus's disciples: one is called Simon Zelotes (Simon *xeloten*) – Simon the Zealot (Luke 6:15). Furthermore, a particularly nasty group of assassins within the Zealot movement were called *Sicarii* after the small curved knife – a *sica* – that they carried to assassinate their opponents; Judas *Iscariot* was clearly Sicarii (whether active or former we do not know). This suggestion of Zealot militancy takes on an added significance when we recall the events preceding the arrest of Jesus in the Garden of Gethsemane. According to Luke's Gospel, as Jesus and his disciples were gathering, Jesus told his immediate entourage to arm themselves: "He that hath no sword, let him sell his garment and buy one." He was told that they had two swords. "It is enough," replied Jesus (Luke 22:36–38). Here Jesus is described in a context defined by the strong and often violent Judaean desire for liberation from Roman rule. To see it as anything but that is to ignore too much of the texts.

It is, in some way, as a representative of this anti-Roman faction that Jesus was sent for crucifixion. Pilate reportedly washed his hands of the entire business, but his insistence that the sign *King of the Jews* remain on the cross reveals that he had *not* washed his hands of Roman law, which was very specific. By its provisions, Pilate's task was clear: he had to crucify Jesus. By placing the sign where he did, he signaled to all people that he knew the truth about the situation.

So we are still left to ask, if Jesus survived the crucifixion, whether by substitution or rescue, who was likeliest to have helped him? Certainly not the Romans – why should they have saved someone opposed to their rule over Judaea? And certainly not the chief priests of the Temple, for Jesus was highly critical, at the least, of their authority. Help, we assume, could only have come from the Zealots.

But as we press on we shall discover that we could not be more wrong.

In 37 B.C., Herod captured Jerusalem. He was not a native of Judaea but came from a southern region called Idumaea. Although he was a competent soldier and administrator, he was also a thug. His friend Mark Antony had provided him with a large Roman army to take Jerusalem, but even with this help it still took a five-month siege to destroy the city's resistance. Immediately upon taking power, Herod executed forty-five of the Sanhedrin, thereby destroying all of its influence. He also arrested Antigonus, the last of the Jewish kings, and dispatched him to Antioch, where Mark Antony was in residence. There the Jewish king was conveniently beheaded. Herod was installed as king in his stead, ruling as "Herod the Great" and remaining a close friend of his backers, the Romans.

Herod remained deeply hostile toward all members of the legitimate royal Jewish bloodline. Although he married a royal princess, he nevertheless had her brother, the high priest, drowned in a swimming pool at the palace in Jericho. Herod later had his own royal wife killed as well. He also had his two sons by this marriage executed. In fact, during his reign he methodically executed all remaining members of the royal dynasty of Israel. He did ultimately rebuild the Temple of Jerusalem, but despite this largesse, he remained hated by most of the Jewish people in the region. When he died in 4 B.C., his final action was to order the burning to death of two Pharisees whose supporters had torn down the golden Roman Eagle that, by Herod's orders, was fixed upon the Temple's front wall.

The only chronicler of this period is the Jewish historian Josephus. He reports that, following the death of Herod, the "people" called for the high priest of the Temple in Jerusalem – a Herodian appointee – to be dismissed. They demanded that a high priest of "greater piety and purity" be appointed.[8] This is the first indication that a significant part of the Jewish population had been deeply concerned about these matters, a point that will be of crucial importance to our understanding of the entire period. But who exactly were these "concerned people"?

Josephus describes three distinct factions in Judaism at the time: the Pharisees, the Sadducees, and the Essenes. The Sadducees maintained the Temple worship and supplied the priests who performed the daily sacrifices. The high priest was also drawn from their ranks. The Pharisees were more concerned with the Jewish tradition, the collection of laws built up by sages past, and were less concerned with the Temple sacrifices. The Essenes, who lived communally, were variously and confusingly described as anti- or pro-Herod, peaceful or warlike, celibate or married, all depending upon which parts of Josephus's works one looks at. This has led to considerable confusion among modern scholars and muddied the waters rather badly. The Essenes were typified, however, by their devotion to the Jewish law; as Josephus mentions, even under severe torture by the Romans, they refused to blaspheme Moses or break any of the law's precepts.[9] They also, Josephus writes, maintained the same doctrine as "the sons of Greece"; perhaps he has in mind the Pythagoreans or the later Platonists in that they too viewed humans as housing an immortal soul within a mortal, perishable body.

In his later work, *Antiquities of the Jews*, Josephus added a fourth group: the Zealots.[10]

Those who wanted a new high priest were not just concerned with intellectual protest. The clamor for the change came at the end of the weeklong mourning period for

Herod. His son Archelaus had every expectation that he would become king in turn, but the decision was in the hands of Augustus Caesar.

Archelaus was in the middle of a grand funeral feast at the Temple prior to his departure for Rome when he heard the noise of an angry mob outside making their demands. The main focus of the clamor – the high priest – must have also been present at the feast. Archelaus was enraged by this noisy demonstration, but he did not wish to inflame the situation, so he sent his military commander to reason with the crowd gathered in the Temple. It was a crowd enlarged by the many who had traveled in from the outlying countryside in preparation for the approaching Passover. But those present stoned the officer before he could even begin to speak. He quickly withdrew.

Archelaus must have panicked, fearing for his own life, because after that point things turned very ugly, very quickly. Moving swiftly, Archelaus ordered a cohort of troops to enter the Temple and arrest the leaders of the crowds who were calling for the changes. This was a sizable force: in the regular Roman army it would have meant six hundred soldiers; for auxiliary forces, which these were most likely to have been, it could have meant anything from five hundred to seven hundred or more soldiers. It is clear that trouble was imminent and Archelaus intended to crack down fast and hard. But his plan didn't work. The people in the crowd were outraged by the sudden appearance of armed troops and attacked them with stones as well. Incredibly, Josephus reports, most of the soldiers were killed, and even the commander was wounded, narrowly escaping death. This was clearly a major battle, indicating that these "people" not only wanted a high priest of "greater piety and purity" but that they were serious, organized, and prepared to fight and die for their beliefs.

Following their defeat of the troops, the crowds proceeded to perform the Temple sacrifices as though nothing untoward had happened. Archelaus took this opportunity to order his entire army into action: his infantry attacked the streets of Jerusalem, while his cavalry attacked the surrounding countryside. It is clear that this opposition to the high priest was far greater, far more structured, and far more widespread than Josephus is prepared to admit. For some reason, Josephus plays down the extent of what was evidently a major insurrection centered in the Temple followed by a major and bloody street battle throughout Jerusalem. Josephus is clear, however, about how he views the event. For him, it was "sedition." Through his use of this derogatory term we can be sure that Josephus took the side of Archelaus and the Romans.

The battle ended with several thousand civilian deaths, including most of those who were in the Temple. Those who survived fled, seeking refuge in the neighboring hills. The funeral feast was promptly ended, and Archelaus, without further delay, departed for Rome. Meanwhile, his brother Antipas contested the will and claimed the throne for himself.

While Archelaus was arguing his case before the emperor in Rome, further revolt erupted in Judaea. On the eve of the Pentecost feast (Shavuot, the fiftieth day after the Passover Sabbath), a huge crowd surrounded the Roman bases, effectively placing them under siege. Fighting broke out in both Jerusalem and the countryside. Galilee especially seemed to be a breeding ground for the most serious organized discontent, and it was from there, in 4 B.C., that the first leader emerged, Judas of Galilee, who raided the royal armory to seize weapons. At the same time, Herod's palace at Jericho was burned down. *Could this act of political heresy have been revenge for the drowning of the last legitimate high priest?* It seems very likely. Moving as rapidly as possible, the Romans gathered three legions and four regiments of cavalry, together with many auxiliaries, and struck back. In the end some two thousand Jews, all leaders of the resistance, were crucified – for sedition, of course.

Meanwhile in Rome, during that same year, Augustus Caesar had decided to divide Judaea among Herod's sons, each of whom would rule with a lesser title than king. He gave the richest half of the kingdom, including Judaea and Samaria, to Archelaus, who ruled as an ethnarch; he divided the other half into two tetrarchies (from the Greek meaning "rule over one-fourth of a territory"), giving one tetrachy each to two other sons, Philip and Herod Antipas. Herod Antipas held Galilee and lands across the Jordan; Philip received lands north and east of Galilee.

Two points need to be noted here: first, while Josephus

seems to suggest on the surface that the demands for a pure and pious high priest came from a loosely gathered, even impromptu mob that was simply part of the usual crowd in the Temple assembled for the coming Passover, it is clear, given the extent of the fighting and the opposition mounted in both Jerusalem and beyond, that this opposition group was well led and its network extensive. It was no accident that they had gathered at the Temple on the day of the funeral feast. They had come deliberately, prepared for trouble. In fact, they must surely have expected trouble. This begs two questions: Who were these people? And what if anything can we glean about their ideology from their deep desire to see a "pure and pious" high priest put in place?

It seems that these events provide an essential context for Jesus's early life: in 4 B.C., when Herod died, Jesus was, according to the most widely held estimates, approximately two years old. Thus, we can be sure that his birth and life occurred against a background of agitation against the corrupt and hated Herodian dynasty. And though his birthplace was Bethlehem, in Judaea, Matthew (2:22–23) records that Jesus was taken to Nazareth in Galilee as a child. After a long period of silence in the gospel record, Jesus is said to have emerged from Galilee to be baptized by John the Baptist. And it is from Galilee that he gathered his disciples – at least two of whom were Zealots. Certainly he was commonly called Jesus of Galilee. As we have seen, Galilee was a hotbed of revolt, and it was from here that Judas, the leader of a large group of rebels, came. What then was the relationship of Jesus with these political agitators, these crowds bent upon sedition? Was he later to become their leader? Clues once again come from Josephus.

The opposition Josephus describes was reaching a wide movement that he takes great pains to play down while at the same time disparaging as "sedition." Yet Josephus also records that the opposition did not end with the vicious slaughter in Jerusalem. In fact, he notes, it became worse with time. Archelaus proved so brutal in his rule that after ten years Caesar exiled him to Vienne in France. The lands of Archelaus were then ruled directly by Rome as the Province of Judaea. Since Philip and Herod Antipas were elsewhere, ruling their respective tetrarchies, a prefect, Coponius, was appointed and dispatched from Rome to rule Archelaus's domains from his capital, the coastal city of Caesarea. Traveling with him was the new governor of Syria, Quirinius. Rome wanted a full accounting of the regions it now had to rule, and so Quirinius undertook a census of the entire country. This census was, to say the least, deeply unpopular. The date was A.D. 6. Trouble was inevitable.

Judas of Galilee led an uprising. He accused all men who paid a tax to Rome of cowardice. He demanded that Jews refuse to acknowledge the emperor as master, claiming that only one master existed and that was God. *This question of the tax was the key means of knowing who was for Judas and who was against him.* At the same time, Josephus reports, the hotheaded Sicarii first appeared. They were the faction behind all the violence. Josephus hints that Judas of Galilee either founded the group or led them, and it is clear from his accounts that Josephus hated them. He accuses them of using their politics as a cloak for their "barbarity and avarice."[11]

Amazingly, a mention of Judas in the New Testament corroborates this profile. "After ... rose up Judas of Galilee in the days of the taxing, and drew away much people after him: he also perished" (Acts 5:37). Josephus further explains that Judas, along with another fighter, Zadok the Pharisee, was responsible for adding a fourth faction to Judaism after the Sadducees, Pharisees, and Essenes: the Zealots, so called because they were "zealous in good undertakings."[12] The term "Zealot" occurs only in the history of Josephus; no other Roman author mentions them, and even Josephus is reluctant to name them. Instead, he prefers to refer to them negatively as *Lestai* (brigands) or *Sicarii* (dagger-men).

This too finds a mention in the New Testament, within the Book of Acts. Speaking of a meeting between Paul and James in Jerusalem after Paul returned from many years of preaching in Greek and Roman cities such as Tarsus, Antioch, Athens, Corinth, and Ephesus, James and his companions mention the "many thousands of Jews" who were all "zealous of the law"(Acts 21, 20). Later in the same book (Acts 21, 38), another more sensitive term is used. Paul was accused of being the leader of "four thousand men who were murderers" by the Romans and then arrested. But when we look at the original Greek text, we find that "murderers" is not what the text says at all. In fact, Paul was being accused of leading four thousand *sicarion* – Sicarii.

Despite the labels – "Zealots" or "murderers" – or maybe even because of them, we are still left to ask: who were these Jews who were prepared to die rather than serve the Romans? Again Josephus would have us believe that they were a small band of hotheaded individuals bent upon sedition. Yet the revolts he chronicles suggest that they fought with fury and vigor and significant manpower. The inherent contradiction leads us to believe that he was not telling the truth about this faction. They were obviously more serious than he wished to admit. And this is crucial to our story and to our understanding.

So why did Josephus hate the Zealots so much? A look at his career makes it quite plain to us: Josephus had actually begun his career as a Zealot. He was even a Zealot military commander. Amazingly, he was in charge of all of Galilee – the Zealot heartland – at the start of the war against Rome. But after the loss of his base, he defected to the Roman side and became a close friend of Emperor Vespasian and his son Titus, the army commander. Finally, Josephus ended up living in Rome within the emperor's very own palace, with a pension and Roman citizenship. But his treachery against his own people cost him dearly. For the rest of his life he had to watch his back because he was hated by even those Jews living in Rome.

In his first book, *The Jewish War* – written around A.D. 75 to 79 for a Roman and Romanized audience – Josephus blames the Zealots for the destruction of the Temple. Although he had access to all the Jewish records that survived the siege and the Temple fires and access to Roman records, we find that we cannot entirely believe what he says. Despite his excellent source material, he had joined the enemy and was writing for the enemy – a Roman Gentile audience. Josephus's writing of *The Jewish War* is analogous to a Nazi writing a history of Poland that justifies the invasion of 1939. Since one man's terrorist is another man's patriot, we need to be careful with our use of his works. We must keep his reporting in perspective.

For now let us turn our attention to an extraordinary event that occurred in 1947. A Bedouin shepherd named Mohammad adh-Dhib was roaming on the northern end of the Dead Sea searching for some lost goats. Thinking that they might be in a cave he had come upon, he threw a rock in to frighten them and drive them out. Instead of the outraged bleat of a goat, he heard the shattering of pottery. Intrigued, he crawled through the small cave entrance to see what was there. Before him lay some large clay pots – one now broken – in which he found the first collection of documents famous ever since as the "Dead Sea Scrolls."

He took them to an antique dealer in Bethlehem, who began peddling them to various parties he thought might be interested. Even so, there is something of a mystery over the full number of scrolls found. Seven were produced and eventually sold to academic institutions, but it seems that several others were found and perhaps held back or passed into the hands of other dealers or private collectors. And at least one found its way to Damascus and, for a brief period, into the hands of the U.S. Central Intelligence Agency.

At that time, the station chief of the CIA in Damascus was Middle Eastern expert Miles Copeland. He related to me that one day a "sly Egyptian merchant" came to the door of his building and offered him a rolled-up ancient text of the type we now know as a Dead Sea Scroll. They were, of course, unknown then, and Copeland was unsure if such battered documents were valuable or even in any way interesting. He certainly could not read Aramaic or Hebrew, but he knew that the head of the CIA in the Middle East, Kermit Roosevelt, who was based in Beirut, was an expert in these ancient languages and would probably be able to read it. He took the scroll onto the roof of the building in Damascus and, with the wind blowing pieces of it into the streets below, unrolled it and photographed it. He took, he said, about thirty frames, and even this was not enough to record the entire text, so we can assume that the text was quite substantial. He sent the photographs off to the CIA station in Beirut.[13] And there they vanished. Searches of CIA holdings under the provisions of the U.S. Freedom of Information Act have failed to find them. Copeland recalls that he heard the text concerned Daniel – but he did not know whether it proved to be a standard text of the Old Testament book or a *pesher*, that is, a commentary on certain key passages from an Old Testament text, like the commentary appearing on several of the other scrolls found in the same

cave. Somewhere out there in the clandestine antique underworld, this valuable text undoubtedly still remains.

The Dead Sea Scrolls that have been studied give us for the
first time direct insight into this large and widespread group
we've been contemplating here – this group who detested
foreign domination, who were single-mindedly concerned
with the purity of the high priest – and king – and who were
totally dedicated to the observance of Jewish law. In fact,
one of the many titles by which they referred to themselves
was *Oseh ha-Torah* – the Doers of the Law.

The Dead Sea Scrolls, it appears, provide original documents from the Zealots. For it was from their community
that they emerged. What is also interesting is that, according to the archaeological evidence, Qumran, the site where
many of the documents were found and where, at first sight,
a Zealot center seems to have been established, was deserted during the time of Herod the Great, who had a palace
just a few miles away in Jericho – the same palace that was
burned down by "Zealots" after his death. It was thereafter
that the occupation of Qumran began.[14]

The Dead Sea Scrolls were written directly by those who
used them, and unusually for religious documents, they remain untouched by later editors or revisionists. What they
tell us we can believe. And what they tell us is very interesting indeed. For one thing, they reveal a deep hatred of foreign domination that verges on the pathological, a hatred
clearly fueled by a desire for revenge following many years

of slaughter, exploitation, and disdain for the Jewish religion by an enemy they term the *Kittim* – this may be generic, but in the first century A.D. it clearly referred to the Romans. The War Scroll proclaims:

> They shall act in accordance with all this rule on this day, when they are positioned opposite the camp of the Kittim. Afterwards, the priest will blow for them the trumpets ... and the gates of battle shall open ... The priests shall blow ... for the attack. When they are at the side of the Kittim line, at throwing distance, each man will take up his weapons of war. The six priests shall blow the trumpets of slaughter with a shrill, staccato note to direct the battle. And the levites and all the throng with ram's horns shall blow the battle call with a deafening noise. And when the sound goes out, they shall set their hand to finish off the severely wounded of the Kittim.[15]

So dreamed the Zealots, who loathed and detested the Romans: they would sooner die than serve the Kittim. They lived only for the day when a messiah would emerge from the Jewish people and lead them in a victorious war against the Romans and their puppet kings and high priests, erasing them from the face of the earth so that once again there might be a pure line of high priests and kings of the Line of David in Israel. In fact, they waited for two messiahs: the high priest and the king. The Rule of the Community, for example, speaks of the future "Messiahs of Aaron and Israel."[16] The Messiah of Aaron refers to the high priest; the Messiah of Israel denotes a king of the Line of David. Further scrolls mention the same figures. Provocatively, from our perspective, some scrolls, such as the Damascus Document, bring these two together and speak of one messiah, a "Messiah of Aaron and Israel."[17] They are revealing a figure who is both high priest and king of Israel.

All these texts make much of the necessity for the line of kings and high priests to be "pure," that is, of the correct lineage. The Temple Scroll states: "From among your brothers you shall set over yourself a king; you shall not set a foreign man who is not your brother over yourself."[18]

Both king and high priest were anointed and were thus a *meshiha*, a messiah. In fact, from as early as the second century B.C. the term "messiah" was used to name a legitimate king of Israel, one of the royal Line of David, who was expected to appear and to rule.[19] This expectation was not, therefore, unique to the Zealots but ran as a strong undercurrent to the Old Testament and the Jewish faith of the second Temple period. It is more prevalent than one might think: it has been pointed out that "the Old Testament books were so edited that they emerge collectively as a messianic document."[20]

The point is, of course, that the Jewish population of Judaea, at least, was expecting a messiah of the Line of David to appear. And with the hardships and horrors of the reign of Herod and the later Roman prefects, the time seemed to

have come. The time for the messiah's appearance had arrived, and that is why we needn't be surprised when we discover that the rebel Zealot movement of Judas of Galilee
and Zadok the Pharisee was, at its heart, messianic.[21]

Who then did they have in mind as the messiah?

The Dead Sea Scrolls provide a context for understanding
the role of Jesus and the political machinations that would
have featured behind his birth, marriage, and active role in
this Zealot aspiration for victory. According to the Gospels,
through his father, Jesus was of the Line of David; through
his mother, he was of the line of Aaron the high priest
(Matthew 1:1, 16; Luke 1:5, 36; 2:4). We suddenly get an understanding of his importance to the Zealot cause when we
realize that because of his lineage he was heir to both lines.
He was a "double" messiah; having inherited both the royal
and priestly lines, he was a "Messiah of Aaron and Israel," a
figure, as we have seen, who was clearly noted in the Dead
Sea Scrolls. And it would appear that he was widely seen as
such. We can take as an expression of this fact Pilate's supposedly ironic sign placed at the foot of the cross: *This is
Jesus the king of the Jews* (Matthew 27, 37).[22]

As high priest and king – as Messiah of the Children of
Israel (in Hebrew, *bani mashiach*) – Jesus would have been
expected to lead the Zealots to victory. He would have
been expected to oppose the Romans at every step and to
hold tightly to the concepts of ritual purity that were so
important to the Zealots. As the Zealot leader, he had a

religious and political role to perform, and as it happens, there was a recognized way for him to perform it: the Old Testament prophet Zechariah had spoken of the arrival in Jerusalem of the king on a donkey (Zechariah 9:9 – 10). Jesus felt it necessary to fulfill this and other prophecies in order to gain public acceptance; indeed, the prophecy of Zechariah is quoted in the New Testament account of Matthew (21:5). So Jesus entered Jerusalem on a donkey. The point was not lost on the crowds who greeted his arrival: "Hosanna to the son of David," they cried as they placed branches of trees and cloaks on the road for him to ride over in spontaneous gestures of acclaim.

Jesus had deliberately chosen his path. And he had been recognized as the king of the Line of David by the crowds of Jerusalem. The die was cast. Or so it seemed.

This deliberate acting out of Old Testament prophecy and its implications were discussed by Hugh Schonfield in his book *The Passover Plot*, which was first published in 1965; reissued many times since, it sold over six million copies in eighteen languages.[23] It was a best-seller by anybody's standards, and yet is today almost forgotten. Recent books do not even mention Schonfield's work.

The matters he raised are certainly controversial but important; the custodians of the orthodox story are constantly trying to keep these alternative ideas out lest they shake the paradigm, lest they cause us to change our attitude toward the Gospels, the figure of Jesus, and the history of the times. Such lessons as Schonfield's need to be repeated, generation after generation, until eventually they are supported by a weight of data so substantial that the paradigm has no alternative but to flip, causing us to approach our history from a very different perspective.

So many factors in Jesus's life – the Zealot revolt, his birth to parents who were descendants of the Line of David and the Line of Aaron, respectively, the Zealot members of his immediate entourage, his deliberate entry into Jerusalem as king – should certainly have ensured Jesus's place in history as the leader of the Jewish nation. But they didn't. So what went wrong?

4

The Son of the Star

Simply put, the Zealot cause failed, utterly and disastrously. It was probably inevitable since, at its heart, it opposed the domination of the Romans, who were the greatest military power the Mediterranean world knew at the time. Although the natural course of the Zealot movement led it to oppose this domination openly and with all the force it could muster, it could never have won. That much was clear to all who looked even a little ahead.

It was evident that there were more Romans than Jews, and Roman power was centered upon an army of disciplined and well-trained professional soldiers who were not averse to feats of creative brutality if the situation demanded it – or if the soldier at hand just happened to feel like it. All this force was backed up by a widespread and formidable command of logistics supported by well-maintained roads and ships, all of which were integrated into a structure that ensured troops and supplies were delivered in strength and on time.

Since the open emergence of the Zealot opposition in A.D. 6, a series of rulers – Roman governors and Jewish high priests alike – had managed, one way or another, to keep a kind of stability in Judaea.

JUDAEA, JESUS, AND CHRISTIANITY

Before 4 B.C.	Birth of Jesus, according to Matthew's Gospel (2:1).
4 B.C.	Death of Herod the Great.
A.D. 6	Birth of Jesus, according to Luke's Gospel (2:1–7). Census of Quirinius, Governor of Syria.
A.D. 27–28	Baptism of Jesus (traditional date) in the fifteenth year of the reign of Emperor Tiberius (Luke 3:1–23).
A.D. 30	Crucifixion of Jesus, according to Catholic scholarship.
c. A.D. 35	Following the marriage of Herod Antipas and Herodias in c. A.D. 34, John the Baptist is executed, following the evidence in Josephus.
A.D. 36	Passover – crucifixion of Jesus, according to Matthew's timetable.
A.D. 36–37	Conversion of Paul on the road to Damascus.

c. A.D. 44   Execution of James, the brother of Jesus.

A.D. 50–52   Paul in Corinth. Writes his first letter (to the Thessalonians).

A.D. 61   Paul in Rome under house arrest.

c. A.D. 65   Paul supposedly executed.

A.D. 66–73   War in Judaea. The Roman army under Vespasian invades Judaea.

c. A.D. 55–120   Life of Tacitus, Roman historian and senator, who mentions Christ.

c. A.D. 61–c. 114 Life of Pliny the Younger, who mentions Christ.

c. A.D. 115   Ignatius, Bishop of Antioch, quotes from letters of Paul.

c. A.D. 117–138   Suetonius, Roman historian, mentions "Chrestus."

c. A.D. 125   Earliest known example of a Christian gospel, John 18: 31–33, Rylands Papyrus, found in Egypt.

c. A.D. 200——   Oldest known fragment of Paul's letters, Chester Beatty Papyrus, found in Egypt.

c. A.D. 200——   Oldest virtually complete gospel (John's), Bodmer Papyrus, found in Egypt.

A.D. 325   Council of Nicaea is convened by the Roman emperor Constantine. The divinity of Jesus is made official dogma by a vote of 217 to 3.

A.D. 393–397   Council of Hippo, formalizing the New Testament, is finalized at Council of Carthage.

THE FIRST CENTURY

4 B.C.	Death of King Herod.
A.D. 6	Zealot uprising, led by Judas of Galilee.
A.D. 26	Pontius Pilate appointed prefect of Judaea (until A.D. 36).
A.D. 36	Pontius Pilate recalled to Rome and exiled.
A.D. 38	Anti-Jewish riots and killings in Alexandria are encouraged by the prefect Flaccus.
A.D. 39	Herod Antipas exiled to the French Pyrenees.
c. A.D. 44	James, the brother of Jesus, is executed.
A.D. 46–48	Tiberius Alexander is prefect of Judaea.
A.D. 64	Burning of Rome under Nero. Arrest of Christians.
A.D. 66	Jewish general in Roman army, Tiberius Alexander, is prefect of Egypt. Sends in his troops to put down revolt in Alexandria. Several thousand Jews are killed.
A.D. 66–73	War in Judaea. Roman army under Vespasian invades through Galilee.
A.D. 67	Josephus, a Jewish military leader in Galilee, defects to the Roman side following a defeat. Writes Jewish histories (*The Jewish War*, A.D. 77–78; *The Antiquities of the Jews*, c. 94) while living in the imperial palace in Rome.
A.D. 69	Vespasian is proclaimed emperor. Places his son Titus in charge of the army. Titus appoints Tiberius Alexander his chief of staff.

A.D. 70   The Temple in Jerusalem is destroyed. After-
                 wards, Vespasian seeks out and executes all mem-
                 bers of the royal Line of David. Jerusalem is
                 renamed Aelia Capitolina, and all Jews are for-
                 bidden to enter the city. The Romans allow the
                 Pharisee Johanan ben Zakkai to establish a reli-
                 gious school and the Sanhedrin at Jabneh, giving
                 rise to rabbinical Judaism. (The school and the
                 Sanhedrin will survive there until A.D. 132)

A.D. 73   Masada is destroyed, and 960 Zealots commit
                 suicide rather than be captured. Jewish temple of
                 Onias in Egypt is closed.

Both sides needed peace and the wealth that arose from it
– conflict never plants seeds or grows crops, and idle land
never produces food or money for the farmers, nor taxes for
the rulers – and Rome relied upon Judaea for the forty tal-
ents it produced each year for the Roman treasury (the ap-
proximate equivalent of 3,750 pounds of silver).[1] Through
careful political husbandry, this unstable balance had lasted
for half of the century. And then suddenly it all fell to pieces.

A group of anti-Roman priests in the Temple in Jerusalem
decided to stop non-Jews from giving offerings. This cessa-
tion of the customary daily sacrifices performed for Caesar
and for Rome in the Temple was a direct and abrupt challenge
to the emperor. There was no turning back. The Zealots and
the anti-Roman priests had led their people across the
threshold of the doorway to hell. As Josephus reports, war
against Rome was inevitable because of this act. The Zealots,

in their misplaced ambition, thought that they would recover control of their nation, but so great was their loss that all such hope was to vanish for nearly two thousand years.

Fighting first erupted in A.D. 66 in the coastal city of Caesarea. Attempts to calm the situation were futile in the face of the frustration and hatred that had fueled the attacks. The Zealots had been waiting for this day, and now they had it. For them, tomorrow had finally come. Thousands were killed: Zealots took the fortress of Masada on the Dead Sea; others took over the lower city of Jerusalem and the Temple, burning down the palace of King Agrippa and that of the high priest. They also burned the official records office.

Leaders emerged from within the Jewish ranks: in Jerusalem the son of the high priest had been in charge. Then Judas of Galilee's son appeared in Masada and looted the armory before returning to Jerusalem like a king, clothed in royal robes, to take over the palace. The official high priest was murdered.

At first, unprepared for such a catastrophic outpouring of hatred toward them, the Romans were readily beaten. The governor of Syria, Cestius Gallus, marched into Judaea from his capital in Antioch at the head of the Twelfth Legion. After destroying many communities and towns, his army besieged Jerusalem. But he was driven off with very heavy losses, including the commander of the Sixth Legion and a Roman tribune. Cestius himself seems to have escaped only by the speed of his retreat. In the debacle, the Zealots seized a great deal of weapons and money. Despite

Administered by Pontius Pilate

Tetrarchy of Herod Antipas

PHOENICIA
(Part of Roman Syria)

Mediterranean Sea

Tyre

GAULANITIS
(Tetrarchy of Philip)

Capernaum · Gamala
Migdal
Tiberias
GALILEE

Caesarea · Pella

DECAPOLIS
(Part of Roman Syria)

SAMARIA

Jordan River

JUDAEA PEREA

Emmaus · Jericho
· Jerusalem
Bethlehem · Qumran

· Machaerus

Dead Sea

Masada ·

IDUMAEA

NABATEAN
KINGDOM

N

ISRAEL
AT THE
TIME OF
JESUS

0   25 km   20 mi

Judea and Galilee

this show of strength, many prescient Jews fled Judaea, as they knew the situation could only get worse.

And they were right: the Romans withdrew, but only to gather their strength. They were to return with brutality and vengeance. Meanwhile, in the absence of the Roman overlords, the Zealots regrouped too. They elected commanders for the various regions, raised troops, and began to train them in Roman military techniques and formations. The first fighting was to be in Galilee, where Josephus – yet to become the historian and friend of the Romans – was commander of the Zealot forces.

The Roman emperor Nero was outraged by the eruption of revolt in Judaea and ordered a respected army veteran, Vespasian, to take charge of regaining control over the country. Vespasian sent his son, Titus, to Alexandria to get the Fifteenth Legion. Vespasian himself marched down from Syria with the Fifth and Tenth Legions, together with twenty-three cohorts of auxiliaries – around eighteen thousand cavalry and infantry.

Vespasian and Titus met in the Syrian port of Ptolemais (now Akko) and, uniting their forces, moved inland, across the border into Galilee. Josephus was caught in his stronghold, Jotapata (now Yodefat), midway between Haifa and the Sea of Galilee. After a forty-seven-day siege, Galilee fell. Josephus escaped but was soon captured, surrendering to a high-ranking Roman officer, a tribune called Nicanor. Josephus describes him as an old friend and in almost the same breath reveals that he was himself "a priest and a descendent of priests."[2] In other words, Josephus was no Galilean hothead but rather a member of the Jerusalem aristocracy with strong links to the Roman administration.

Immediately after his capture, Josephus was imprisoned by the commander, Vespasian. But Josephus, in an action that clearly revealed his high-level association with the Romans, asked for a private meeting. Vespasian obliged, asking all but Titus and two friends to leave them. One of those two was probably Titus's military chief of staff, Tiberius Alexander, who was Jewish and a nephew of the famous philosopher Philo of Alexandria.[3] Tiberius Alexander had his own reasons for this meeting, which we shall see. What ensued was clearly a bit of well-contrived theater, with Josephus and Tiberius Alexander each playing a prominent part.

"You suppose, sir," Josephus addressed Vespasian, clearly aware that this was a pivotal moment in his life and that the next few minutes would determine his future, "that in capturing me you have merely secured a prisoner, but I come as a messenger of the greatness that awaits you." He explained, to give added importance to his words, that he was "sent by God Himself," and then continued,

> You, Vespasian, are Caesar and Emperor ... you are master not only of me, Caesar, but of land and sea and all the human race; and I ask to be kept in closer confinement as my penalty if I am taking the name of God in vain.

Of course, with Nero still ruling in Rome, what Josephus was suggesting was high treason. But Vespasian, according to Josephus – and we should remember that he was writing this in Vespasian's palace in Rome long after these events – was already thinking along these dangerous lines. Vespasian was reportedly skeptical of Josephus's claims at first – and he should also have been outraged at the treason uttered against his emperor and should have ordered Josephus to be executed immediately. Yet he did not. In his book, Josephus provides a reason: "God was already awakening in him imperial ambitions and foreshadowing the sceptre by other portents."[4]

This talk of "the sceptre," meaning royal status, reveals a link to a crucial prophecy of "the Star" – referring to the expected messianic leader – which was, as stated earlier, the catalyst for the outbreak of war. References to "the Star" and the "sceptre" were contained in a prophecy made by Balaam the seer, as reported in the Old Testament. Balaam proclaimed his oracle:

> I see him... I behold him – but not close at hand. A star from Jacob takes the leadership. A sceptre arises from Israel. (Numbers 24:17)

This "star from Jacob" clearly establishes that the messianic leader was expected to be born of the Line of David. Josephus states explicitly that this prophecy was the cause for the timing of the violence:

Their chief inducement to go to war was an equivocal
oracle also found in their sacred writings, announcing
that at that time a man from their country would become monarch of the whole world.

It was this prophecy that Josephus told to Vespasian. He also
no doubt added – but didn't reveal in the report of his meeting with the Roman commander – that the Zealots in
Jerusalem took this "to mean the triumph of their own
race." They were certain that they would win in their war
against the Romans because of this very religious oracle.
But, Josephus adds later in his book, they were "wildly out
in their interpretation. In fact," he states bluntly and obse-
quiously, "the oracle pointed to the accession of Vespasian;
for it was in Judaea he was proclaimed emperor."[5]

Roman historians too were aware of this prediction: Suetonius writes that "an ancient superstition was current in
the East; that out of Judaea at this time would come the
rulers of the world. This prediction, as the event later
proved, referred to a Roman Emperor, but the rebellious
Jews ... read it as referring to themselves."[6]

Tacitus also mentions it: he explains that

the majority were convinced that the ancient scriptures of their priests alluded to the present as the very
time when the Orient would triumph and from Judaea
would go forth men destined to rule the world. This
mysterious prophecy really referred to Vespasian and

Titus, but the common people ... thought that this mighty destiny was reserved for them, and not even their calamities opened their eyes to the truth.[7]

Then Nero was murdered. After him, two emperors came and went in quick succession. Finally, in A.D. 69, Vespasian was proclaimed emperor by his army. He called off the siege of Jerusalem in order to concentrate on his power base and shore up his imperial ambitions. He wanted, above all, to dominate Egypt. Luckily, his supporter and friend, the Jewish general Tiberius Alexander, was prefect of Egypt and in charge of the two legions stationed there. Vespasian wrote to Tiberius Alexander explaining his desire to seek the imperial throne; Tiberius Alexander read the letter aloud to all, then called for troops and civilians to swear an oath to Vespasian. Omens had foretold Vespasian's reign, and he "specially remembered the words of Josephus, who while Nero was still alive had dared to address him as Emperor."[8] Josephus was immediately released from captivity. Vespasian put his son Titus in charge of the army, and Titus appointed Tiberius Alexander as his chief of staff.

As a Jew, Tiberius Alexander would have been well aware of the "Star" prophecy, so it is conceivable that he contrived to apply it to Vespasian. The Roman historian Dio Cassius reports that while Vespasian was in Alexandria he was said to have healed a blind man and another man with a crippled hand; both had been told in a dream to approach Vespasian.[9] Long ago, the great scholar Robert Eisler suggested that only Tiberius Alexander, with his knowledge of Jewish prophecy and his desire to see the triumph of Vespasian, would have thought to manipulate circumstances so that the prophecy of Isaiah would come true – the prophecy that states the day when God heals the earth, the day when "the eyes of the blind shall be opened, the ears of the deaf unsealed, then the lame shall leap like a deer" (Isaiah 35:5–6). Only Tiberius Alexander, Eisler noted, would have contrived to send the blind man and the cripple to Vespasian so that he could perform his "messianic miracle."[10]

Tiberius Alexander would also have been aware of another part of the prophecies of Isaiah – the destruction of the Temple in Jerusalem. Isaiah wrote that God said: "I will tell you what I am going to do to my vineyard ... knock down its wall for it to be trampled on." Two verses later, he explained, "Yes, the vineyard ... is the House of David" (Isaiah 5:5, 7). For Tiberius Alexander, Vespasian was the messiah. Josephus agreed, writing, "In fact the oracle pointed to the accession of Vespasian."[11] To both these Romanized Jews, Vespasian was the messiah who had been foretold long ago in their sacred scriptures. For both, the Line of David was as defunct as the Temple was soon to be.

Nevertheless, Vespasian must have felt that even if the prophecy were true, he had a shaky hold over the identification since he certainly hadn't descended "from Jacob." There was no blood from the Line of David coursing through his veins. So, after he had won the war and destroyed Jerusalem, he sought out all surviving members of the Line of David and executed them. Vespasian respected the power of the oracle and was not about to take any chances. He wanted "to ensure that no member of the royal house should be left among the Jews."[12] But as history would later reveal, a number of the members of that ancient royal house had escaped his clutches.

With all this talk of stars, it is inevitable that we should address the Star of Bethlehem. The star is the messianic symbol of the Line of David. The Star of Bethlehem can also be termed "the Messiah of Bethlehem." This would suggest that we need not look for astronomical supernovae or stellar conjunctions to explain the arrival of the Magi in Bethlehem, a stronghold of the Line of David. It was a matter of dynasty rather than astronomy. And the Magi knew where to go to find their king.

But there has always been a mystery over the story of Joseph and Mary taking the infant Jesus from Bethlehem to Egypt to escape Herod – as noted by Matthew. Luke explains that Jesus was born in Bethlehem, having been taken there as a member of the Line of David for the census. The only census known was that of Quirinius in A.D. 6, after Rome had taken over Judaea. But this is always thought of as too late for Jesus's birth because the Gospels put him at around thirty years old at his crucifixion.

However, these calculations do not work very well and do not match the data given in the Gospels. Hugh Schonfield proposed a very provocative alternative.

The usual date for the crucifixion is given, with the Vatican's imprimatur by a chronological table at the end of The Jerusalem Bible, as on the eve of the Passover, 8 April A.D. 30.[13] The reasoning is this: John's Gospel contains some rather precise dating, citing the first Passover following Jesus's baptism as that of A.D. 28 (John 2:13, 20).[14] John mentions two more Passovers, the third of which sees the crucifixion, which thus must have occurred before the Passover of A.D. 30. Can this be correct?

We have only two sources of hard data beyond the New Testament. First, Tacitus states that "Christ had been executed in Tiberius' reign by the governor ... Pontius Pilate."[15] We know that Pilate was prefect of Judaea from A.D. 26 to 36, so that gives us a range within which we must stay. Second, although Josephus mentions the same incident, there is no general agreement that his passages mentioning Christ are original rather than later insertions by Christian editors.

The Gospel of Luke (3:1, 23) states that Jesus was about thirty years old at the time of his baptism by John, and this was after the fifteenth year of the reign of Tiberius (as calculated in Syria) – A.D. 27. But he was baptized not long before John the Baptist was executed, and after John's death the Gospel of Matthew (14:13) describes Jesus as seeking refuge in the desert, perhaps fearing for his own life. What then was the date of the execution? It could not have been A.D. 27, for Matthew and Mark report that John the Baptist was arrested by Herod Antipas for criticizing his marriage to Herodias – the wife of his brother, whom she had divorced

– a marriage outlawed by Jewish law and also by one of the texts of the Dead Sea Scrolls, the Temple Scroll.[16] Following this public criticism, John was executed. So far as can be ascertained, the marriage of Herod Antipas and Herodias took place in A.D. 35. Hence, John the Baptist was executed in A.D. 35. So Jesus must still have been alive at this date.

The last Passover attended by Pilate was A.D. 36. In other words, since Jesus is said in the Gospels to have been executed *after* John the Baptist's death and by the decision of Pilate, it must have been the Passover of A.D. 36 during which Jesus was crucified.[17] This is later than most experts have placed the event, but if Jesus was born at the time of the census in A.D. 6, as stated by Luke (2:2), and if he was aged about thirty, A.D. 36 is just about the right time of the crucifixion – the crucifixion of the "Star of Bethlehem."

In fact, early Christians were well aware of the connection between the messianic "Star of Bethlehem," the prophecy of the "Star" as relayed by Balaam in Numbers, and Jesus. The Christian writer Justin Martyr, who taught and wrote in Rome and died in approximately A.D. 165, argued with a Jewish teacher, Trypho, that Jesus was the messiah. Justin explained that the rising of the Star of Bethlehem was the rising star predicted by Balaam; again we can see that the star was messianic rather than astronomical.[18]

Faced with the inevitability of total destruction, many fled Judaea. The Church historian Eusebius reports that the early "Christian" community – that is, the messianic community – after the execution of James around A.D. 44 and before the outbreak of war, left Jerusalem for Pella across the Jordan in Roman-controlled Syria.[19] But this was prob ably the first stage on a longer journey north to Edessa, the capital of a kingdom that is described by Eusebius as being the first ever to convert to Christianity.[20] It is certainly true that by the second century A.D. Edessa was a strong Christian center. It cannot be a coincidence that the king of Edessa in the early second century was the son of a king of Abiadene (a state that lay a little to the east), part of a royal family with close links to the messianic Jewish cause. In fact, Queen Helen of Abiadene and her son converted to Judaism.[21] Moreover, we know for sure that her son converted to *messianic* Judaism – in other words, to the Zealot cause.[22] This alliance was maintained by others as well. At least two relatives of the king of Abiadene were prominent Zealots in the opening battles of the revolt against the Romans in A.D. 66.[23]

Still, there were Jews who remained in Judaea who opposed the Zealots. In Jerusalem, Zealot factions began fighting other Jewish factions. Many deserted to the Roman side – according to Josephus at least, though we must remember that he had a strong reason to accentuate this fact, as he strongly believed the Zealots were responsible for the war and the destruction of the Temple. Despite his bias, he may well be right, given what we now know about the ruthless determination of the Zealots. Nevertheless, the fury of the fighting was such that we have to conclude that support for the Zealots was widespread and that Josephus was at pains to diminish it. For one thing, there was the business of the suicides.

Running constantly throughout Josephus's accounts is talk of Zealots, soldiers and civilians alike, committing suicide rather than fall into the hands of the Romans. The most famous case is that of the mass suicide at Masada, where 960 people killed themselves. The ideology was widespread; armed resistance to Roman rule was a corollary. Even Josephus was involved in a suicide pact – which he managed, by treachery, to survive. But there were also accounts such as the one at Gamala, where *five thousand* people killed themselves. To kill yourself is one thing; however, to kill your wife, your children, and then yourself is something much greater. What was going on here?

The Zealots believed that if they died in a state of ritual purity, they would be resurrected together in accordance with the prophecy of Ezekiel: "I mean to raise you from your graves ... and lead you back to the soil of Israel" (Ezekiel 37:12 –14).[24] Further, they believed that those who died together would be resurrected together. So the Zealot warriors chose not just to die but to die in the company of their family. Had they been captured, they would have been separated, and the women and boys would have been dispatched to the brothels, where they would have lost their ritual purity, preventing them from any hope of resurrection.[25]

Jerusalem was besieged by the legions of Titus. Little mutual respect or chivalry was evident on either side. All fighters captured were crucified, and when that became commonplace, the soldiers amused themselves by nailing up their victims in various strange attitudes. So many were executed that the Romans ran out of room for the crosses and ran out of wood to make them.

On 29 August A.D. 70, and in line with the prophecy of Isaiah, the Temple was destroyed in a display of butchery without restraint. Over the following days the rest of the city was taken. Once the Romans held Jerusalem, they burned the remaining houses and tore down the defensive walls. The city was completely destroyed. All captured fighters were slated to be executed, civilians over seventeen were sent to labor in Egypt, and those younger were sold. Great numbers of the fighters were reserved for death in the Roman arenas. Many were exported to the Roman provinces to die as gladiators or to be torn to pieces by wild animals, to the delight of idle crowds; others were taken by Titus on his leisurely march up the coast. At every town he held displays in the arena where his Jewish prisoners were set upon by animals or forced to die in large battles for the spectators' entertainment.

During the siege of Jerusalem, Vespasian had been traveling, showing himself as emperor. He returned after the fall of the city and shortly after his return celebrated his brother's birthday with the death of over 2,500 Jewish prisoners in the arena. Later, in Beirut, he celebrated his father's birthday with even more deaths. All the while he was planning his triumphal entry to Rome bearing treasures and prisoners, including some of the leaders of the revolt whom he would have executed. The times were harsh.

For the Jewish people, this was a disaster of such a magnitude that even they, having once stood amid the smoking ruins of their Temple, could not even begin to comprehend it. In a religious sense, it was a second exile; the Temple, the House of God, the central bulwark of their religion, was gone. Jerusalem itself was lost too; Jews were not even allowed into the city, which had been renamed Aelia Capitolina. It seemed as if God had abandoned them. All around the world anti-Jewish feeling mounted, and rioting and killing destroyed the influence, power, and respect that Jewish merchants, philosophers, and politicians had once held. Even well-established communities suffered a terminal decline as tens of thousands were killed, and so those who had managed to survive kept their heads down. Some sicarii were able to flee to Alexandria, where they foolishly tried to encourage anti-Roman strife. So determined were they that they murdered some prominent members of the Jewish community who opposed them. In retaliation, the Jewish community rounded up the sicarii and gave them over to the Romans, who tortured them to death.

A small flame flickered on, however, in the town of Jabneh on the coastal plains of Judaea. There, under Johanan ben Zakkai, a leading Pharisee who had escaped Jerusalem and had requested rule of the town from Vespasian, the Sanhedrin was re-formed and a school was established. It was there that rabbinical Judaism was born. This significant favor from the emperor reveals that Johanan, like Josephus, was prepared to reach an accommodation with the invaders – something the Zealots had refused to do. Furthermore, Johanan is reported to have also proclaimed that the messianic "Star" prophecy referred to Vespasian.[26]

The scholars at Jabneh revived the *halakhah* – the legal side of Judaism comprising the law handed to Moses on Mount Sinai and the interpretation of the law that had been handed down through the ages – the study of which was crucial in a Judaism without the Temple. Between A.D. 70 and 132, after the destruction of Jerusalem, Jabneh served as the capital of the Jewish administration as well as the center of Judaism and Jewish scholarship. There the canon of texts in the Bible – the Old Testament to Christians – was fixed. This centralization of the faith helped establish some sense of national unity after the terrible destructions wrought by the war.

However, resistance continued, in small but important ways. Jewish prisoners were put to work as slaves, laboring on building projects, making weapons for the army, striking coins for the administration. The coins that were struck this time all emphasized the humiliation of Judaea. Some had *iudaea capta* – which means "Judaea Conquered" – on one side and a soldier, a palm tree, and a sorrowful figure representing Judaea on the other side. Other coins featured Vespasian with his imperial titles, including P.M. for *Pontifex Maximus,* or High Priest. And still others included the words *victoria aug[ustus]* – meaning "Victory of the Sacred Emperor." They were a constant reminder for the Jewish population of their total subjugation. But one hardy Jewish slave working in the Roman mint had other ideas.

Once, while I was visiting a dealer in Middle Eastern antiquities, he said, with a slight smile, "Look at this," and handed me a coin from one of his cabinets. It was a coin issued by the Roman mint of Vespasian, but this coin had one difference: on the palm tree side it had been struck *iudaea august* – "Sacred Judaea." A brave or foolhardy Jewish slave had mixed the striking punches. I turned the coin over; it had been struck with the head of Vespasian as usual. But there was a difference on this side too – a prominent dent had been smashed into the temple of Vespasian's head by a rounded punch. The point had very literally been made.

This is the only such coin ever found. It remains in a private collection.

In the summer of A.D. 115, the Jews outside of Judaea – especially those in Cyrene, Libya, and Alexandria, Egypt – rose in revolt. This insurrection then spread up the Nile to many other towns in Egypt. Vespasian might have tried to destroy all the members of the Line of David, but he had failed. Another descendant appeared in Egypt. His name was Lucuas, and he was described as the king of the Jews. He was the man who led the revolt.[27] This uprising too had a definite messianic orientation.[28] It implies that Lucuas very likely had, or claimed, a Davidic descent, but yet we know very little about the events because there was no historian equivalent to Josephus to write about them. It was a brutal two years of which we only know the outcome. This revolt entirely destroyed the position of Jews in Egypt. After this time they no longer had any power, influence, or even harmony. What's more, the Romans took a very strong view of this revolt. Egypt was supremely important to the empire, and a successful coup there could have held Rome ransom. Ceasing shipments of grain to Italy from Egypt could have caused the Italian people to starve. Rome could never allow such a danger to exist. In response, the revolt was ruthlessly suppressed. At its end, in August 117, there had been a comprehensive destruction of the Jewish community in Alexandria.[29] And in all the rest of Egypt, the cost to Judaism was mounting.

But the Jews had not yet given up hope that they might regain their independence, either through military prowess or from divine intervention – or both. Almost sixty years after the destruction of the Temple, during the rule of the emperor Hadrian, a second attempt to buck Roman authority was made.

This attempt had been well planned over a long period of time. The strategy needed to be developed in great secrecy. So a network of underground bases was constructed in subterranean caverns both natural and man-made. At least six such sites have been found in the Judaean foothills; one at Ailabo in Galilee had a purposefully excavated cavern beneath the ground sixty-five meters long, with vents in the roof that let in light and air.[30] Places such as this served for both planning and training. Those in charge knew that they had to avoid the mistakes of the earlier war, in which the Zealots had allowed themselves to be trapped behind the defensive walls of towns and cities only to be picked off and destroyed, one by one, by Roman armies that were masters of siege-craft. This time they intended to attack the Romans fast and hard and then disappear back into their underground redoubts just as swiftly; they saw mobility as the key to victory.

It is important to note that this time the Jewish fighters were united under a single strong leader named Simon Bar Koseba, later to become known as Bar Kochba — "the Son of the Star," revealing his messianic status. He too had the prophecy from Numbers 24 applied to him ("a star from Jacob takes the leadership, a sceptre arises from Israel"), and so, it would seem, he must also have carried the royal blood of David in his veins. Professor Robert Eisenman, a historian of the Dead Sea Scrolls, is intrigued by the possibility that Simon was related not just "figuratively but physically" to earlier messianic leaders in Judaea.[31]

Bar Kochba recruited military experts from overseas. Lists of names in Greek have been found, each name carrying the title *Adelphos*, or "Brother," like the later chivalric orders such as the Templars or the Knights of St. John.[32] Here were men with military experience who had come from the Jewish diaspora beyond Judaea where Greek was spoken and Aramaic or Hebrew unknown. These same men either served on the planning staff or, by virtue of their experience with the Roman forces, helped with the training of the secret Jewish army.

Bar Kochba knew that his men were facing the best disciplined army in the world with a potential manpower far exceeding his own: it has been estimated that the Roman standing army topped 375,000 well-trained men. There were two legions in Judaea, the Sixth and the Tenth, providing roughly 12,000 men together with an equal number of auxiliaries. Additionally, in the surrounding Roman provinces of Syria, Arabia, and Egypt, there were another five to seven legions and auxiliaries. The Jews could, at the most, raise 60,000 men, none of whom would have had military experience. Training was a necessity, and Bar Kochba devoted much time and effort to it.

He and his men needed weapons. So they devised an inventive way of ensuring a supply that is described by the Roman historian Dio Cassius, writing from A.D. 194 to 216. Because many or most of the workers in the arms industry in Judaea were Jewish, "they purposely did not forge up to standard those weapons which they had been ordered to furnish, so that the Romans might reject them, and they might thus have use of them themselves."[33]

The war broke out in A.D. 131 and was immediately successful. Roman civilians fled Jerusalem and the Tenth Legion retreated. The Twenty-second Legion from Egypt is unaccounted for in the military records of the time. It is assumed that it was rushed from its base in Egypt to Judaea but was there overwhelmed and totally annihilated. Jerusalem was recaptured from the Romans, its walls were repaired, and a Jewish civilian administration was established. For almost two years Judaea was free of Romans. But, of course, the Romans were gathering soldiers in order to return with overwhelming force.

This time Hadrian himself was in command. With him was the former governor of Britain, Julius Severus, whom he considered the finest of all his generals. In A.D. 133, nine, perhaps twelve, Roman legions and auxiliaries drawn from as far away as Britain – some sixty thousand to eighty thousand soldiers – invaded Galilee from the west and from across the Jordan river in the east. But they found it tough going. The Jewish fighters mounted a very flexible defense. The former high-ranking army officer Professor Mordechai Gichon wrote of Bar Kochba's long-term strategy: "The tangible Jewish hope lay in drawing out the war long enough to bait hostile forces from within and without, to take up arms, and to exhaust the Roman will to win this war at any cost."[34] But they lost. Simon Bar Kochba was killed in the summer of A.D. 135 while defending the town of Bethar. His great campaign was over.

Hadrian, wanting to eradicate Judaea from memory, changed the name of Judaea to Palaestina (now Palestine). But two generations later, the population was finally granted considerable autonomy – including being excused from "any duty that clashes with the observance of their religious rules and beliefs."[35]

It seems that the Romans still recalled the rivers of blood that their reconquest of Judaea had cost. And it still hurt.

I became friendly with Mordechai Gichon in Israel during a period when I was regularly involved in archaeological work with Robert Eisenman and his team from California State University in Long Beach. Gichon's extensive knowledge of Bar Kochba fascinated me, and he was intrigued and interested by the thesis in *Holy Blood, Holy Grail*, which he had read. He once took me – along with some of the students and volunteers helping our excavation efforts at the Dead Sea – to visit one of the last Bar Kochba fortresses to be taken by the Roman troops. It was a forlorn ruin near Emmaus in the Judaean foothills, halfway between Jerusalem and the coast. It had never been excavated, and Professor Gichon wanted the chance to do so. I was soon to find out why.

Under the stone-paved platform of the fortress was a warren of tunnels. After the fall of the fortress to the Romans, the defenders retreated to these tunnels, which we crawled along on our hands and knees. They would have been able to hear the Romans talking just a few feet above them. A curiosity of the site lay in the design of the cisterns: those supplying the fortress were accessible from above through a hole in the paved platform, rather like a well. But these cisterns were roughly circular and bulbous, that is, water stretched beyond the access hole for some yards underneath the paved platform. The tunnels beneath allowed the former defenders access to the edge of the bulbous cisterns out of sight of the Romans so that they were able to live beneath the fortress for some weeks, drawing water without the Romans suspecting their presence. But their main refuge was even deeper in the hill, in underground tunnels reached by only one entrance from the upper level of tunnels. The Bar Kochba fighters and their families would probably have come up only to draw water.

When the Romans finally discovered what was happening beneath their feet, they filled the cisterns with stones, destroying the water source. Then they broke into the tunnel complex and crawled in seeking to destroy the Bar Kochba fighters who had fled down to the deeper levels.

Gichon asked me to follow him as he crawled along ahead of me through the claustrophobic tunnels. We then reached one that turned down into the rocky hillside at a steep angle. It had been sealed up with stone and mortar.

"The Romans sealed this up permanently," he explained to me. He paused for a moment. "This tunnel has never been opened. All the defenders are still down there."

It took me a moment to realize the magnitude of what he was saying. And then I was struck by the scene of tragedy and horror that would await the first archaeologist to remove the stonework and crawl down into the tunnel. I have never forgotten that small bricked-up entrance to the refuge that, in a few minutes almost 1,900 years ago, became a sealed tomb for the living.

This, then, was the world within which Jesus, his followers, and at least the first of his later biographers lived. It was also the world out of which Christianity emerged. And it is the connection between these two parts of that world that is so contentious. It was, as we have seen, a time when belief was everything and the wrong belief in the wrong context could bring a sudden death, either from the Romans via crucifixion or from the zealous Sicarii via lethal dagger.

Few of these events have found their way into the Gospels. Instead of history, our New Testament gives us a sanitized, censored, and often inverted view of the times. But even those who brought us the New Testament were unable to entirely cut away the world in which their characters moved. Jesus was born and spent his formative years in the era of the early Zealot movement. When he began his ministry around the age of thirty, some of his closest followers were known to be members of this messianic movement, a movement in which Jesus was born to play an important role. In the New Testament, we can see the arguments against the Romans, and we can pick up a dulled sense of the violence that permeated the era – a sense that sharpens, of course, when we reach the end of the story with the crucifixion of Jesus.

But this crucifixion in their telling has quite deliberately had its political context expunged. This is proof that later censors made a concerted attempt to separate Jesus and his life from the historical times in which he was born, lived, and died – however he eventually met his death. In so doing, these later censors did something far more pernicious:

they removed Jesus from his Jewish context. And today a large number of Christians remain completely unaware that Jesus was never a Christian; he was born, and lived, a Jew.

A generation after the crucifixion of Jesus – or, at least, the removal of him from the scene – Jerusalem and the Temple were lost to Judaism. The faith was instead centered upon the rabbinical school at Jabneh. At the same time began the manipulation of Jesus's story that ultimately created a tradition centered upon Jesus rather than upon God. This was a point upon which many early chroniclers did not agree but one that would eventually take over all alternative explanations. The Jewish origins of Jesus became subsumed within an increasingly influential pagan context introduced by converts to Christianity from among the Greeks and Romans. This pagan influence drew Christianity and its view of Jesus a long way from Judaism in the succeeding centuries.

The audience for the Christian message had clearly changed: it was no longer intended for Jews but rather addressed pagans – believers in gods and goddesses like Mithras, Dionysius, Isis, and Demeter – and as such it needed to be presented in a new package, one laced with an anti-Jewish flavor. The field was ripe for the reinterpretation of history and the beginning of the triumph of the artificial "Jesus of faith" over the true "Jesus of history" – a man who spoke of God, who expressed a divine message, but who did not himself claim to be God.

In what is probably a true miracle, one of the Gospels, while creating a distance between Jesus and his Jewish

context, still maintains elements of the Jesus of history and
the inclusiveness of his teaching on divinity:

> The Jews fetched stones to stone him, so Jesus said to
> them, "I have done many good works for you to see ...
> for which of these are you stoning me?" The Jews an-
> swered him, "We are not stoning you for doing a good
> work but for blasphemy: you are only a man and you
> claim to be God." Jesus answered, "Is it not written in
> your Law: I said, you are gods? So the Law uses the
> word gods of those to whom the word of God was ad-
> dressed." (John 10:31–35)

Between the time these words were spoken and committed to writing, perhaps near the end of the first century A.D.,
Jesus had been made a Christian. And to be a Christian
meant to follow teachings far removed from those of
Judaism. This is clearly evident in a recorded dialogue between the second-century church father Justin Martyr and
a Jewish teacher named Trypho. The latter makes the very
reasonable point that "those who affirm [Jesus] to have
been a man, and to have been anointed by election, and then
to have become Christ, appear to me to speak more plausibly."[36] To further his point he poses a challenge to Justin:
"Answer me then, first, how you can show that there is
another God besides the Maker of all things; and then
you will show, [further,] that He submitted to be born of
the Virgin."[37]

Leaving aside the particulars of the debate and Justin's responses – ambiguous and weak, according to Trypho – what is clear is that a distance had evolved between the two religions that was now unbridgeable. There was little point of compromise left among those who were marching resolutely into that horizon that would become Christian orthodoxy. For Justin, only belief in Christ mattered, and such belief could bring salvation to anyone, "even although they neither keep the Sabbath, nor are circumcised, nor observe the feasts."[38]

As we can see, the Jewish law had been left far behind – along with the true history of Jesus.

JUDAEA, JESUS, AND CHRISTIANITY

Before 4 B.C.	Birth of Jesus, according to Matthew's Gospel (2:1).
4 B.C.	Death of Herod the Great.
A.D. 6	Birth of Jesus, according to Luke's Gospel (2:1–7). Census of Quirinius, Governor of Syria.
A.D. 27–28	Baptism of Jesus (traditional date) in the fifteenth year of the reign of Emperor Tiberius (Luke 3:1–23).
A.D. 30	Crucifixion of Jesus, according to Catholic scholarship.
c. A.D. 35	Following the marriage of Herod Antipas and Herodias in c. A.D. 34, John the Baptist is executed, following the evidence in Josephus.

A.D. 36   Passover – crucifixion of Jesus, according to Matthew's timetable.

A.D. 36–37   Conversion of Paul on the road to Damascus.

c. A.D. 44   Execution of James, the brother of Jesus.

A.D. 50–52   Paul in Corinth. Writes his first letter (to the Thessalonians).

A.D. 61   Paul in Rome under house arrest.

c. A.D. 65   Paul supposedly executed.

A.D. 66–73   War in Judaea. The Roman army under Vespasian invades Judaea.

c. A.D. 55–120   Life of Tacitus, Roman historian and senator, who mentions Christ.

c. A.D. 61–c. 114 Life of Pliny the Younger, who mentions Christ.

c. A.D. 115   Ignatius, Bishop of Antioch, quotes from letters of Paul.

c. A.D. 117–138   Suetonius, Roman historian, mentions "Chrestus."

c. A.D. 125   Earliest known example of a Christian gospel, John 18: 31–33, Rylands Papyrus, found in Egypt.

c. A.D. 200——   Oldest known fragment of Paul's letters, Chester Beatty Papyrus, found in Egypt.

c. A.D. 200——   Oldest virtually complete gospel (John's), Bodmer Papyrus, found in Egypt.

A.D. 325   Council of Nicaea is convened by the Roman emperor Constantine. The divinity of Jesus is made official dogma by a vote of 217 to 3.

A.D. 393–397   Council of Hippo, formalizing the New Testament, is finalized at Council of Carthage.

THE SECOND CENTURY

c. A.D. 55 – 120 Life of Tacitus, Roman historian and senator, who mentions Christ.

c. A.D. 61 – c. 114 Life of Pliny the Younger, who mentions Christ.

c. A.D. 115 Ignatius, bishop of Antioch, quotes from letters of Paul.

A.D. 115 Revolt in Alexandria is led by Lucuas, the "King of the Jews." The Jewish community in Egypt is destroyed.

c. A.D. 117 – 138 Writing years of Suetonius, Roman historian, who mentions "Chrestus."

c. A.D. 120 The Gnostic teacher Valentinus is educated in Alexandria.

A.D. 131 – 135 Simon Bar Kochba leads revolt in Judaea.

A.D. 133 Nine to twelve Roman legions invade Judaea from the north.

A.D. 135 Jewish forces are defeated. The Roman emperor Hadrian changes the name of Judaea to Palaestina (now Palestine).

c. A.D. 135 The Christian theologian Justin Martyr argues with the Jewish intellectual Trypho.

c. A.D. 140 Marcion arrives in Rome and begins teaching. He rejects the Old Testament and uses only Luke's Gospel and some of Paul's letters.

c. A.D. 150 First Christian writers begin to condemn the Gnostics.

A.D. 154 Justin Martyr names Simon Magus (mid-first-century A.D.) the source of all heresies.

c. A.D. 180   Irenaeus, bishop of Lyons, writes against the Gnostics. Produces the first list of texts for a canonical New Testament.

c. A.D. 195   Clement, bishop of Alexandria, writes about the secret Gospel of Mark and against the Gnostics, but maintains a sympathy for the secrets, mysteries, and initiations within Alexandrian Christianity.

c. A.D. 197   Tertullian converts to Christianity; is militantly opposed to heresy and to women in leadership roles in the Church.

5

Creating the Jesus of Faith

Modern Christian illustrations depict the popular image of Jesus wandering around ancient Israel – the sun gilding his blond hair yet never burning his fair skin. They portray him as a Christian missionary accompanied by his disciples, some of whom were already scribbling down their Gospels in order to record the sacred words of a living god.

We have already pointed out the obvious flaw in this picture: Jesus was a Jew. He was a dark Palestinian, not a fair northern European. But there is another profound error in this image, one equally significant but less well known: there was no such thing as a gospel at the time, let alone a "New Testament"; there was no "Christianity." The sacred books that Jesus and his disciples used were those of Judaism – as is immediately apparent to anyone who reads the New

Testament and notes how familiar Jesus was with the
Judaic scriptures, the ease with which he quoted from them,
and the assumption of familiarity on the part of his audience – presuming, of course, that the events depicted in the
Gospels actually happened.

Because we've always been told with such confidence that
the various Gospels had been written by the latter part of
the first century A.D., it is a surprise to discover that there
wasn't a New Testament in existence at the beginning of the
second century A.D. Or even by the end of that century, although by that time some theologians, nervous about what
they considered to be the "truth," were attempting to create one. Despite these theologians' best efforts, Christians
had to wait almost two more centuries for an agreed-upon
text. So what was it that they were really waiting for?

This delay in arriving at an official collection of Christian texts calls into serious question the widespread Christian belief over the last 1,500 years that every word in the
New Testament is a faithful transmission from God himself. To an independent observer, it seems more likely not
only that the New Testament was deliberately imposed
upon a god who was actually quite happy with a wide expression of teachings, but that it was deliberately imposed
by a group of people who wished to control the divine expression for their own profit and power.

The delay, as it happens, occurred while the theology was
catching up with the demand for a centralized orthodoxy.
Until key decisions were made with regard to the divinity

of Jesus, the leaders of the Church lacked the officially sanctioned criteria by which to choose the texts designed to represent their newly created religion.

Even more crucially, many people today consider the New Testament texts sacrosanct. They believe them to be the divine words of God written as the only means by which we might be saved, words that cannot be changed or taken in any other way than literally. No one has ever told them that this was not the intention of the early compilers of the traditions about Jesus that make up the collection. In fact, for the first 150 years of the Christian tradition the only authoritative writings were those books now called the "Old Testament."[1]

A good example of the early attitude toward scripture is given by the second-century Christian writer Justin Martyr. For him our so-called Gospels were simply memoirs of the various apostles that could be read in church and used in support of the faith but were never considered as "Holy Scripture." The term "Holy Scripture" was reserved for the books of the law and the prophets – that is, the Old Testament. Bluntly, Justin Martyr "never considers the 'Gospels' or the 'Memoirs of the Apostles' as inspired writings."[2] Justin reached the pinnacle of sainthood, but his position would be considered radical if held by any member of the Christian Church today.

It is certainly true, however, that during the later first century and the entire second century A.D., traditions about Jesus began to be recorded. Sayings and stories about the events of his life were collected, but none were deemed the official or authorized collection at that time. It is also true that the texts that now appear in our New Testament were written in that span. During the late first and second centuries A.D., the whole concept of "Christianity" crystallized out of messianic Judaism, and this leads us immediately to a number of logistical challenges, some of them quite radical.

A curious phenomenon began in the second century B.C.: the Aramaic word *meshíha* – messiah – which is otherwise devoid of any explanation, began to be used as the name of the true ruler of Israel. In particular, it denoted the expected king of the royal Line of David.[3] A general hope that a descendant of King David would arrive found expression in the books of the prophets in the Old Testament. Thus, the Christian use of the term *christos*, or "Christ," a Greek translation of the Aramaic *meshíha*, along with the transliteration into Greek *Messías* – now "messiah" – came from a Jewish context and usage that was already well understood by Jesus's day.[4]

The most radical logistical challenge is answering a charge that has regularly been made, particularly over the last 150 years: that Jesus didn't exist at all and the stories about him are simply tales of various messianic leaders that were later gathered together in order to justify, first a Pauline position, and later, a Roman-centered tradition wherein the Jewish messiah was turned into a deified imperial figure, a kind of royal angel. William Horbury, reader in Jewish and Early Christian Studies at Cambridge

University, recently noted, "A cult of angels ... accompanied the development of the cult of Christ."[5]

Can we really be sure that Jesus existed? Is there any proof of his reality beyond the New Testament? If not, if the New Testament was put together long after his time, how do we know that the whole concept of Jesus Christ is not just an ancient myth given a new spin? Perhaps it was some rewriting of the Adonis myth or the Osiris myth or the Mithras myth: all three were born of a virgin and raised from the dead – a familiar story to Christians.

There is considerable reason, according to Horbury, for seeing, within early Christianity, "a cult of Christ, comparable with the cults of Graeco-Roman heroes, sovereigns and divinities."[6] And as mentioned earlier, this cult was accompanied by a cult of angels. Horbury explains that it appears likely that the title given to Jesus, "Son of man," linked him with "an angel-like messiah."[7] In fact, "Christ, precisely in his capacity as messiah, could be considered an angelic spirit... It seems likely that messianism formed the principal medium through which angelology impinged on nascent Christology, and that Christ, precisely as messiah, was envisaged as an angel-like spiritual being."[8] So are we dealing solely with an ancient myth revisited for the purposes of Christianity?

We have seen that the word "Jesus" derives simply from the Aramaic *Yeshua*, which can mean Joshua but also can mean "the deliverer," the "savior." Therefore, it could just be a title. We've also noted that "Christ" comes from *chris-tos*, the Greek translation of the Aramaic *meshiha*, meaning "the anointed one." So we are dealing with a double title: "The deliverer (or savior), the anointed one." In that case, what was his name? We really don't know – someone "ben David" we would assume, but that is all we can glean.

We cannot appeal to the New Testament for evidence because we have no idea how much history and how much fantasy is incorporated into the texts. And in any case, the earliest fragments we have are from the second century A.D. – around A.D. 125 for some pieces of John's Gospel. But what about the letters of Paul? After all, they were written before the first war against the Romans. The earliest – Paul's first letter to the Thessalonians – was written while he was resident in Corinth from the winter of A.D. 50 to the summer of 52.[9] The rest of his letters were written between A.D. 56 and 60, perhaps even later when he was in Rome and supposedly executed around A.D. 65 – although no one knows the truth about this since the Book of Acts, our only source for details of Paul's travels, breaks off with him under house arrest in Rome.

Unfortunately, we cannot be sure about the authenticity of all Paul's letters within the New Testament either, since the earliest copies we have date from the early third century.[10] In the letters written in A.D. 115 by Ignatius, Bishop of Antioch, on his way to Rome, he quotes from various letters of Paul, so we know that some were in existence by this time, but we do not know whether they might have been edited, before or after. In any case, Paul did not know Jesus, and unlike the Gospels, he did not show any great concern about what Jesus may have said or done. We get no information about Jesus from Paul, whose letters proclaim the gospel of, well, Paul: that the crucifixion and resurrection of Jesus marked the beginning of a new age in the history of the world, the most immediate practical effect being the end of the Jewish law – quite a different stance to that taken by Jesus in the Sermon on the Mount: "Think not that I am come to destroy the law, or the prophets: I am not come to destroy, but to fulfill" (Matthew 5:17).

No records from Pilate have survived either; there are also no records from Herod, and no records from the Roman military or other administrative bodies. But this is not surprising, as the records office of the Herodian kings in Jerusalem was burned during the war. The official Roman records would have been in their administrative capital, Caesarea, and it too was caught up in the fighting. Copies and reports would have gone back to Rome, but even if they survived the various destructions by later emperors like Domitian, they would have been lost in the sack of Rome by the Goths in A.D. 405, when so many official archives were destroyed – those that had not been taken to Constantinople. Of course, by that time Rome was Christian, and so we can be certain that any documents that compromised the developing story of Christ would have already been extracted and destroyed. And there is good reason to think that Pilate's reports would have been among such documents.

But all is not lost: Josephus certainly had access to Roman records, and if Jesus had been mentioned, he would have been able to read of him. In fact, Josephus does mention Jesus, but in such a manner as to lead everyone who has looked at the text to consider it a later Christian insertion, although there is probably a kernel of truth in his discussion somewhere. But Josephus cannot help us entirely, for he has proven to be an unreliable witness and chronicler. Our other Jewish chronicler and philosopher, Philo of Alexandria, who died around A.D. 50, does not even mention Jesus. This is a curiosity for which there is no good explanation beyond taking it as evidence either for the lack of Jesus's reality or for his irrelevance to the lives of educated Jewish Alexandrians.

However, there are surviving works of two Roman historians who both enjoyed access to Roman records and who had occasion to investigate the Christians long before any orthodoxy developed in the Church. Their testimony is therefore very important. Based on their accounts, the fact that official reports mentioning the Christians existed in the Roman archives cannot be denied. The first of these historians was the early church writer Tertullian (c. A.D. 160 – 225), who wrote of these records as an acknowledged fact, although it does not seem that he had access to any.[11]

The historian Tacitus (c. A.D. 55 – 120) was a Roman senator during the time of Domitian and was later governor of western Anatolia in Turkey; in the latter capacity, he had ample opportunity to interrogate Christians – called *Chrestiani* – who were hauled into his courtrooms. Writing of the burning of Rome during the reign of Nero, he explains:

> Nero fabricated scapegoats – and punished with every refinement the notoriously depraved Christians (as they were popularly called). Their originator, Christ, had been executed in Tiberius' reign by the governor of Judaea, Pontius Pilate. But in spite of this temporary setback the deadly superstition had broken out afresh, not only in Judaea (where the mischief had started) but even in Rome.

Because, he adds in a sarcastic aside, "All degraded and shameful practices collect and flourish in the capital."[12]

Tacitus's friend and student, Pliny the Younger, also mentions the Christians. He had occasion to interrogate a number of them formally and reported back to Rome that they sang hymns to "Christus" as if he were a god.[13]

The second-century pagan writers Lucian and Celsus portray Jesus as a sorcerer and a "fomenter of rebellion"[14] – both of which activities were crimes under Roman law and carried the death penalty. We have also the later quote, which we have already noted, from the historian Suetonius, who, writing around 117–38, explains that during the rule of Claudius the Jews rioted in Rome at the instigation of "Chrestus."[15]

There is then little doubt that Jesus *Christos* – the messiah – existed, since these Roman writers are rather matter of fact about it. Not only that, but these Roman writers all concur that the records showed this messiah was tried and "executed" for political actions.

But we mustn't be too confident: what specifically is it that the writers know? Who is it they are speaking of? They may be speaking of "Christos" or "Chrestos" – that is, the "messiah" – but we still do not know his name. We can only be certain that Pontius Pilate, during the time of Tiberius, executed a Jewish "messiah" who was a political rebel against Rome and thus merited the sentence of crucifixion. From this "messiah" a movement grew that, by the end of the century at least, was called "Christian."

Try as we might, we cannot get away from the importance of the second century A.D. for the beginning of the recording of the cult of Jesus. The earliest fragment of any part of the New Testament we have is part of the Gospel of John written about A.D. 125 in Egypt (now held in the John Rylands Library in Manchester, England), but the text or tradition from which it was written clearly dates back to an even earlier time. By the end of the century, we have hundreds of documents representing many different texts, from Gospels to various Acts. Harvard University's Professor Helmut Koester analyzes quite a few of these works in his book *Ancient Christian Gospels*. There are a surprisingly large number of them – the Gospel of Peter, the Gospel of

Thomas, the Secret Gospel of Mark, the Gospel according to the Egyptians, then the letters of Clement, Bishop of Rome, others of Peter, and documents such as the Apocryphon of James, the Dialogue of the Savior, the unknown texts recorded in the Egerton Papyrus No. 2 in the British Museum, and a number of infancy stories. All were current in the second century A.D., and all have a very good chance of carrying some original and valid information about Jesus deriving from either the oral record or various very early compilations of "sayings."

With such a wide range of "Jesus memoirs" having been recorded, it is not surprising that some very different approaches had developed. Furthermore, it is also not surprising that one particular strain attempted to dominate: that based upon the work of Paul, which was supported by those Christians with a pagan, rather than a Jewish, background.

Paul's letters in the New Testament are very different from the Gospels. For one thing, Paul does not provide any Jesus stories. Paul provides only Paul stories. Paul did not know Jesus personally – so far as we know – and his teaching was aimed at those potential pagan converts, the Gentiles. It is significant that the Jewish Christian leadership in Jerusalem under the guidance of James, the brother of Jesus, managed to get Paul out of Israel, sending him away, up the coast to Antioch and elsewhere. They must have known that he was not on their side. James and the others were very concerned about the maintenance of Jewish law, while Paul suggested that the law had little relevance at that point – that Gentiles could become Christians without buying into the totality of the law. This idea was anathema to James, as his letter says: "For whosoever shall keep the whole law, and yet offend in one point, he is guilty of all" (James 2:10).

Paul's approach, by contrast, was "circumcision of the heart, not of the flesh" (Romans 2:29). He held to a flexibility with regard to the Jewish law. "A man is justified by faith," wrote Paul, "without the deeds of the law." He asked, "Do we then make void the law through faith?" Then he answered his rhetorical question: "God forbid; ... we establish the law" (Romans 3:28 – 31).

This brings us to the basic fault line that separated two strong traditions as Christianity moved into the second century A.D.: on the one side were those who sought knowledge, and on the other were those who were content with belief. It is important that we distinguish between the two since this fault line is one of the primary forces that ultimately crystallized the orthodox Christian position.

"Faith is the substance of things hoped for, the evidence of things not seen." So wrote Paul in his Letter to the Hebrews (11:1). But faith is a lesser thing than knowledge. I have always regarded that as self-evident, but let me explain with an example.

One can be afraid of fire because one believes that by placing a hand in the flames, it will be burned and pain will be the result. One can have faith that this is true. But until this is actually done – until one's hand is actually placed in the flames and the pain from burning is caused – one cannot truly *know* what such pain is like. This experiential knowledge – different from knowing, for example, that two plus two is four – is called *gnosis* in Greek. For this very reason, members of the mystical groups within Christianity who wished to experience God for themselves called themselves Gnostics. It is not known when this idea began within Christianity, but such a mystical approach based upon profound personal experience had long been common in the pagan religions. The second century A.D. saw this approach rapidly increase in popularity throughout the Christian Church.

The Gnostics, despite the complexity of much of their literature, were concerned less about the facts *about* Jesus and God, less concerned about faith in the various scriptures and memoirs, than they were concerned about *knowing*, directly, for themselves, through experience, what God was. They were concerned less about faith in Jesus's words and more about becoming just like him and, like him, about *knowing* God. As one of the Gnostic texts found at Nag Hammadi, the Gospel of Thomas, expresses it: "When you come to know yourselves, then you will become known, and you will realize that it is you who are the sons of the living Father."[16]

It cannot be stressed enough that the material used to support any of the myriad emerging viewpoints was selected by using theological criteria: someone, some group, sat down and decided – from their perspective and understanding – that this book should be considered "authentic" and that book should be considered "false," that is, as "orthodox" or as "heretical." That theological grounds were used does not, of course, automatically justify the decisions made despite all the appeals to divine guidance that were put forth. Very human decisions were made, based upon very human priorities – mostly concerning control and power. As Koester writes, "In the earliest period of Christianity, the epithets 'heretical' and 'orthodox' are meaningless."[17] What is even greater nonsense is to think that the books we have in our New Testament are the only authentic traditions about Jesus. Once again, Koester's comment is blunt: "Only dogmatic prejudice can assert that the canonical writings have an exclusive claim to apostolic origin and thus to historical priority."[18] In fact, our New Testament was not settled until the Councils of Hippo and Carthage in A.D. 393 and 397 – over 360 years after the events they refer to.

Around A.D. 140, a wealthy shipowner and convert to Christianity, Marcion, traveled from his home of Pontus and went to Rome, where he formed his own community and from which he established communities all over the Roman empire. All of his writings have been lost, but according to his critics, he claimed that only Paul knew the truth: he regarded the other disciples as too influenced by Judaism. He rejected the "Old Testament" totally and used only certain of the Pauline letters together with an edited version of

Luke, which he referred to as a "gospel." He was, it appears, the earliest person to use this term in relation to a written text. His organization was the first Christian church to have its own sacred scripture.[19] For him, Christianity had to irrevocably replace everything deriving from the Jewish "Old Testament" tradition, including the books of the prophets. He was perhaps the greatest danger to the Church in the mid to latter first century, and in A.D. 144 he was formally excommunicated from the Church at Rome.

But the effect of Marcion's use of the texts was to force the growing Christian tradition to leave behind the oral tradition and begin a written tradition based upon "gospels" whose authorship was attributed to various apostles in order to establish an acceptable official canon of sacred "New Testament" literature. This desire to formulate an official list of texts was first put into form by Irenaeus, Bishop of Lyons, the capital of Roman Gaul.

He and his fellow guardians of orthodoxy would have no part of any deviation from what they held to be "the truth." They were not impressed with the obsessive Paulism of Marcion; neither did they carry any affection whatsoever for the Gnostics, who held that direct knowledge of the Divine was superior to any faith or belief. Taking the lead against this position, Irenaeus, about A.D. 180, wrote a monumental work in five books attacking the Gnostics, his famous *Against Heresies*.

Irenaeus was clearly having considerable trouble from the Gnostics. They were, he says, leading away members of his flock "under a pretence of superior knowledge."[20] He complains about their attacking him with arguments, parables, and tendentious questions.[21] After reading some of their literature and speaking with various Gnostics about their beliefs, he resolved to find a way to attack and disprove their teachings, which he truly abhorred.[22] During the course of his long assault in *Against Heresies* he gives much information about them and about the beliefs of the emerging orthodoxy in the late second century A.D.

He is aware of the Gnostics' claim to be privy to some secret information: they declare, he says, "that Jesus spoke in a mystery to his disciples and apostles privately."[23] He also points out that this suggestion of an esoteric understanding passed down from the previous century is somehow connected with the resurrection of the dead. The Gnostics, Irenaeus explains, do not take the resurrection literally; in fact, they see much in the scriptures, especially the parables, as symbolic – as stories that need interpretation in order to glean the underlying message.[24] For them, the resurrection from the dead is a symbolic means of presenting someone who has experienced the "Truth" taught by Gnosticism.[25]

Curiously, Irenaeus uses this as one of his points to refute the Gnostics: raising from the dead in the Church had been performed both in the past and during his own day. He mentions in two places at least one incident of a dead man being brought back to life that seems to have been personally known by him. On this occasion the dead man remained alive for many years afterwards. It's a fascinating story, sadly not developed further, but serves as evidence that Irenaeus had somewhat missed the point.[26]

But whether he missed the point or not, Irenaeus was the torchbearer for orthodoxy during those tricky times when Gnosticism could have taken over the Church. He made it clear which gospels were to be used and which were to be rejected. He first drew together the four gospels of Matthew, Mark, Luke, and John. In effect, he created the identification of the one Divine God Jesus, both Son and eternal Creator.[27] He also made it clear that the central unified organization of the Church was a measure of its universal appeal, nature, and truth. Thus, centralization and orthodoxy were established as proofs of validity and rectitude: physical power was one of the proofs of God's support. Conversely, decentralization was a proof of error. As there was one God, so too there could be only one Church and one truth. A simple but specious argument, it nevertheless convinced many. And even today it has its supporters in the Vatican, one, of course, being the pope.

While theologians were attempting to create a centralized orthodoxy of faith and belief, others were trying to centralize the physical structure of the Church, maintaining that it was better to rule from a position of centralized power. Political concerns – fueled, of course, by the persecutions, which we cannot forget – were as important as theological concerns in shaping the emerging Christianity.

About the same time as Irenaeus was arguing his version

of Christianity, the way that the Church ruled itself was changing. Previously, local churches had been governed by a group of men – presbyter-bishops – but these governing structures were gradually centralized. The group was being replaced by a single bishop who represented the power in each diocese. This process seems to have begun in Rome in the mid-second century and was completed by the early third century. Of course – and we should not be surprised – the bishop of Rome was clear that he was the most important of all these bishops. He wished to be recognized as the supreme ruler of the Church on earth as the representative of the messiah. Pope Stephen I (254–57) was the first bishop of Rome to justify this claim of preeminence among all bishops from his succession to the apostle Peter. He based his claim upon the Gospel of Matthew (16:18): "Thou art Peter and upon this rock I will build my church." It was further claimed that Peter came to Rome and, around the late second century he was identified as the first Christian bishop in the city.[28]

However, in 258, Emperor Valerian ordered the immediate execution of all Christian bishops, priests, and deacons. Many were executed, but many survived. The advantages of centralized power would have been very apparent to the leaders of the Christian Church, who must have felt that should they ever get the opportunity, they would take such power for themselves.

Their first opportunity came during the reign of Constantine. Although he was not baptized a Christian until he was on his deathbed, at least under his rule Christianity was allowed to flourish. Constantine wanted unity; he called the Council of Nicaea to oppose the ideas of the heretic Arius. The aim was to get support for the idea that Jesus Christ was "of one being" with God the Father, a claim that Arius and others disputed; for them, Jesus was not divine. As Princeton's Professor Elaine Pagels dryly observes, "Those who opposed this phrase pointed out that it occurs neither in the Scriptures nor in Christian tradition."[29] But the objections proved of no consequence to the politically ruthless theologians who traveled to Nicaea with a set agenda in mind.

The Council was clearly loaded against the views of Arius, but the presence of his supporters made for stormy meetings and heated discussions. In fact, it appears possible that during one angry exchange the bishop of Myra physically assaulted the emaciated and ascetic Arius, as depicted in traditional pictures of the proceedings. The arguments spilled out of the Council and into the streets of Nicaea: parodies of the disputes were played for laughs in the public theaters, and everywhere about the city the disputes were argued by the market traders, the shop-keepers, the money-changers. "Inquire the price of bread, and you are told, 'The Son is subordinate to the Father.' Ask if the bath is ready, and you are told, 'The Son arose out of nothing.'"[30]

In the end, a vote was taken. The exact numbers are disputed, but it is known that Arius and two of his colleagues voted against the decree; the accepted figure is that the proposition was carried by a vote of 217 to 3. Arius and his two colleagues were exiled to the Danube area.

In a curious, even bizarre, appendix to this episode, when, on his deathbed, Constantine was baptized, the ceremony was performed by a member of the heretical Arian church. This reveals that for Constantine details of theology were less important than adopting any idea that best served unity, which, for him, was stability, and that was his overriding concern.

By this decision, the Council of Nicaea created the literally fantastic Jesus of faith and adopted the pretense that this was a historically accurate rendering. Its actions also established the criteria by which the New Testament books would later be chosen. The Council of Nicaea produced a world of Christianity where a code of belief was held in common. Anything different was to be deemed heresy and to be rejected and, if possible, exterminated.

We are still suffering from this today. In an unusual move for an academic, Pagels, an expert on the Gnostic texts, introduces a personal note in her book *Beyond Belief: The Secret Gospel of Thomas*. The note addresses a crucial point with far-reaching consequences: what she cannot love in the Church, she explained, is "the tendency to identify Christianity with a single authorized set of beliefs ... coupled with the conviction that Christian belief alone offers access to God."

Realizing the high cost of failure, subsequent bishops of Rome consolidated power – and none more so than Pope

Damasus I (366–84), who hired a group of killers to spend three days massacring his opponents. When Damasus had seized back control, he termed Rome "the apostolic see" – in other words, the only place in the entire Church that might claim a continuous succession from the apostles, thereby maintaining and acting as heir to their authority and function. Of course, this claim left Jerusalem out of the loop. Any Zealot follower of Jesus would have found this claim preposterous and self-evidently untrue.

Ignoring any such implications, Damasus claimed to be the true and direct successor to Peter and so rightfully inherited the Church that Christ had founded upon him. As ultimate authority on earth, Damasus also established the principle that the true measure of any creed to be considered orthodox was whether it received papal endorsement. In such a blatant manner was the claim of apostolic succession enforced.

The next pope, Siricius (384–99), imitated the imperial chancery by issuing decrees – commands that were considered beyond discussion, commands that were to be immediately obeyed. Under his dogmatic authority, the canon of the New Testament was finally settled at the Council of Hippo in A.D. 393 and the Council of Carthage in A.D. 397.

This overt process of taking and centralizing power continued: Pope Innocent I (401–17) presented the claim, now inevitable, that as the apostolic see, Rome represented supreme authority in the Christian Church. But the greatest of the power-taking popes was Leo I (440–61). He established finally, without compromise, the claim that persists today: that Christ gave supreme authority over the Church to Peter; that this authority was transmitted from Peter to each succeeding bishop of Rome; and that the bishop of Rome, the pope, was "the primate of all the bishops" in the Church and acted as the "mystical embodiment" of Peter. It remained only for his successor, Pope Gelasius I (492–521), to enunciate the most arrogant of all statements: he wrote to the emperor explaining that the world was governed by two great powers – the spiritual authority vested in the pope and the temporal authority vested in the emperor. Of the two, he explained, the pope's authority was superior because it "provided for the salvation of the temporal." At the synod held in Rome on 13 May 495, Gelasius was the first pope to be called "Vicar of Christ."

At the same time as theological dominance was being coveted and seized, in a psychologically astute move the Church began taking physical possession of pagan sites and festivals – that of the Birth of Mithras on 25 December being just one that is still with us today. The Church's reasoning was clearly expressed by Pope Gregory I (590–604) in A.D. 601 in his instructions to an abbot about to depart for Britain. "We have come to the conclusion," the pope wrote,

> that the temples of the idols among that people should on no account be destroyed. The idols are to be destroyed, but the temples themselves are to be aspersed

with holy water, altars set up in them, and relics deposited there. For if these temples are well-built, they must be purified from the worship of demons and dedicated to the service of the true god. In this way, we hope that the people, seeing that their temples are not destroyed, may abandon their error and, flocking more readily to their accustomed resorts, may come to know and adore the true god. And since they have a custom of sacrificing many oxen to demons, let some other solemnity be substituted in its place, such as a day of Dedication or the Festivals of the holy martyrs whose relics are enshrined there.[31]

Although the Church, in support of the growing orthodoxy, may have left the altars intact, they certainly did not shy away from the destruction or forging of documents. So just how did the people feel about this?

Let us turn our attention to Eunapius to find out. Eunapius was a Greek teacher of rhetoric who lived from around 345 until around A.D. 420. Rhetoric is the art of persuasive and impressive expression, either in writing or via speech. Our modern spin doctor is an heir to techniques perfected by the ancients. At the age of sixteen, Eunapius went to study in Athens. While there, he was initiated into the Eleusinian Mysteries, becoming a priest of the College of Eumolpidae just outside Athens. The Eumolpidae were one of the "families" of priests who experienced and taught the Mysteries of Demeter and Persephone at Eleusis to the select few – both men and women – who had proven ready to learn these mysteries. These few were referred to as initiates.

After five years in Athens, Eunapius returned to his hometown of Sardis in Turkey and fell in with a local group of Platonic philosophers, learning medicine and theurgy – a very practical working *with* the divine powers by means of ritual, dance, and music.[32] He was alive when the emperor Theodosius banned all pagan religions in A.D. 391, but despite the dangers, Eunapius fiercely criticized Christianity in his writings.

Eunapius wrote biographical histories of contemporary philosophers. He also delved into general history, writing a supplement to a published history by another writer. Eunapius added details to this book covering the years A.D. 270 to 404. He finished around A.D. 414. Unfortunately, only small pieces of this history have survived. But there is a mystery about this loss.

Emperor Constantine reigned from A.D. 306 to 337, and it was during his time that the Council of Nicaea was convened to proclaim Jesus to be "God." It was during his time that Christianity became the official religion of the Roman empire – against the wishes of many. With his interest in unifying the empire, Constantine seems to have taken a solely political view of the religion. Indeed, as we have seen, he was only converted to Christianity himself on his deathbed.

Eunapius, as a believer in what was perceived by Christians to be a pagan religion, can be relied upon to dislike these changes in general and Christianity in particular. We can be certain that his history of the reign of Constantine was treated very critically, with hostility, perhaps even with anger in his supplement to the published history of the time. This would have been very damaging for the emerging Christian orthodoxy of the early fifth century. Eunapius, as a follower of theurgy, would also have had some interesting things to say on the subject of the emperor Julian (A.D. 361 – 63), who was also a devotee of the ritual technique and who tried to return the empire to paganism, specifically to the Platonic thought of one of the greatest and most underrated philosophers of late classical times, the teacher of theurgy, Iamblichus of Apamea (c. A.D. 240 – c. 325).

Eunapius's history would be a very interesting text to have today. Sadly, we would have had a copy were it not for the Vatican and its relentless need to protect its fraudulent picture of Christ and Christianity, for a copy of Eunapius's book existed in the all too often impenetrable Vatican library as late as the sixteenth century.

This was reported by the classical scholar Marc-Antoine de Muret, who in 1563 was lecturing at the University in Rome. There he saw a copy of Eunapius's *History* in the Vatican library. He found it so interesting that he asked Cardinal Sirlet, one of the leading scholars at the Vatican, to arrange for a copy to be made. But Sirlet declined and, with the pope's support, stated that this book of Eunapius's was "impious and wicked." Once attention had been drawn to this work, the authorities sought a solution to the problem. It was very simple: a learned Jesuit scholar later reported that Eunapius's *History* "had perished by an act of Divine providence."[33] Undoubtedly providence acted through the less than divine agency of men.

The Vatican has a history of obtaining – and destroying – writings that run counter to the myth it is promulgating as true history. How much else has been destroyed over the years? And how much else is out there that might have escaped the Vatican's relentless and single-minded pursuit of the heretical? No one can be certain.

By the fifth century A.D., the victory of the Jesus of faith over the Jesus of history was, in all practical matters, complete. The myth that the two are the same became theologically justified and as such an accepted truth. However, the protectors of orthodoxy could not rest, of course, because, like corrosion and decay, heresy, in their minds, never sleeps. They ruthlessly protected the faith by doing to other Christians what the pagan emperors had done previously. In A.D. 386 they executed Priscillian, bishop of Ávila, on the grounds of heresy. This was the first execution ordered by the Church in order to defend its position.

All roads may have led to Rome, but over the succeeding centuries, so did an increasing number of rivulets of blood. The price of theological unity was paid not just in gold –

although that would always find a welcome home in the hands of the Church – but in lives as well.

Priscillian's death was a tragic precedent. Sadly, it was to be oft repeated – all in the name of a Jewish messiah who preached peace.

Judaea, Jesus, and Christianity

Before 4 B.C.	Birth of Jesus, according to Matthew's Gospel (2:1).
4 B.C.	Death of Herod the Great.
A.D. 6	Birth of Jesus, according to Luke's Gospel (2:1–7). Census of Quirinius, Governor of Syria.
A.D. 27–28	Baptism of Jesus (traditional date) in the fifteenth year of the reign of Emperor Tiberius (Luke 3:1–23).
A.D. 30	Crucifixion of Jesus, according to Catholic scholarship.
c. A.D. 35	Following the marriage of Herod Antipas and Herodias in c. A.D. 34, John the Baptist is executed, following the evidence in Josephus.
A.D. 36	Passover – crucifixion of Jesus, according to Matthew's timetable.
A.D. 36–37	Conversion of Paul on the road to Damascus.
c. A.D. 44	Execution of James, the brother of Jesus.
A.D. 50–52	Paul in Corinth. Writes his first letter (to the Thessalonians).
A.D. 61	Paul in Rome under house arrest.

c. A.D. 65	Paul supposedly executed.
A.D. 66–73	War in Judaea. The Roman army under Vespasian invades Judaea.
c. A.D. 55–120	Life of Tacitus, Roman historian and senator, who mentions Christ.
c. A.D. 61–c. 114	Life of Pliny the Younger, who mentions Christ.
c. A.D. 115	Ignatius, Bishop of Antioch, quotes from letters of Paul.
c. A.D. 117–138	Suetonius, Roman historian, mentions "Chrestus."
c. A.D. 125	Earliest known example of a Christian gospel, John 18: 31–33, Rylands Papyrus, found in Egypt.
c. A.D. 200—	Oldest known fragment of Paul's letters, Chester Beatty Papyrus, found in Egypt.
c. A.D. 200—	Oldest virtually complete gospel (John's), Bodmer Papyrus, found in Egypt.
A.D. 325	Council of Nicaea is convened by the Roman emperor Constantine. The divinity of Jesus is made official dogma by a vote of 217 to 3.
A.D. 393–397	Council of Hippo, formalizing the New Testament, is finalized at Council of Carthage.

THE THIRD TO FIFTH CENTURIES

A.D. 250	Christians are persecuted under the Roman emperor Decius, beginning with the execution of Bishop Fabian of Rome.
A.D. 254–257	Reign of Pope Stephen I, the first bishop of Rome

to claim Rome's primacy over all other Christian bishops owing to the succession from the apostle Peter.

A.D. 258   The Roman emperor Valerian orders the execution of all Christian clergy.

A.D. 303   The beginning of the persecution of Christians by the Roman emperor Diocletian will be followed by widespread deaths and destruction.

A.D. 313   Edict of Milan by the Roman emperor Constantine declares religious freedom for all Christians.

A.D. 324   Emperor Constantine makes Constantinople (now Istanbul) the capital of the Roman empire. All administrative records are based there.

A.D. 337   Emperor Constantine dies.

A.D. 366–384   Pope Damasus I terms Rome "the apostolic see" – the only place that can claim a continuous descent from the apostles. Orders his secretary, Jerome, to revise the text of the Bible.

A.D. 367   Athanasius, bishop of Alexandria, declares that all "non-canonical" books in Egypt be destroyed.

A.D. 386   Priscillian, bishop of Ávila, Spain, is executed for heresy, the first such execution ordered because of heresy against Church doctrine.

A.D. 390   An army of Gauls lays siege to and destroys much of Rome.

A.D. 401–417   Pope Innocent I establishes the claim that Rome has supreme authority in the Christian Church.

A.D. 410   The Visigoths sack and destroy Rome.

A.D. 440–461   Pope Leo I formally establishes the primacy of

Rome on the basis of the inherited authority of the apostle Peter and the concept of the pope as the "mystical embodiment" of Peter.

How far had the faith fallen into the hands of the self-proclaimed heirs of Christ? The popes of Rome later took it upon themselves to ritually anoint the emperors into their exalted office as part of the ceremony of coronation, as if a pope should have the power to create a messiah. As if they alone had a monopoly over the pathway to truth.

6

Rome's Greatest Fear

It was 5 August 1234. A poor woman lay on her deathbed in a house in Toulouse owned by her son-in-law. She belonged to a mysterious Christian religion that was widespread in the south of France at the time, the Cathars. This religion was both despised and feared by Rome. And the Cathars held Rome in equally low regard. For many Cathars, the pope himself was the Antichrist and the Church of Rome, they said, was "the harlot of the Apocalypse" or "the church of wolves."[1]

On that day, some Cathar priests had visited the woman to give her the faith's most sacred rite, the *consolamentum*, initiating her into the "last rites" of their religion – a common enough occurrence on the deathbed of believers. But their arrival was noted by an informer hostile to their religion.

Perhaps the woman was being spied upon, for she was known as a Cathar supporter by the townsfolk, and her son-in-law acted as a courier for the Toulouse Cathars. The informer rushed to give word to the prior of the house of the Inquisitors.

The Dominican Inquisitors were with the bishop of Toulouse, who had just said mass. It was the day on which the canonization of their founder, Dominic de Guzman, had been proclaimed in Toulouse. The monks were about to have a celebratory meal. Then, by "divine providence," the prior was told of this dying heretic openly accepting the Cathar rites. The prior quickly notified the bishop, who was adamant that the Inquisitors deal with this outrage to the "true" religion without delay, and so, ignoring their meal, the Inquisitors, accompanied by the bishop, rushed to the dying woman's house. They entered her room so suddenly that even a warning call from a concerned friend came too late to avert the impending tragedy.

The bishop sat down beside the ill woman and calmly began to chat with her about her beliefs. She felt no alarm – perhaps she did not know who was visiting her. Perhaps she thought he was a Cathar dignitary instead of one representing Rome. Evidently unconcerned, believing herself to be in sympathetic company, she spoke freely, contented that she had been finally received into the Cathar rites before her death, which was obviously not far off. In fact, her death was closer than she thought.

The bishop led her on, encouraging her to talk: "You must

not lie," he said, feigning sympathy. "I say that you are to be steadfast in your belief, nor in fear of death ought you to confess anything other than what you believe and hold firmly in your heart."[2]

The dying woman, thankful and comfortable in her Cathar faith, replied with considerable composure and dignity. "My lord, what I say I believe, and I shall not change my commitment out of concern for the miserable remnant of my life."[3]

At this, the bishop's countenance abruptly darkened. "Therefore you are a heretic!" he cried loudly to all in the room. "For what you have confessed is the faith of the heretics... Accept what the Roman and Catholic Church believes."

Showing considerable courage, the dying woman refused. So the bishop, invoking Jesus Christ, formally pronounced her a heretic and by so doing, condemned her to death. She was immediately picked up and carried, still on her bed, to a meadow outside the city owned by the count of Toulouse where, on that balmy summer's day, she was immediately burned to death.

The bishop and his Dominican associates then jubilantly made their way back through the streets of Toulouse to their monastic house and, thanking God and their saintly founder, "ate with rejoicing what had been prepared for them." As the chronicler of these events, a Dominican monk who was present in the room, concluded: "God performed these works on the first feast day of the Blessed

Dominic, to the glory and praise of His name ... to the exaltation of the faith and to the discomfiture of the heretics."[4]

The "Blessed Dominic" was a cruel and fanatical Spanish monk, Dominic de Guzman. He had joined the anti-Cathar crusade from the very first, and such was the fame of his zeal that in 1216 his Order of the Dominicans was established by the pope. Their brief was to destroy heresy, utterly and finally, by whatever means proved necessary. Dominic died in 1221, and in 1234, the year the woman of Toulouse was burned alive, he was created a saint by one of his friends who had been elected pope the previous year.

During the twelfth century, particularly in the south of France, the Church had become overtaken by corruption. There was hardly even any pretense at piety among those who ruled the parishes and dioceses and who were more concerned with administering their properties and increasing their incomes than with taking care of their parishioners' souls. Secular amusements, such as cavorting with mistresses, gambling, and hunting, and secular occupations, such as money-lending and charging fees for ecclesiastical office, permitting illegal marriages, and acting as lawyers, were all so common and blatant that finally Pope Innocent III, from his election in 1198, found himself moved to condemn these ecclesiastical practices. The leading ecclesiastic of the Languedoc, the archbishop of Narbonne, at the turn of the thirteenth century was, according to the pope, worshiping at the altar of only one god – that of money. He charged substantial fees for consecrating bishops, took the income from vacant positions, let monks marry, and condoned other practices contrary to church law.[5] The pope dismissed him, along with another archbishop and seven bishops. Even the families of some Catholic clergy turned away from Rome. The bishop of Carcassonne, from 1209 to 1212, maintained his Catholicism while his mother, sister, and three of his brothers all took the consolamentum.[6]

The nobles, especially the rural nobility, were constantly in dispute with the Church over matters of property and income; staunchly loyal to their region, they formed close alliances with the Cathars. Indeed, some members of the nobility went further, taking the consolamentum to become fully professed Cathars. The wife of the count of Foix in the twelfth century, for example, became a "Perfect," as did the count's sister, Esclamonde, after the death of her husband.

The Cathars were a group of holy men and women who embraced a life of renunciation, spirituality, and simplicity – *les Bonhommes*, they called themselves, "the Good Men" or "the Good Christians." They served a population who craved personal religious experience but whose needs were hardly served by the established church, which had abdicated its spiritual role for one more commercial and venal. The Cathars' rejection of worldly gifts served to highlight the avarice of Rome's ecclesiastics and fuel implacable opposition from those whose power they threatened.

The Cathars' opponents termed them "perfected" heretics, the "Perfects." Full members of the faith were those who had taken the central rite, the consolamentum, which has been described as "baptism, confirmation, ordination, and, if received at death's door, extreme unction all rolled into one."[7]

By taking this rite, they distanced themselves from daily life and maintained a disdain for worldly possessions. Thereafter, they lived a very simple existence of prayer and teaching – which they did in the local language, not in Latin. They were vegetarian, they traveled about in pairs and administered spiritual comfort, and for those who wished to know more, they gave the rite of the consolamentum. They represented honesty and truth to those who had had enough of lies and deceit.

In practice, owing to the great responsibility and change of life entailed in taking the consolamentum, most took it only on their deathbed. But all could partake, men and women. Unlike the Catholic Church, there was no male dominance in this movement. The Perfect were of both genders; there was no hierarchy or organization – at least at first.

The Church recognized the challenge posed by these simple and benevolent spiritual teachers, and one of the first to take it up was Bernard of Clairvaux, the shining light of the monastic Order of the Cistercians. He and his Order were, like the Cathars, dedicated to the simple life. Bernard traveled extensively in the south of France in 1145, debating with Cathar Perfects in town squares. Recognizing their piety and appreciating their honesty and simplicity – while condemning their heresy – he found that he was unable to stop the movement, which was continuing to grow in strength and, as a result of these public debates, creating a more formal organization, which was in place by the late twelfth century.

Many of the regional nobles supported the Cathars because they saw the movement as one centered upon their own lands in the Languedoc rather than in Rome, as the Church was. Inevitably, Rome was not happy.

In 1209 it launched a crusade against the Cathars, and mayhem ensued. Northern armies of knights and adventurers descended upon the Languedoc, destroying many of the cities and towns, burning thousands of Cathars alive, sometimes hundreds at once in huge conflagrations. By this time the dilapidated castle of Montségur, perched upon its apparently impregnable rocky hilltop, had been rebuilt as a base for the Cathar church. After the destructions in the lower valleys, in 1232 it became the center of the faith and the seat of a "bishop" of the Cathars. A small village for Cathar Perfects was built between the castle and the precipitously high cliffs to the north, the remains of which can be seen clutching to the hillside to this day.

Accompanying the northern armies was the young Spanish cleric Dominic de Guzman. Little is known of his involvement in the wholesale sacrifice of the Cathars during the first years of fighting, but it was certainly close. During the bitter campaign, he realized that a new organization would be needed to combat what he saw as an evil heresy –

a new order of monks with a new approach. Dominic founded the monastic Order of Dominicans, and together they created what is now the infamous Inquisition. Dominic had burned and tortured; his Dominicans followed his example, ravaging their way through southern France. Such was the Church's need for discipline and control over those heretics who had dared to ignore Rome. A cold horror swept the land. Dominic's Inquisitors were feared and hated everywhere. Many were beaten or murdered, but the Order continued its relentless pursuit of heretics. For the Cathars, it was a battle they could not win.

The Inquisition's methods were simple: those suspected of heresy were "put to the question," a euphemism that hid – even sought to excuse – the reality that no simple interrogation would ensue but rather a process of pain-centered information extraction that even the notorious Gestapo would have admired for its cold and ruthless efficiency.

The suspect was arrested following a denunciation or confession. There was no haste in bringing matters to a conclusion, for the Dominicans had a solid understanding of psychology and knew that incarceration and fear could do much of the work for them. The process inexorably moved on to torture. Owing to a "sensitivity" toward the shedding of blood, the instruments used by the hooded torturers tended to be blunt, red-hot, and restrictive; bones could be broken, and limbs dislocated or distorted, so that any blood spilled was by "accident" rather than design and thus acceptable according to the rules the Church had devised.

Once the victim was in a mind to confess – to anything probably, if only the nightmare would stop – Dominican lawyers and clerks would take down the testimony and often record in detail the events they had witnessed. The victim was then taken to a nearby room and asked to confirm that his or her confession was "free and spontaneous." If the confessors were to be sentenced to death, then they were passed over to the secular authorities for execution. The Church, as a Christian institution, did not execute – or so it claimed, apparently unconcerned by the level of hypocrisy involved.

By means of these testimonies, the Dominicans created an institutional memory, a vast archive that held data on all they came into contact with. While they burned thousands of those whom they condemned as heretics, they usually did so only after an extensive interrogation. They wished always to maintain and augment this collective memory that formed the heart of their power, for, pragmatic as always, they believed that "a convert who would betray his friends was more useful than a roasted corpse."[8]

The Inquisition was the intelligence agency of the thirteenth century in that it maintained an extensive, sophisticated database for its time. It investigated suspected heretics, recorded testimonies, denunciations, and confessions in intricate and legal detail, and maintained archives of these records so that information could be retrieved long afterwards. In one example, these records show that a woman who was arrested for heresy in 1316 had been arrested before, in 1268 – forty-eight years earlier. This kind of information retrieval was ominous. It represented a malevolent memory system in the service of the dominating power of the Church.

The Inquisitors became the Church's killers – their army of secret informers, ruthless interrogators, and cold judges, all acting in the name of Christ. The historical messiah had been long forgotten; what mattered now was the Vatican's Christ. And this pathetically crucified figure became the justification of last resort for an exponentially increasing number of rules and regulations that affected every life and every part of life.

The first major battle was won by the Inquisition when the heart of the Cathar church was finally torn out in a blood-letting that echoed the sacrifices of the Aztec cult in the New World. In March 1244, the center of the Cathar church, the castle of Montsègur, fell to the invading forces. Two hundred or more Cathars were burned alive at the foot of the hill. But the Inquisition saw this not as the end of its activities but merely as the beginning of another stage. The Inquisitors now monitored the region with their archives and their informers. The Inquisition was there to stay in order to support Rome's power.

And it has stayed until the present day. It has, of course, rather sanitized itself: in 1908 the Inquisition was renamed the Sacred Congregation of the Holy Office. Then, in a further change, it became the Congregation for the Doctrine of the Faith in 1965: calm, even soft, words for the title of a dogmatic and unbending institution whose unchanged role in the Church is to maintain the orthodoxy of belief.

The current head of the Congregation – called the "Prefect" and effectively the current Grand Inquisitor, appointed on 13 May 2005, is the Californian-born Monsignor William Levada, formerly the archbishop of San Francisco. His immediate predecessor, Cardinal Joseph Ratzinger, was elected pope in April 2005. Ratzinger is quite clear about the Church's doctrine: there is no flexibility with regard to its precepts.

"Revelation terminated with Jesus Christ," Ratzinger has stated bluntly, throwing out a direct challenge to those who might think that truth is there to be discovered even today.[9] And conveniently forgetting the vote at the Council of Nicaea that deified Jesus, he is dismissive of those who think of the Church as being anything other than divine: "Even with some theologians," he grumbles with apparent surprise at their impertinence, "the Church appears to be a human construction."[10] But he has the answer for those who might – horror of horrors – think that the man-made Church has created its theology by putting ideas to the vote. "Truth cannot be created through ballots," he states.[11] In any other context, one would tend to agree with him, but in this particular argument he has moved beyond what is reasonable and beyond what is historically supportable, since what he claims to be truth was itself created through ballots. Ratzinger has added to this dogmatism: "One cannot establish the truth by resolution but can only recognize and accept it."[12] Hence, he explains, it follows that "the Church ... the bearer of faith does not sin."[13] History is clearly not Ratzinger's strong point; dogmatic public relations spinning is.

There is nothing in Ratzinger's statements that leads one to hope the Vatican might pull back from its stance that it provides the only path to truth – a path built up through a desire for power and control; a path steeped in blood; a path centered upon a mythical figure of Jesus Christ that bears little relationship to the historical messiah Jesus who was crucified as a political agitator by Pontius Pilate.

The Congregation for the Doctrine of the Faith cleverly maintains the stance of its ancestor, the Inquisition. In shoring up the boundaries of belief and placing limits on the discovery of truth, it serves, in effect, as the center of the Vatican's command and control department.

This department's whole reason for being is to keep at bay the Vatican's greatest and most secret fear: that evidence might emerge that would irretrievably prize apart the Jesus of history and the Jesus of faith and thereby reveal that the Vatican's entire existence is founded upon a fraud. They fear the appearance of evidence that Jesus was not God, as the Council of Nicaea declared – not God, but a man.

Once the Cathars had been destroyed, the Inquisition looked about for other heresies to combat. They found that the Knights Templar were needing their guiding hand. Inquisition torturers were sent all over Europe to eradicate the military Order that had served the Christian nations for almost two hundred years.

Then, in the early fourteenth century, the Inquisition turned upon the Franciscans who, because of their determined simplicity and poverty, were assumed to be infected with heresy. Many of them were consigned to the flames. A hundred years later, the Inquisitors turned upon the Jews and the Muslims in Spain, in particular those who had converted to Catholicism and were suspected of secretly returning to their previous faith. Burnings erupted with a new vigor. In Seville, 288 innocent victims were burned alive between February and November 1481. And this was just the beginning of a new period of sustained human sacrifice in the name of Christianity. Yet despite the cost, an opposition to this tyranny continued. In 1485, in Saragossa, the Inquisitor was murdered in the cathedral while he knelt in prayer at the high altar. Brutal reprisals followed, resulting in the loss of even more lives.[14]

The bloodletting slowed only as the slaughter inevitably reduced the number of potential victims. That is, until a whole new catchment of victims was discovered by an obsession of the fifteenth century: witchcraft. This was a masterstroke of ecclesiastical duplicity. The Church had always considered witchcraft a fraud or a delusion, and belief in it had long been considered a *sin*. But in 1484 the Church's attitude abruptly changed: the pope issued a bull condemning witchcraft and demanding that its reality be recognized, with any denial of this new demonic reality being itself *heretical* and subject to all the penalties the Church had devised. The same bull empowered the Inquisition to interrogate, imprison, and punish any witches it might discover.[15] The Dominicans needed little encouragement to act.

All over Europe the Dominican hunt charged through both urban and rural populations – except, interestingly, in Spain, where the Inquisition leadership felt that the entire witch craze was a fraud best ignored. They believed that the obsession with finding witches to burn was itself responsible for creating the mass hysteria that, in turn, actually produced those witches. Nevertheless, despite this regional outbreak of sanity, elsewhere in Europe women were arrested, tortured, and burned. The Inquisition boasted that over the course of 150 years it burned approximately thirty thousand women – all innocent victims of a Church-sanctioned pathological fantasy.

So organized and enthusiastic were the Dominicans that they produced a manual for those Inquisitors and civil authorities who found themselves dealing with witches. This is one of the most infamous books in history: the *Malleus Maleficarum* ("The Hammer of the Witches") is a prime example of high scholarship placed in the service of madness. It was written in 1486 by two highly educated German Dominicans – monks who feared all things feminine like the devil, it is said, fears the crucifix.

There was no question that for them women were the source of all that was demonic in the world. The two experts found the very worst wickedness to be vested in females. Women to them were incorrigibly imperfect and always sought to deceive. They were weaker than men and thus more likely to be corrupted and to corrupt others. They lacked discipline and were "beautiful to look upon, contaminating to the touch, and deadly to keep."[16] These two earnest interrogators concluded that "all witchcraft comes from carnal lust, which is in women insatiable."[17]

Why was it that the Church saw the feminine as destructive, demonic, and inhuman? Why were they terrified of women? What had led to this extreme reaction?

It had to do particularly with sex. The Church was terrified of it. "Sexual pleasure can never be without sin," states the *Responsum Gregorii*, which is attributed, perhaps wrongly, to Pope Gregory I.[18] The early fifth-century church father John Chrysostom is very clear about where the danger lies:

> There are in the world a great many situations that weaken the conscientiousness of the soul. First and foremost of these is dealings [*sic*] with women... For the eye of woman touches and disturbs our soul, and not only the eye of the unbridled woman, but that of the decent one as well.[19]

Faced with such unrelenting hostility, some modern women theologians have simply ceased treating such statements with any form of scholastic deference. Uta Ranke-Heinemann, professor of the history of religion at the

University of Essen, resorts to forthright language rarely encountered in academic circles: "All in all, considering the repression, defamation, and demonization of women, the whole of church history adds up to one long arbitrary, narrow-minded masculine despotism over the female sex. And this despotism continues today, uninterrupted."[20]

She is, of course, correct. Take, for example, the sound and fury that erupts over any suggestion that women might be ordained as priests.

Where did this fear and the consequent sexual despotism come from?

It has to do with the Church's obsession with perpetual virginity and celibacy.

So long as she never knew a man, the Church has loved the mother of Christ, the so-called Virgin Mary. She gave birth to Jesus through the unlimited power of God. In other words, the implication is drawn "that God is a kind of man."[21] Furthermore, the late Pope John Paul II, in his 1987 encyclical *Redemptoris Mater*, ruled that her hymen remained intact.[22] It was a miracle.

At least, it would have been had it been true. But unfortunately, like so much attributed to the Jesus of faith, this story does not stand up to even the slightest confrontation with the Jesus of history.

Of the four Gospels, assuming that they contain a basis of historical information, only two, Matthew and Luke, even mention the Virgin Birth. And Luke (2:48) rather compromises the theological understanding when he describes Mary and Joseph as Jesus's parents, and Joseph explicitly as Jesus's father. John in his Gospel (1:45, 6:42) also states that Jesus was the son of Joseph (see also Matthew 13:55).

The earliest New Testament writings are the letters of Paul, but there is no trace of the Virgin Birth to be found in them. In fact, Paul explicitly denies it in his letter to the Romans (1:3), in which he states that Jesus "was made of the seed of David according to the flesh." The earliest Gospel is generally accepted to be that of Mark, who also fails to mention such a miracle and is more interested in Jesus's baptism by John than in his birth.

The notion of a virgin birth arose when the Hebrew Bible – the Christians' Old Testament – was translated into Greek in the third century B.C. Isaiah (7:14) had prophesied that a "young woman" would bear a son and that this son would be called Immanuel. The Hebrew word for "young woman," *alma*, was translated into the Greek Bible as "virgin," *parthenos*. When Matthew first mentions Jesus's birth, he stresses that it fulfills the words of "the prophet" – that is, Isaiah. Then he speaks of a virgin, *parthenos,* becoming pregnant and bearing a son. But all that was actually needed to fulfill the prophecy of Isaiah was for a young woman to bear a child; such an event, one can say, is a kind of a miracle, but one that is hardly unique and does not need to postulate a sexually active deity. In fact, Matthew's story (1:22 – 23) is quite clearly metaphorical.[23] But its implications have been, dare I say, seminal.

The Church proceeded to make a cult of virginity, and this cult attracted many men who could at best be described as "disturbed," and at worst as pathological pedants – men like the church father Origen, who castrated himself at age eighteen in order that he might become a more perfect Christian, or like Augustine, who hated all pleasure, especially that encouraged by sex. A succession of these men struggled to introduce compulsory celibacy for all teachers of the faith, a task that finally achieved success in 1139 when marriage and sex were forbidden to priests in the Roman Church.

But Jesus never mentioned celibacy, and Paul indicates that there was not even any unwritten testimony to that effect. "Now concerning virgins," he writes, "I have no commandment of the Lord" (1 Corinthians 7:25).

Moreover, the apostle Peter, the supposed founder of the Catholic Church who was retrospectively designated as the first pope, was certainly married and traveled about with his wife. Paul's first letter to the Corinthians (9:5) makes that clear, as it does his own marital status and that of all or most of the other disciples and brothers of Jesus.[24] The memory of Paul's married state persisted until the end of the second century A.D., when it was last mentioned by Bishop Clement of Alexandria.[25] Thereafter, Paul was gradually and inexorably moved into the status of a celibate. As the male virgins took over the faith, women were excluded from its expression.

By any independent view of the fragments that have survived of Jesus's life and times, it seems increasingly likely
that Jesus too was married. My colleagues and I argue in
Holy Blood, Holy Grail that Jesus was married to Mary Magdalene and that the marriage at Cana, for which the New
Testament records him bearing some responsibility, was
his own.[26]

At the time, the position of the Pharisees, one of the major groups within Judaism in the first century A.D., was that
"it was a man's unconditional duty to marry."[27] The contemporary Rabbi Eliezer is credited with stating: "Whoever
does not engage in procreation is like someone who spills
blood."[28] So if Jesus was unmarried, as the Church would
have us believe, why didn't his Pharisee opponents – of
which there were many noted in the New Testament – use
his unmarried state as a further criticism of him and his
teachings? Why didn't the disciples who were married ask
Jesus to explain his failure to marry?

Paul, before he became a Christian, was a Pharisee – if
Jesus was not married, if Jesus was celibate, why didn't
Paul mention it? Ranke-Heinemann makes a crucial
point: when Paul was writing about celibacy, saying that
he knew no commandment by Jesus on the subject and
so could only give his personal opinion, "there is no way
he would have failed to mention the unusual example set
by Jesus' own life – if Jesus had set it."[29] Elaine Pagels, interviewed on a television program in 2005, commented
that "it's certainly true that most Jewish men got married

and Rabbis in particular. And it could well be that Jesus was married."[30]

But a virginal birth and a virginal life were important for the growing orthodoxy of Christianity, especially as it left its origins within Judaism and sought converts among the Gentiles. Celibacy had, of course, been highly rated by many philosophers in the pagan world, especially the Stoics. It seems that part of the original impetus for Christian virginity was a desire, in the fight for respect within a pagan-dominated world, to demonstrate that Christians too could climb the apparent moral heights of the pagan philosophers. And they certainly achieved some respect for this: Marcus Aurelius's doctor, Galen, wrote in the second century A.D. of the Christians,

> For they have not only men but women too who live their entire lives sexually continent. Their numbers include individuals who have reached a stage in their self-discipline and their self-control which is not inferior to that of genuine philosophers.[31]

But in a prescient comment in a letter to the bishop of Smyrna, Bishop Ignatius of Antioch – who later died in the arena around A.D. 110, torn to pieces by wild animals for the entertainment of Romans – noted that there were Christians who "live in chastity to honour the flesh of our Lord," then revealingly admitted that he did not admire them. In fact, he stated, he deplored their "arrogance" and warned that if they boasted about their virginal state, they would be lost.[32] Unfortunately, those who were successful in establishing the Church's orthodoxy and instrumental in obtaining the deification of Jesus were also those who wished to introduce perpetual virginity for the rulers of the Church and in the same breath to exclude women from any important role. They grew apoplectic at the thought of women teaching. They were forgetting that even Paul mentions – with support and admiration – the role of women as teachers in the Church.

In his letter to the Romans (16:1–12), Paul praises eight women who were either deacons or "helpers in Jesus Christ" (and so teachers): Phoebe, Priscilla, Aquila, Mary, Junia, Tryphena, Tryphosa, and Persis. He further mentions, in his first letter to the Corinthians (11:5), that both women and men were "praying or prophesying" in church. Ranke-Heinemann points out that "prophesying" indicates "an act of official proclamation, best translated as 'preaching.'"[33] Yet at the same time, Paul writes that women in the congregation should "remain quiet at meetings since they have no permission to speak; they must keep in the background... If they have any questions to ask, they should ask their husbands at home" (1 Corinthians 14:34–35).

But by the late second century A.D., any involvement of women in Christian teaching was becoming a thing of the past. Those who disliked women in the Church already had their long fingers clutching at the levers of control – in particular, Tertullian. Educated in Carthage before converting to Christianity by A.D. 197, he ranted against women: "You are the devil's gateway: you are the unsealer of that [forbidden] tree: you are the first deserter of the divine law... On account of your desert – that is, death – even the Son of God had to die."[34]

Naturally, given the blame attached to women for all the ills of humanity and for the crucifixion of Jesus, it was not going to sit well with Tertullian if they were to be found performing any divine office in the churches. "For how credible would it seem, that he [Paul] who has not permitted a woman even to learn with over-boldness, should give a female the power of teaching and baptizing. 'Let them be silent,' he says, 'and at home consult their own husbands.'"[35]

Although this posture is most predictable, we still need to pause here and ask: what does this outburst mean? It means that somewhere in the Christian Church known to Tertullian women were exercising the roles described by Paul and more. It means that women were acting as priests, conducting Holy Communion, preaching, and baptizing converts into the new religion. But where might this have been occurring? How prevalent might this have been? Tertullian is silent on these points. Like many of the church fathers, he penned an attack on heresy, but in his criticism he never mentions any groups that allowed women an opportunity equal to that of men to exercise the priestly office. He is keeping this matter rather quiet. One needs to ask why.

At stake here, of course, was a matter of great importance by this time. Rome was beginning to assert itself. The entire concept of "apostolic succession" – one of the most important bases upon which the argument of Rome's primacy and the validity of priestly succession rests – was beginning to be established.

According to the Gospel of Matthew (16:18), Peter was the rock upon which Christ's church was built.[36] Ignoring the difficult question of why a good Jew would want to found a church, Vatican tradition insists that by this statement – not mentioned by any of the other gospel writers – Christ transferred to Peter the supreme right to rule over the Christian Church. All subsequent bishops of Rome have this right transferred on to them specifically. Peter was, according to this tradition, the first bishop of Rome, and as we have noted, the bishop of Rome elected in A.D. 440, Pope Leo I, claimed that this heritage gave Rome the right to lead Christendom. This is crucial to the Vatican's assumption of spiritual validity. Without this claim – if it should be shown to be nonsense – the entire edifice of the Vatican and the papacy would crumble into dust. And further, built upon this claim is the truly extraordinary assertion that the Catholic Church is the only path to truth and that the pope is Christ's – that is, God's – primary representative on earth. The historical Jesus would have been appalled at what was spawned in his name.

We can argue, with good reason, that Jesus was married and that Mary Magdalene was his wife. But we are short of evidence – all that we have is circumstantial. However, when it comes to pointing out the difference between the attitude of Rome toward women and the attitude of Jesus toward women, we are on much surer ground. Jesus, as is made abundantly clear in the Gospels, had an easy and close rapport with his female followers – so easy and close that the male disciples on occasion complained. The Gospel of John describes an episode when Jesus was traveling through Samaria. His disciples had all departed to buy meat. Jesus was left alone and, tired from his long journey, he sat next to a well. An unmarried woman came to draw water, and she and Jesus began a discussion. When the disciples returned, they were shocked that he was talking with the woman, and yet, John adds, none of them challenged Jesus (John 4:27). It was understood that discourse, in Jesus's view, was for everyone.

Since the publication in 1977 of the Nag Hammadi texts, the close relationship of Jesus and Mary Magdalene has been the cause of much academic and popular debate. The crucial text in the Gospel of Philip has certain words reconstructed – placed within brackets in the translation – but even without these, the close and very special relationship between the two is clear.

And the companion of the [Savior is] Mary Magdalene. [But Christ loved] her more than [all] the disciples [and used to] kiss her [often] on her [mouth]. The rest of [the disciples were offended] by it [and expressed disapproval].[37]

But there is more here than an emotional or sexual relationship. If we look further into this Gospel and into others that also date from around the second century A.D. and have been similarly excluded by the Church, we find that Mary Magdalene had a special knowledge of Jesus's teaching – an insight, or understanding, not necessarily shared by the other disciples. The Gospel of Philip, after mentioning Jesus's close relationship with her, goes on to explain his relationship with the disciples:

> They said to him, "Why do you love her more than all of us?" The Savior answered and said to them, "Why do I not love you like her? When a blind man and one who sees are both together in darkness, they are no different from one another. When the light comes, then he who sees will see the light, and he who is blind will remain in darkness."[38]

Jesus is implying that Mary Magdalene is able to "see the light" whereas the disciples are not. She, in other words, understands fully what Jesus is teaching; the others do not.

This point is also expressed in another of the early texts found in Egypt, the Gospel of Mary. Here the disciples want to learn; Peter is recorded as asking Mary Magdalene, "Sister, we know that the Savior loved you more than all other women. Tell us the words of the Savior that you remember, the things which you know that we don't."

And Mary replies, "I will teach you about what is hidden

from you."[39] But after she does so, the male disciples complain about her explanation, and Andrew declares, "I do not believe that the Savior said these things, for indeed these teachings are strange ideas." And Peter, rather disgruntled, comments on Jesus, "Did he, then, speak with a woman in private without our knowing about it? Are we to turn around and listen to her? Did he choose her over us?"[40]

Here is the source of the problem: this relationship between Jesus and Mary is tangled up with secrets about Jesus that the Church is at pains to conceal, and at pains to keep concealing; these are secrets that the disciples are depicted in the Gospel of Mary as willfully ignoring or denying.

What were these secrets? Who and what, then, was Jesus?

We need to revisit the world of the Romans and the bitterly divided inhabitants of Judaea to ask some sharper questions and demand some better answers than those with which we have been satisfied until now.

We must return to Jerusalem.

7

Surviving the Crucifixion

Jesus entered Jerusalem on a donkey. This seems an incidental fragment of information. Earlier, on his journey from Jericho up to Jerusalem for the Passover, Jesus had paused on the Mount of Olives. He asked two of his followers to go and find him this donkey. It was important to him, and Matthew (21:4) explains why: "This took place to fulfill the prophecy." Unfortunately, Matthew's bare statement covers much more than it reveals. We need to try to prize it open a bit.

The Old Testament prophets were very concerned about the messiah. They described in detail how he would arrive in Jerusalem to take his kingdom and free his people. They also described how he would act: the prophet Zechariah (9:9) predicted that the king of Israel would arrive, triumphant yet humble, riding upon an animal as lowly as a donkey. Jesus would follow this prediction, it is related, to the letter. On the day Jesus arrived in Jerusalem, crowds gathered to watch him enter the city gate and ride through the crowded streets leading to the Temple. The chant of "Hosanna to the Son of David" erupted from them as he passed by. The entry of Jesus into the city rapidly became a public event. Crowds filled the street in front of him. Other crowds followed him in procession. The city itself is described as having been in "turmoil." Clearly both the populace and the administration were aware of what was occurring and, furthermore, aware of its importance. The promised liberator of Israel was, before their very eyes, riding through Jerusalem on his way to the Temple, where, so far as they knew – or perhaps expected – he would take control.

To have been aware of this event, these crowds must have been informed beforehand, but nothing is recorded in the New Testament about how this would have occurred. There, the public acclamation is described in such a way as to make us think it was spontaneous, but we can be sure that Jesus's arrival had already been announced and the acclamation encouraged.

A slight hint of this planning does appear in John's Gospel (11:56 – 57). He writes that many people who had come to Jerusalem for the Passover "looked out for Jesus," wondering whether or not he would come to the Temple for the Passover, because it was generally known that orders for his arrest had been issued by the leading priests. Evidently he was already seen as a threat to the establishment. John further reveals (12:12–13) that, on the day when those in the city "heard that Jesus was coming to Jerusalem," they took up palm branches and went out to greet him. He was certainly expected – as was trouble.

Jesus, with his ever-increasing entourage filling the streets, processed to the Temple, where, in a well-known incident, he threw out the money changers. This act too was to demonstrate another of the marks of the king of Israel, the *meshiha*, given by the ancient prophets: Isaiah (56:7) had spoken of the Temple as a pure "house of prayer," and Jeremiah (7:11) cried out the words of God, "Do you take this Temple that bears my name for a robber's den?" Again this prophecy is explicitly quoted in the account given by Matthew (21, 13). There is no getting away from it: Jesus entered Jerusalem quite deliberately, pressing all the right buttons in order to put himself forward as the chosen Messiah of Israel, the anointed king, whose arrival had been foretold by the prophets.

He knew it. He was open about it.

But all messiahs were, by definition, anointed. When, then, was Jesus anointed? In the Gospels of Matthew, Mark, and Luke, there is no mention of any anointment prior to his entry into Jerusalem, so, according to them, it would appear that he was not, technically speaking, the messiah at that point. Rather, according to their account, it seems that he was intent upon establishing the final pieces of his claim, for which reason he needed public recognition and support.

After Jesus ejected the money changers from the Temple, we are told, the blind and the lame approached him asking that they be healed, and children took up the cry, "Hosanna to the Son of David." This was the third time that he fulfilled the traditional requirements of messianic leadership, that of healing the maimed and being acclaimed by children ("your majesty chanted by the mouths of children" [Psalm 8:1–2] and "for Wisdom opened the mouths of the dumb and gave speech to the tongues of babes" [Wisdom 10:21]). Matthew (21:16) describes Jesus himself as referring back to these two texts when challenged.[1] Then, following this third demonstration of his destined role, Jesus left Jerusalem and traveled to Bethany, where he was to spend the night.

When morning came, he returned to Jerusalem. This time he began to teach in the Temple, narrating parables to the crowds who had come to listen and, by so doing, irritating the hostile priests who were intent on monitoring his activities. It was during this second day that a crucial event occurred, one that directly concerned a vitally important problem in Judaea: the question of paying taxes to Caesar.

Jesus knew well the reality of the political situation in Judaea under the domination of the Romans. The later writers of the Gospels also knew the sensitive nature of this issue. According to Matthew's account (22:17), the Pharisees and Herodians – both supporters of the pro-Roman establishment – went up to Jesus and asked him bluntly and plainly:

"Is it permissible to pay taxes to Caesar or not?"

Now, we must be clear, this was an extremely loaded question. In the context of the times, it was fundamental, even explosive. It had been the question of tax and the refusal to pay it that triggered the first rebellion against the Romans in A.D. 6 by Judas of Galilee; that rebellion had opened up half a century of bloodletting. To the Zealots – and to many less committed Jews – the tax was the symbol of all that was wrong with Rome. We can be certain that Jesus knew the implications of the answer – as would have the later readers of the Gospel accounts. Jesus would have had to tread carefully, since whatever answer he gave was going to get him in trouble with one or the other faction. To answer yes would get him in trouble with the Zealots, and to answer no would bring condemnation from the Romans and their supporters among the priesthood.

So what did Jesus do? We all know the answer. He asked for a coin. They gave him a Roman denarius. Jesus looked at the coin and asked, "Whose head is this? Whose name?"

"Caesar's," they replied.

"Very well," replied Jesus. "Give back to Caesar what belongs to Caesar – and to God what belongs to God" (Matthew 22:19–22).

At that time, and at that place, this was not just a clever and cute retort – the Judaean equivalent of a modern sound bite – but an outrageous and provocative challenge to the Zealots.

Imagine the problem: the Zealots, whose entire focus was

the removal or destruction of Rome's hold over Judaea, had organized a dynastic marriage between Joseph, a man of the royal line of David, and Mary, of the priestly line of Aaron, in order to have a child, Jesus – the "Savior" of Israel – who was both rightful king and high priest.

Jesus is brought up to fulfill his role, he enters Jerusalem as a messiah, he acts in accordance with all the prophecies, he does everything that is expected of him – until this crucial moment. Up until this point, the Zealots would have been very pleased with the way events were going. But then, in an unexpected move, their messiah abruptly switches gear: "Pay the tax," he is saying. "It means nothing." For his true kingdom – as he often stressed – was not of this world.

The Zealot supporters of Jesus must have been apoplectic with rage, speechless at this sudden and public turn of events. Their carefully constructed messiah had rejected them – had betrayed them. And so, in fury, they would reject him.

After this second day in the Temple, Jesus again returned to Bethany for the night; according to Matthew's Gospel (26:6), the Passover was but two nights away, and Jesus was staying in the house of "Simon the Leper." But John's Gospel (11:1–2, 12:3) states that he was staying at the house of Mary, Martha, and Lazarus. One of these Gospels is wrong – that much is clear – but whichever house Jesus was staying in, an extraordinary event occurred there: Jesus was anointed. Was this his recognition and confirmation as the Messiah of Israel? It would seem that it was.

The Gospel of Matthew (26:7) describes "a woman" anointing Jesus on his head with "precious ointment" that she took from an "alabaster box" – a very expensive item at the time.[2] This ointment and its container were not something that would have been lying around the house of a peasant farmer or artisan. The entire incident hints of a shadowy source of wealth behind those close to Jesus. Mark (14:3) mentions the same incident and adds that the expensive oil was spikenard – one of the spices used in the Temple incense. John (11:2), as ever the source of interesting detail, names the woman: she was, he said, Mary of Bethany, the sister of Lazarus.

Most modern readers of the Gospels have no great knowledge of the politics and practices of the time, and so for them this anointing seems incidental, a mark of respect perhaps, or as some church commentators have argued, an ornate ceremony for greeting an honored guest. Perhaps, but in the context such an explanation is hardly convincing. For those of the first century A.D., the implication of this action would have been unmistakable: this was a royal anointing. Traditionally, the priests and kings of Israel were anointed with expensive oil: with kings, it was poured around the head as a symbolic wreath, while a priest's head was anointed with a diagonal cross.

Furthermore, we should note, Matthew states that after this anointment Judas immediately reported to the "chief priests" in order to arrange for the betrayal of Jesus. This event is so suspiciously close in time to the anointment that we must consider a direct connection between the two. This act by a woman close to Jesus obviously triggered official alarm. We may now be clear where the Gospel is obtuse: Matthew, however hesitantly, is indicating that Jesus was being recognized and proclaimed in his role as messiah.

Curiously, in 1988 a small jug — containing a mysterious oil that has never been identified — dating from Herodian times, wrapped protectively in palm fibers, was found close to Qumran near the Dead Sea.[3] Archaeologists speculated that it might be balsam oil, for which the area was famous in antiquity and which was also expensive — double its weight in silver — and used for royal anointing. This jug may have been hidden there from Jerusalem, or it may have been used in Qumran itself for anointing an "alternative" high priest: the Temple Scroll makes it clear that the Qumran community retained a critical interest in the Temple, for the entire scroll describes at length and in intricate detail the correct procedures to be observed at that sacred site.[4]

But the method of his anointing raises another deep mystery — as if there were not enough mystery about Jesus already. One would expect such a ceremony to be performed by a group of top officials, perhaps priests, perhaps representatives of the Sanhedrin, whether the "official" one or some Zealot "alternative" one — if any Zealots were still talking to Jesus after the incident with the denarius.

But no such person was present. Jesus was, according to Matthew's account, simply anointed by "a woman" — identified in John's Gospel (12:3) as Mary "of Bethany" — and

the event took place in the home she shared with her sister
and her brother Lazarus, who had been recently "raised
from the dead." In the history of royal or priestly confirma-
tions by a male-dominated organization, this is unprecedented: the anointment ceremony presided over by a
woman? A woman confirming and acclaiming Jesus as
meshiha? Exactly what kind of ceremony was it that has left
its brief, perhaps garbled, trace in the Gospels like a comet
obscured by dark clouds?[5]

This event remains unexplained to this day, yet it cannot
be ignored. It was of such importance in the Christian movement, and knowledge of it evidently so widespread, that it
could not later be removed from the record. It continued to
be included in those memories that survived to become written down as our Gospels. It was downgraded and distorted,
but at least it remains, even if unexplained and mysterious.
Furthermore, it is curious that a woman, Mary of Bethany,
should perform this role rather than the woman who was far
more prominent in the circle of disciples: Mary Magdalene.
Unless, of course, the two were the same – unless Mary of
Bethany was, in fact, Mary Magdalene.

A distinction between the two seems to be made in the
New Testament, but there was certainly a tradition com-
bining the two, a tradition that was put into the faith during the sixth century by Pope Gregory I. Evidence is lacking,
however, and this identification is no longer maintained by
the Vatican. However, as we shall see, that is not the end of
the matter.

A very interesting – and persuasive – perspective was published by Margaret Starbird in her 1993 work *The Woman with the Alabaster Jar*. As we have discovered, all the important actions of Jesus in the few days preceding the crucifixion were carried out in accordance with Old Testament prophecy. Even the anointment of Jesus itself can be seen as fitting in with the acclamation of the Jewish *meshíha* whose coming had been foretold. Starbird suggests that we can find the origins of Mary Magdalene in one of these prophecies.[6] She points to the Old Testament prophet Micah (4:8), who wrote: "And you, Tower of the Flock, Ophel of the daughter of Zion, to you shall be given back your former sovereignty, and royal power over the House of Israel."

The phrase "Tower of the Flock" means a high place from which the shepherd might watch over his flock. Here, though, according to the official Vatican translation (the Jerusalem Bible), it refers to Jerusalem.[7] "The Flock" refers to the faithful of God. The addition of the reference to "Ophel" reinforces this explanation, since Ophel was the district in Jerusalem where the king had his residence. As the Jerusalem Bible also explains, "Tower of the Flock" is *Migdal-eder* in Hebrew; *Migdal* means "tower," but it also carries the meaning of "great." Starbird suggests, very plausibly, that here we have the origins of the epithet "the Magdalene" rather than any possible town called Magdala. In other words, if this explanation is correct, Mary of Bethany, "the Magdalene," the wife of the messiah, was known as "Mary the Great."[8]

In the same way that Jesus's entry into Jerusalem was arranged to pick up on the statements of the Old Testament prophets about the coming of the messiah, Mary "the Magdalene" also connects us to an Old Testament messianic prophecy about the reinstatement of royal power to Israel.

Suggesting, of course, that Jesus was anointed as messiah by his wife!

For some reason, it was in her power and by her authority. This gives those advocates of the primacy of male apostolic authority in the Church another enigma to worry about. Clearly authority in Jesus's movement was *not* exclusively vested in the male disciples.

What are the implications? It has been suggested that this ceremony of annointment represents a sacred marriage. But this is unlikely: anointment was not a feature of the classical Mystery traditions.[9] Neither was it a feature of the Mesopotamian religions.[10] Apart from Judaism, there was only one earlier tradition in the area in which anointment with holy oil was significant, and that was in ancient Egypt. There the priests were consecrated with holy oil poured on their head.

Certainly the New Testament is bad history. This is impossible to deny. The texts are inconsistent, incomplete, garbled, and biased. It is possible to deconstruct the New Testament to the point where nothing remains but a heavily biased, dogmatic Christian mythology – in which case we could argue that the account of Jesus supporting the payment of taxes to Caesar was simply a later addition to reassure the mostly Greco-Roman Gentile converts to Christianity that there was nothing politically dangerous about the new faith, that it was never a political threat to Roman power.

On the other hand, if we accept that these stories contain some history, however garbled, we need to seek those facts that might have survived beneath the later mythological edifice. As mentioned earlier, the pagan historians themselves, in particular Tacitus and Pliny the Younger, while sparse in their information, do report – and by so doing confirm – that a Jewish messiah was crucified during the period when Pontius Pilate was prefect of Judaea, and further, that a religious movement, centered upon and named after this particular messiah, was in existence by the end of the first century A.D. Consequently, we must admit that there is some real history in the Gospels, but how much of it is there? How we judge the extent of the Gospels' truth ultimately depends upon the perspective we bring to them.

It is here that the inconsistencies in the Gospels become important. One in particular is crucial.

We have mentioned that Jesus was not anointed until two days after his entry into Jerusalem, when, in the house in Bethany, Lazarus's sister Mary anointed him with very costly ointment, spikenard. Thus, when Jesus entered Jerusalem for the Passover as messiah, he had not yet been anointed. He was not, technically speaking, the messiah – that was yet to come.

But John's Gospel (12:1–3) gives us a very different story. In this, Jesus was anointed six days *before* the Passover, *prior to* his entry into Jerusalem. So in John's Gospel, when Jesus entered Jerusalem and was acclaimed as messiah, this acclamation was correct, for he had already received the sacred anointing. Who is telling the truth? John or the other three evangelists? We cannot tell. All we can say is that John's story makes sense of the triumphant entry into Jerusalem in a way that the other Gospels do not. It is more plausible, and interestingly it is John alone who identifies the consecrating woman for us as Mary, the sister of Lazarus.

We need to take a further look at the hypothesis we are posing here: it is not hard to imagine that the Zealots, enraged over Jesus's acceptance of the messianic anointment and subsequent rejection of any political role, would embark on a major exercise in damage control. They had to get rid of Jesus so that a more amenable leader could take over – perhaps his brother James, who was more in tune with the political aspirations of the Zealots. Certainly, after the removal of Jesus from the scene, James was leading the community of messianic Jews in Jerusalem.[11]

It is also not hard to suppose that the Zealots set Jesus up – if they couldn't have a leader, then at least they could have a martyr. He knew they had to betray him – and it is interesting that the man who has been recorded as the traitor, Judas Iscariot, was undoubtedly a Zealot *Sicarii*. He was, we can suggest, a traitor to Jesus but a patriot to the

Zealots. He did what they wanted. He pointed out Jesus to the armed guards who came to make the arrest. And as he was arrested in the Garden of Gethsemane, Jesus asked (as rendered in the original Greek), "Am I a *Zealot*, that you had to set out to capture me with swords and clubs?" (Matthew 26:55).[12] Jesus thus reveals – and incidentally, so does the writer of the Gospel of Matthew – that he knew the political reality of the time.

If the Sadducee priesthood wanted to be rid of Jesus because they saw him as a messiah and a threat to their power, and if the Zealots too, for different reasons, wanted to be rid of Jesus, then word of this would have reached Pilate. And this intelligence would have put him in a very difficult position. Pilate was Rome's official representative in Judaea, and Rome's main argument with the Jews was that they declined to pay their tax to Caesar. Yet here was a leading Jew – the legitimate king no less – telling his people to pay the tax. How could Pilate try, let alone condemn, such a man who, on the face of it, was supporting Roman policy? Pilate would himself be charged with dereliction of duty should he proceed with the condemnation of such a supporter.

The New Testament represents "the Jews" as baying for Jesus's blood. And this apparent guilt of the Jews stuck for millennia – it was only acknowledged as fraudulent by the Vatican and excised from the teachings as late as 1960. But as should now be clear, it was not "the Jews" in general who were calling for Jesus's arrest and execution, but the militant

Zealots, those who hated the Romans and would sacrifice even one of their own for their political aims. In the scenario presented here, Pilate would have found himself in a serious dilemma: to keep the peace he had to try, condemn, and execute a Jew who was supporting Rome but whose existence was causing public disorder, the flames of which were being fanned by the disgruntled Zealots. Pilate needed to try to square the circle on this; he desperately needed a deal.

And the deal, I suggest, was this: that he try Jesus and condemn him as a political agitator, thus appeasing the Zealots, who threatened widespread disorder. This was the last thing Pilate needed on his watch, especially since he was aware that he was falling out of favor with the Roman authorities. But while he condemned Jesus and had to go through with the required sentence of crucifixion, he could not dare have it reported to Rome that Jesus had actually died. So Pilate took steps to ensure that Jesus would survive. He spoke with a member of the Sanhedrin and friend of Jesus, the wealthy Joseph of Arimathea.

Technically, how could a crucifixion have been faked? Just how could Jesus have survived? Was it possible at all to survive a crucifixion of any length of time?

Crucifixion was not so much an execution as a torturing to death. The procedure was very simple: the victim was tied, hanging to the crossbar, while his feet were supported on a block at the base of the cross. His feet were also usually tied at the block, although at least one example recovered by archaeologists reveals that a nail might be driven through each ankle.[13] The weight of the hanging body made breathing very difficult and could be managed only by constantly pushing upwards with the legs and feet to relieve the tension in the chest. Eventually, of course, weariness and weakness overcame the ability to keep pushing. When this happened, the body slumped, breathing became impossible, and the crucified person died – by asphyxiation. This was reckoned to take about three days.[14]

As an act of mercy – only the brutal Romans could come up with such a definition – the legs of the victim were often broken and so deprived of any strength whatsoever to maintain the weight of the body. The body would drop, and death by asphyxiation rapidly followed. We can see this in the New Testament. John reports that the legs of the two Zealots crucified beside Jesus were broken, but when they came to break Jesus's legs, "he was dead already" (John 19:31–33).

Clearly it would be difficult to survive a crucifixion, but it was not impossible. Josephus, for example, reports that he came upon three of his former colleagues among a large group of crucified captives. He went to Titus asking for mercy, begging that they might be taken down. Titus agreed, and the three men were brought down from the cross. Despite professional medical attention, two of them died, but the third survived.[15]

Could Jesus have survived just like the survivor in Josephus's report? There are traditions in Islam that say so. The Koran's statement "They did not crucify him" could as well be translated as "They did not cause his death on the cross."[16] But the Koran is a very late text, even though it undoubtedly uses earlier documents and traditions. Perhaps more relevant for us is a statement by Irenaeus in the late second century; in a complaint about the beliefs of an Egyptian Gnostic, Basilides, he explains that this heretic taught that Jesus had been substituted during the journey to Golgotha and that this substitute, Simon of Cyrene, had died in Jesus's stead.

But if Jesus survived without being substituted, how could it have happened? Hugh Schonfield, in his *The Passover Plot*, suggests that Jesus was drugged – sedated on the cross such that he appeared dead but could be revived later, after he had been taken down.[17] This is by no means such a wild idea, and it has received a sympathetic hearing. For example, in a television program on the crucifixion broadcast by the BBC in 2004 called *Did Jesus Die?* Elaine Pagels referred to Schonfield's book, which, she noted, suggested that Jesus "had been sedated on the cross; that he was removed quite early and therefore could well have survived." And, she concluded, "that's certainly a possibility."[18]

There is a curious incident recorded in the Gospels that may be explained by this hypothesis: while on the cross, Jesus complained that he was thirsty. A sponge soaked in vinegar was placed on the end of a long reed and held up to him. But far from reviving Jesus, the drink from this sponge apparently caused him to die. This is a curious reaction and suggests that the sponge was soaked not in vinegar, a substance that would have revived Jesus, but rather in something that would have caused him to lose consciousness — some sort of drug, for example. And there was just this type of drug available in the Middle East.

It was known that a sponge soaked in a mixture of opium and other compounds such as belladonna and hashish served as a good anesthetic. Such sponges would be soaked in the mixture, then dried for storage or transport. When it was necessary to induce unconsciousness — for surgery, for example — the sponge would be soaked in water to activate the drugs and then placed over the nose and mouth of the subject, who would promptly lose consciousness. Given the description of the events on the cross and the rapid apparent "death" of Jesus, it is a plausible suggestion that this use of a drugged sponge was the cause. No matter how carefully a "staged" crucifixion might have been carried out (one intended for Jesus to survive), there was no way to anticipate the effect that shock might have had upon him. Crucifixion was, after all, a traumatic experience, both physically and mentally. To be rendered unconscious would reduce the effect of the trauma and thus increase the chance of survival, so the drug would have been a further benefit in that regard too.

There are some further points that are striking: John's Gospel mentions that a spear was thrust into Jesus's side and that blood came out. Taken at face value, we can conclude two things from this observation: first, that the spear was not thrust into the brain or heart and so was not necessarily immediately life-threatening. And second, that the flow of blood would seem to indicate that Jesus was still alive.

All that remained then was for Jesus to be taken down from the cross, apparently lifeless but in reality unconscious, and taken to a private tomb where medicines could be used to revive him. He would then be whisked away from the scene. And this is precisely what is described in the Gospels: Luke (23:53) and Mark (15:46) report that Jesus was placed in a new tomb nearby. Matthew (27:6) adds that the tomb was owned by the wealthy and influential Joseph of Arimathea. John (19:41−42), who generally gives us so many extra details, adds that there was a garden around this tomb, implying that the grounds were privately owned, perhaps also by Joseph of Arimathea.

John also stresses that Jesus was taken down quickly and put into this new tomb. Then, in a very curious addition, he reports that Joseph of Arimathea and a colleague, Nicodemus, visited the tomb *during the night* and brought with them a very large amount of spices: myrrh and aloes (John 19:39). These, it is true, could be used simply as a perfume, but there could be another equally plausible explanation. Both substances have a medicinal use − most notably, myrrh has been used as an aid to stop bleeding. Neither drug is known to have a role in embalming dead bodies. Mark (16:1) and Luke (23:56) touch obliquely on this theme as well, adding to their story of the tomb that the women − Mary Magdalene and Mary, "mother of James" − brought spices and ointments with them when they came to the tomb after the Sabbath had ended.

It is also curious that Jesus just happens to have been crucified next to a garden and a tomb, the latter at least owned by Joseph of Arimathea. This is all rather convenient to say the least. Could it be that the crucifixion itself was private? Perhaps in order to control witnesses to what was occurring? Luke (23:49) informs us that the crowds watching were standing at a distance. Perhaps they were *kept* at a distance? In fact, the description of the events of Golgotha suggests that the site of the crucifixion was actually in the Kidron valley, where there are many rock-cut tombs to this day and where is also located the Garden of Gethsemane, which may well have been the private garden involved and one with which Jesus was familiar.

But there is yet another oddity that we need to note: in the Gospel of Mark, Joseph of Arimathea is described as visiting Pilate and requesting the body of Jesus. Pilate asks if Jesus is dead and is surprised when told that he is indeed, for his demise seems very rapid to Pilate. But since Jesus is dead, Pilate allows Joseph to take the body down. If we look at the original Greek text, we see an important point being made: when Joseph asks Pilate for Jesus's body, the word used for "body" is *soma*. In Greek this denotes a living body. When Pilate agrees that Joseph can take the body down from the cross, the word he uses for "body" is *ptoma* (Mark 15:43 – 45). This means a fallen body, a corpse or carcass. In other words, the Greek text of Mark's Gospel is making it clear that while Joseph is asking for the living body of Jesus, Pilate grants him what he believes to be the corpse. Jesus's survival is revealed right there in the actual Gospel account.

If the writer of this Gospel had wished to hide that fact, it would have been very easy for him simply to use one word for both statements – to have both Joseph and Pilate speaking of the *ptoma*, the corpse. But the writer chose not to be consistent. Could this be because it was too well known a fact for him to get away with any manipulation of it? This had to wait for the translation of the New Testament from Greek into Latin: in the Latin Bible – the Vulgate – the word *corpus* is used by both Pilate and Joseph of Arimathea, and this simply means "body" as well as "corpse." The hiding of the secret of the crucifixion was completed.

Again, it takes only a slight shift of perspective, a standing aside from the theological dogma, to see the crucifixion in a new way. That is, to see how Jesus could very well have survived.

"My kingdom is not of this world," said Jesus to Pontius Pilate during his interrogation (John 18:36). Jesus explained, "If my kingdom were of this world, then would my servants fight." This is another statement, like that of the advice to pay taxes, that would have been sure to enrage the hard-line Zealots.

But what does this statement really mean? And even more curiously, where did he learn this approach that so differed from that of his politically active colleagues and contemporaries?

Jesus cannot have learned his trade in Galilee, for Galilee was the Zealot heartland. The Zealots would have controlled his training and learning, especially given the destiny they had planned for him. And even if, for some reason, he had, despite all, adopted such a mystical perspective and a political approach that accommodated Roman demands, then his Zealot teachers would have known of his change of heart and so have prevented him from entering Jerusalem as the prospective messiah.

All this suggests that Jesus was working to his own plan – one that not only involved his being anointed as messiah by a woman close to him but ensured that the Zealots would not suspect the truth until it was too late. We have to conclude that Jesus had learned his trade elsewhere.

A clue can be discerned in a very curious statement by Jesus reported in one of the Gospels. He says, "When thine eye is single, thy whole body also is full of light" (Luke 11:34).

This is pure mysticism of a type not otherwise found in the New Testament; nor is it found in the Zealot teachings we find expressed in the Dead Sea Scrolls. This is unique in a Judaean context. We are forced to conclude that Jesus had, as it were, been initiated somewhere else. He had had an experience of the Divine Light that mystics all through the ages have reported.

We need to understand this statement more fully, for it is crucial. It is the very pivot around which the truth about Jesus revolves. If we can understand this statement, then we can understand Jesus; we can understand why he broke with the Zealots, and why the Church has pushed lies about him ever since. The Church had to perpetuate such lies, for clearly if it told the truth about Jesus, it would be finished. It is really *that* important.

There was only one place where Jesus could have learned this approach. Only one place among the Jewish residents where these kinds of mystical concepts were discussed and taught, where the political obsessions current in Judaea were either absent or much muted. And that place was Egypt.

It is impossible to understand Jesus, his teaching, and the events of first-century Judaea without understanding the Jewish experience in Egypt.

8

Jesus in Egypt

Exactly where Jesus lived from his early teens until he emerged out of Galilee to be baptized in the Jordan is a complete mystery. Luke (3:1–23) dates this baptism to the fifteenth year of the Emperor Tiberius – which would be A.D. 27 to 28 — and adds that Jesus was about thirty years old at the time. We can be certain of only one thing: wherever it was that Jesus lived, it could not have been in Israel.

This certainty is guided by the logic of the Gospels: had Jesus been living in Judaea, Galilee, or Samaria, this fact would have been mentioned along with extraordinary, even miraculous, indications of his impending greatness in exactly the same way that incidents both in his youth and following his baptism were lovingly described by Matthew, Mark, Luke, and John.

Although it is true that the Gospels are primarily concerned with Jesus's mission following his baptism, they also
provide details about his birth, the travels of his family, and,
significantly, his debating with priests in the Temple when
he was twelve (Luke 2:41–47). Surely at least one of the
Gospels, having established such early evidence of his religious insight, would have noted further incidents of this
kind, especially as Jesus moved into adulthood. It would be
deeply suspicious if there were no such incidents. But that
is precisely the case: a search of the New Testament reveals
nothing of the next eighteen years or so, the prime of
Jesus's life.

There is one further curiosity: Matthew, Mark, and Luke
all say that Jesus was living in the town of Nazareth in
Galilee. Luke gives a little more information, adding that
Jesus grew to maturity there and that every year his parents
would go to Jerusalem to celebrate the Passover. It was during one of these visits that Jesus was discovered sitting in the
Temple with learned scholars and questioning them on
matters of religion. Unfortunately, there is no evidence
whatsoever that Nazareth even existed in Jesus's day. The
first mention of it appears no earlier than the third century
A.D.[1] Could this mention of an exchange at the Temple have
been placed here as some kind of cover story for a period in
Jesus's life that was otherwise unaccounted for?

As far as the Gospels were concerned, Jesus appears to
have vanished during his youth and early adulthood. But it
was during those years that he learned the ideas, the beliefs,

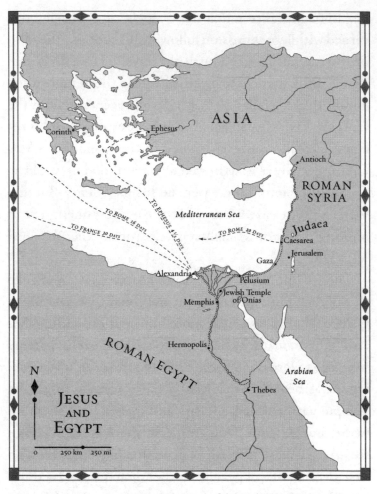

Main roads leading into Egypt at the time of the Holy Family's migration

and the knowledge that he later taught. So where exactly was he? And why have his whereabouts been kept hidden? Had he been "talent-scouted" by priests or rabbis and whisked away for almost two decades of secret training? Surely the disciples must have known where Jesus had been. But what could have possibly been at stake, what problem could have arisen, through sharing this information? In fact, we cannot avoid asking, what were the writers of the Gospels intent on concealing?

This gap in the account of Jesus's life has been noted by scholars for many years and has opened the way for much speculation. There are arguments of varying degrees of plausibility for his traveling to the East, far beyond the jurisdiction of the Romans, to Parthia, Persia, or beyond, to Afghanistan or India. Even today there are many who believe that the shrine of Yus Asaph in Kashmir is that of Jesus himself who, after surviving the crucifixion, returned home to the East to live and ultimately die. There are also suggestions that he studied as a child under Buddhists – this would explain, it is said, the parallels that can be found between the teachings of Jesus and those of the Buddha. And we have the very early Christian community, centered in Malabar on the west coast of India, which claims to have been founded by the apostle Thomas. Surely where Thomas went then so too could have Jesus gone?[2]

On the surface the argument that Jesus moved east has, in its various forms, much merit, but it remains rather difficult to prove. Hugh Schonfield explored the Kashmir beliefs in his work *The Essene Odyssey*, first published in 1984. What he discovered was that a branch or leader of the messianic Jewish group – the Zealot group – had indeed fled the areas under the control of the Romans and moved northeast, eventually reaching the Indian subcontinent.

Schonfield firmly believed that documents existed to support this exodus. In a personal statement to me before his death in 1988, he explained that he had narrowed the search for crucial evidence to a Nestorian monastery in the region of Mosul, Iraq, but the monks there – now called Assyrian Christians – would never allow him access to them. He wouldn't give me any specific details of which monastery and which documents. I believe he was still hoping to get his hands on them and thus was keeping the information close to his chest. But a clue appears in *The Essene Odyssey*, where he refers to an Arab historian, 'Abd al-Jabbar, who seems to have access to important Judeo-Christian documents dating from the sixth or seventh centuries A.D. These documents were located in monasteries, apparently Nestorian, in the Mosul area.[3] Of course, this was long before the two wars against Iraq's Saddam Hussein. Whether anything remains of the monasteries or the documents is anybody's guess.

These messianic Jews who left Palestine, according to Schonfield and others, did so because of persecution from the authorities that became increasingly violent as the first century progressed. One can understand the desire to simply move to a more peaceful place where the community's beliefs could be maintained without hindrance. However, Jesus does not easily fall into this pattern. Before he was baptized and began his mission, he had not yet come to the attention of either the Romans or the pro-Roman Jewish authorities. In any case, there were already many other Zealots happy to cause trouble, especially as the Romans continued their attempts to place images of the emperor in the Temple in Jerusalem. The unwavering Jewish opposition to these moves showed that there was no lessening of sensitivity to Roman demands. Whatever Jesus was doing at that time, he was not recorded as being involved in this opposition, which bears all the hallmarks of Zealot activity. So there would have been no need for Jesus to flee Roman jurisdiction. Any move he made out of Judaea or Galilee must have been by choice rather than by coercion. But where would he have ventured, and why?

There is a single clue in the Bible, one in the Old Testament that is echoed in the New. As we have seen, it was important for Jesus to follow, to act out quite specifically, the predictions made by the Old Testament prophets in describing the coming of the messiah. We have already seen the very literal expression of these predictions during Jesus's entry into Jerusalem when he finally went public with his messianic claims. We can therefore be confident in expecting that every messianic prediction in the Old Testament would be pressed into use in this manner.

In a real sense these predictions by the prophets *limited* Jesus. They provided a set of boundaries within which his messianic mission needed to express itself. A particularly interesting prediction was given by the prophet Hosea (11:1): "When Israel was a child I loved him, and I called my son out of Egypt." Matthew (2:15) picks up on this in one of the earliest prophetic predictions he mentions: in a garbled historical account, he records that the Holy Family fled into Egypt when Jesus was still a baby, explaining, "This was to fulfill what the Lord has spoken through the prophet: 'I called my son out of Egypt.'"

At this point, we cannot help but ask, why Egypt? This is a minor detail in Matthew's Gospel and is treated as such in the Roman Church. But for the Egyptian Coptic Church, which separated from Rome in 451 following the Council of Chalcedon, it is a matter of considerable importance indeed. For almost a thousand years it has maintained a legend about the journey the Holy Family made into Egypt, all the sites they visited or resided at, and all the miracles that accompanied the presence of Jesus. This legend is called "The Vision of Theophilus." Theophilus was patriarch of Alexandria and leader of the Egyptian church from A.D. 385 to 412, but the Vision seems not to have been written down until the eleventh or twelfth century.

Given the highly devotional nature of the story and the very obvious use made of it to justify Jesus's uniqueness and divinity, we can locate its theology far beyond the beliefs of the Jewish community in Egypt – the community that would have been giving refuge to Jesus's family. What's more, these same factors place the origins of the theology in an era following the dogmatic decisions of the Council of Nicaea in A.D. 325. It seems fairly evident that the Vision – at the very least – is a product of Christian thought in the fourth century A.D. or later, and certainly not of Judaism or Judeo-Christianity. It therefore cannot be an accurate account of any such journey, although it may very well contain some elements of a real journey. Thus, we need to ask, who does the story serve? Who would have benefited from its telling?

Despite its strictly Christian context, *the Vision* reveals that as late as the Crusade period, a time when Egypt had been under Muslim rule for several hundred years, there were those who wished to link Jesus with Egypt. Could the story have possibly been created to encourage the Crusaders to invade Egypt and liberate the Christian Coptic Church from Islam? Perhaps, but this argument seems less tenable as we look deeper: the Coptic Church had been at odds with Rome for over six hundred years, and its faith was at least tolerated by the Muslim rulers. The most obvious beneficiary that emerges then is the Gospel of Matthew: its statements about the flight of the Holy Family are greatly supported by the story. But the Coptic Church may also have been a less obvious beneficiary. If the Gospel of Matthew is given greater credence, then it stands to reason that various Egyptian holy places within the story would also be validated, thereby opening up a whole new pilgrim route that would include Egypt. With pilgrims, of course, came trade and gold.

Despite its deficiencies, the tale gives every appearance of picking up on local oral tradition or legend. And local legend is dismissed at one's own peril, for local memories are long. There had certainly been a very ancient and widespread Jewish presence in Egypt – extensive enough to justify the story's telling well into Islamic times.

The Jewish community in Egypt was not just large but extremely influential. As allies of the Greek conquerors, the Ptolemies, they enjoyed a social status higher than that of the native Egyptians, who, after the conquest, were considered "subjects," second-class citizens in their own country, a social disability that few, if any, escaped. The Ptolemies, in fact, never sought to learn Egyptian until the very end. Cleopatra, the last ruler, was the only one able to speak the native language of the land she ruled. Inevitably, the resentment caused by the invasion bred insurrection. Significant revolts occurred in Thebes (now Luxor) from the late third century when two native Egyptian pharaohs were declared, one after another. This nationalistic revolt was soon stamped out, but all through the second century B.C. there were a number of serious attempts at a coup.

Nevertheless, a small number of conquerors can rule over a large indigenous population by means of innumerable regulations and restrictions coupled with a pervasive and psychologically degrading social disdain that destroys the self-confidence and self-assurance of the native population.

This technique was used by the British with sophistication and success much later in India.

Jewish immigration into Egypt was extensive, encouraged particularly by the removal of all boundaries between Egypt and Israel from 302 B.C. until 198 B.C., a period when Israel formed part of the Ptolemaic empire. These immigrants quickly became absorbed into the prevailing Greek culture; they learned Greek, took Greek names, and adopted many traits of Greek commercial and social customs, such as forming trade associations whose meetings were held in the synagogues. In fact, Hebrew became virtually forgotten as Greek became the daily language of choice for the Egyptian Jews. In many synagogues even the services were conducted in Greek.

This can all be ascribed to the influence of Alexander the Great. He took Egypt in 332 B.C., and following a visit to the Temple of Amun at Siwa Oasis veiled in secrecy, he was declared "Son of God" and created pharaoh. He founded Alexandria in 331 B.C. as a Hellenistic city *in* Egypt but not actually *of* it. He was never to see its success as the greatest Greek city in the Hellenistic world; indeed, it would become larger and more important even than Athens.[4] Alexander died mysteriously on campaign in Babylon in 323 B.C. His empire was then split among his Greek generals: Ptolemy received Egypt and began the illustrious Ptolemaic dynasty of kings and queens that ended only with the death of the famous Cleopatra in 60 B.C. In due course Seleucis received Syria and based himself at Antioch.

Under the Greek Ptolemaic rulers, Egypt enjoyed massive commercial success. For one thing, it was the source of grain supplies for Rome, and it is no exaggeration to say that the fate of the emperors was entangled with the continued success of this trade. Such success allowed the Ptolemies to support powerful army and naval forces. The region prospered greatly – the annual revenues were the rough equivalent of 288 tons of gold. A royal bank based in Alexandria took deposits and arranged mortgages and money lending. Cultural life also prospered, greatly encouraged by the region's extraordinary library, the largest in the world. Passengers on every ship visiting Alexandria were searched for books and any found were copied; the originals were then taken and put in the library while the copies were given to the former owners. In addition, libraries from all over the known world were purchased by the Ptolemies until, it was said, the holdings in Alexandria comprised some seven hundred thousand scrolls, most of which were deposited on the shelves of the seven great halls in the main library, the Mouseion, and a little over forty thousand were deposited in a smaller library in the Temple of Serapis.

As a result of this dynamic energy, there was a rapid growth of new towns in Egypt, and additions were made to existing ones. Alexandria probably held the largest Jewish community of any city in the Roman empire beyond the bounds of Israel. Around three hundred thousand Jews lived in Egypt: half resided in the provincial cities or in the country as landowners, and the other half lived in Alexandria.

The Jewish community was based in its own quarter on the eastern side of Alexandria; this was not a ghetto, however, for Jews also resided in other parts of the city, and members of the Jewish community enjoyed great prestige. This community operated semi-independently of the rest of Alexandria. It ran its own courts under the presidency of an ethnarch, and its sophisticated members rose to high positions within the country. In fact, during the reign of Ptolemy VI and Cleopatra II, in the second century B.C., the administration of all Egypt and the overall control of the army and navy were given to two Jews, Onias and Dositheus. Later there were also two Jewish generals in the army of Cleopatra III, who ruled from 115 to 101 B.C.[5]

Of course, there was a long history of Jewish contacts with Egypt predating this time – even setting aside whatever reality there may have been behind the stories of Joseph and Moses. But we are on surer ground when we note that Jewish soldiers served the later pharaohs, perhaps as early as the seventh century B.C., especially in the southern expeditions in Nubia. Jeremiah (44:1), raging bitterly in the seventh century B.C. against the Jewish colonies in Egypt, specifically noted that Memphis, the capital of Egypt at the time, was host to one of these expeditions, and he mentioned other sites in Upper and Lower Egypt as well.

By the fifth century B.C., according to papyrus documents that have been recovered, a Jewish military colony had been established on Elephantine Island in the Nile – off the modern city of Aswan – an island which guarded the southern frontier of Egypt.[6] The colony included a fortress, a customs post, and a township for soldiers and their families, who were given land on which to live when they retired from active service.

The Egyptians had a temple of the god Khnum on the island; for the Jewish community, there was a temple of Yahweh. The two temples were close to each other. In fact, for the greater part of the sixth century B.C. after the Temple in Jerusalem had been destroyed and the population taken in captivity to Babylonia, the temple on Elephantine Island was the sole functioning Jewish temple keeping the religion alive by conducting the required sacrifices.

Unfortunately, tension prevailed between the Jews and the Egyptians, and during the time of Darius (522–486 B.C.), when the Persians controlled Egypt, the Elephantine Egyptians destroyed the Temple of Yahweh. Imperial authorization for its reconstruction was not forthcoming until 406 B.C.; by 401 B.C. it was rebuilt. But it was soon again destroyed, and nothing more is heard of it or the Jewish military colony after that date.[7] Around 400 B.C., Egypt threw off the Persian conquerors, and a new pharaoh was enthroned. The nationalistic resurgence was very likely to have been a major factor in the demise of the Jewish colony.

The remains of the large Jewish community there are still being excavated by the German archaeological school in Cairo. Their discoveries are officially downplayed – the small museum on Elephantine Island ignores the Jewish nature of the settlement – but the archaeologists actually doing the excavation are more forthcoming.

On a visit to the site I was struck by how extensive and impressive the remains of this Jewish town are: the blackened mud-brick ruins of multistory houses, separated by narrow streets, are perched on high ground at the southern tip of the island, gazing down at the Nile as feluccas pass, their white sails like gull wings between the blue water, the rocky islands, and the great golden dunes of the arid western bank.

Archaeologists working on the site explained to me that they had been finding ostraca – broken potsherds recycled as writing material – that held Aramaic text and recorded Jewish names and streets. The remains showed that when the end of the Jewish community came, it was final: all the houses were destroyed by fire. The same fate is presumed for the Temple of Yahweh. The present ruined Temple of Khnum dates back from Ptolemaic times and is thought to have been built on top of the earlier Jewish structure. Certainly it is right beside the ruined Jewish town, which seems a strange place to build a non-Jewish temple. However, the Temple of Yahweh on Elephantine Island was not to be the last Jewish sanctuary in Egypt.

It is almost a secret. It is certainly kept discreet. During the lifetime of Jesus, there was a functioning Jewish temple in Egypt, a temple in which Jewish priests carried out the required daily sacrifices in just the same manner as was done in Jerusalem. This temple, moreover, claimed to be the only one in the Jewish world to be served by legitimate priests, and it survived, for a few years at least, the destruction of the Temple in Jerusalem.

Its claim to legitimacy as the sole temple served by the true priesthood of the Jewish faith finds support in much of the surviving evidence. Almost every source agrees that its priests, unlike those in Jerusalem, were of the true "Zadokite" priesthood – that is, they were legitimate descendents or heirs of the Levitical priests, "the sons of Zadok," described in Ezekiel (44:15–16) as having God's permission to enter into the divine presence in order to serve and perform the sacred liturgy. We find that this heritage is of vital importance to the members of the group who produced the Dead Sea Scrolls: one of the terms of self-description they used was *benei Zadok*, the "Sons of Zadok"; they took this responsibility very seriously. In fact, one of the scrolls, the Damascus Document, earlier called "A Zadokite Work," proclaims: "The sons of Zadok are the chosen of Israel."[8]

Professor Joan Taylor of New Zealand's Waikato University, one of the few modern scholars to have studied this temple, explained that it was certainly to be considered a Zadokite institution.[9] This links the temple with the milieu of the Dead Sea Scrolls and draws it closer into our story.

One of the many enigmas surrounding the Dead Sea Scrolls concerns Cave 7 at Qumran: all the texts found in this cave – parts of Exodus, part of the Letter of Jeremiah,

and seventeen small fragments that have not been identified – were written in Greek and on papyrus. All of the
scrolls found in the other caves were written in Hebrew or
Aramaic on parchment. Given that the Qumran sect was
vehemently opposed to foreigners, it is impossible that any
Greeks would have been members of their group. The only
explanation is that there were Zealots whose native language was Greek and *who could not speak Hebrew or Aramaic*.
Where could such Jews who were also Zealots have lived?
As we now know, they could have lived in Egypt.

It is incredible to think that even today this temple's existence remains a sensitive matter. Long ago the historian
Josephus, for his own reasons, conspired to relegate it to ob-
scurity as a schismatic institution operating contrary to Jewish law. This judgement, it is said, rendered illegitimate any
temple other than the one in Jerusalem. Even the modern
Encyclopaedia Judaica concurs with this dismissive attitude,
stating, "The temple fulfilled no religious function in the
Jewish community of Egypt whose loyalties were solely to
the Temple in Jerusalem."[10] Scholarly consensus endorses
this view: the Oxford historian Professor Geza Vermes is
happy to describe the temple as an illegitimate structure
erected "in direct breach of biblical law." He declares – with
no evidence whatsoever – that this foundation "must have
scandalized every Palestinian conservative, even those
priests who belonged, or were allied, to the Zadokite
dynasty."[11] We can be forgiven for wondering what on earth
he is talking about.

The story behind the foundation of this Jewish temple in Egypt is very simple: at first the Ptolemaic dynasty ruled both Egypt and Israel. So long as the taxes were paid, the Egyptian rulers were happy to leave Israel under the jurisdiction of the high priest and his council. The high priest served as a kind of viceroy. In that capacity, he commanded the Jewish army, which he placed at the disposal of the Ptolemies.

Around 200 B.C., the Seleucid ruler of Syria conquered Israel. In 175 B.C., Antiochus Epiphanes succeeded as ruler; resolved to increase his influence in Judaea and Egypt, he attacked Jerusalem and Egypt in 170 B.C. The Zadokite high priest, Onias III, a close friend of Ptolemy VI's, led his Jewish forces in support of the Egyptian army against the Seleucids. But the Syrian forces prevailed, and Onias was forced to flee into Egypt around the same date with many of his priests. Meanwhile, the Temple in Jerusalem was taken over by non-Zadokite priests allied to the Syrian ruler.

In 169 B.C., Antiochus again invaded and this time seized the treasures in the Temple. He moved on into Egypt again the next year, but the increasingly powerful Romans ordered Antiochus out. They wished to protect the all-important grain supplies to Rome. Antiochus then, in 167 B.C., forbade further Jewish worship in the Temple and instead dedicated the sanctuary to Zeus. It was this act that finally drove the Jews left in Israel to insurrection, led by the Maccabees.

Once in exile, Onias sought to maintain the legitimate temple service. He found a long-ruined temple of Bubastis in the Egyptian delta and asked Ptolemy if he could take it over and rebuild it as a Jewish temple; Ptolemy granted his request. The temple, we are told, was built on the same design as that in Jerusalem. Significantly, after services began, only this temple was served by priests of the legitimate Zadokite lineage. To that extent it is true that this was the sole legitimate Jewish temple. But since it was outside Judaea, its status was ambiguous. In fact, it would appear most likely that the intention was for these legitimate services to be maintained in Egypt only until the Temple in Jerusalem could be returned to the legitimate priesthood; when that happened, the priests would be immediately available and ready to move back. Unfortunately, this never happened, and so this temple and its Zadokite priesthood maintained services for the next two hundred years or so.

It is therefore by no means clear-cut that this Egyptian foundation was illegitimate and contrary to Jewish law. Rabbinical tradition records debates on the temple, in particular discourse on whether it was correct to fulfill vows at the Egyptian temple rather than in Jerusalem and whether it was possible for a priest from the Egyptian temple to serve in the Jerusalem temple.[12] These debates reveal that religious experts closer to the period than the scholars of today found support for both viewpoints. In other words, whatever the Torah might have said on the subject, nothing constituted a clear denunciation of Onias's temple.

It is right, then, that we should look at the history of this temple and try to understand why its existence is considered so sensitive that it has had to be marginalized to the point that very few people today have even heard of it. And why, since 1929, have no archaeologists shown any interest in the site? Why too has it *never* been systematically excavated, despite the fact that part of an inscription written in ancient Hebrew has been found there?[13] The archaeologist Flinders Petrie also reported finding there Jewish tombstones and a fragment of text bearing the name Abram.[14]

One immediate possibility is that political concerns have made the site an unwelcome addition to Egyptology. Sadly, this challenge may make it easier for those who wish to bury the site forever to do so. The site, Tell el-Yehoudieh (the "Mound of Judaea"), about twenty miles from Cairo, has been heavily vandalized and will soon be covered by the suburbs of the expanding modern town of Shibin al Qanatir. Time for any action is fast running out.

The story of this temple is given by the Jewish historian Josephus. In his earliest work, *The Jewish War*, he describes the building of the temple in Egypt by the high priest Onias, son of a former priest, Simon, and a friend of Ptolemy VI's. This then is the priest known to history as Onias III, who was of the legitimate Zadokite line.[15]

Approximately fifteen years later, Josephus wrote his *Antiquities of the Jews*. But in this work he changed details of the story: he attributed the building of the temple in Egypt to Onias IV – the *son* of Onias III. Not only does this serve to move the building of the temple to a later date, but more importantly for Josephus's purpose, it places someone who was *not* a high priest of the Zadokite line as the founder. Onias IV was a military commander in the Egyptian army, as were his two sons after him. By changing the attribution, Josephus *has removed the legitimacy of the Jewish temple in Egypt.* Why would he want to do this?

This error has been perpetrated to the present day. Oxford's Geza Vermes states explicitly that it was Onias IV who founded the Egyptian temple, thus maintaining the exclusion of this temple from serious academic consideration.[16] In this example, the process is clear: if history chooses to accept Onias III as the founder, then this temple is legitimate and Jerusalem's temple is not. If history chooses to accept Onias IV as the founder, then it is the Egyptian temple that is illegitimate. But on the evidence of Josephus's *Jewish War* and, interestingly, early rabbinical tradition, Onias III was the builder of this temple, and so we must conclude that the Egyptian temple was indeed the legitimate one.[17]

The Greek papyrus manuscripts found in Cave 7 at Qumran attest to a close connection between overseas Jewish Zealots, of which Egypt was the most probable source, and those Zealots active within Judaea and Galilee. Both were, it seems, members of the community of the Sons of Zadok. But there are closer links that, significantly, draw the Temple of Onias into the Zealot milieu. This can be demonstrated by means of the calendar in use.

Most of Judaism maintained a lunar calendar in which the new month was determined by the day the new moon first became visible, and the day was measured from sunset. This was a very unreliable calendar, however, and could be kept practical only by adding extra days when necessary. The Zealot authors of the Dead Sea Scrolls, who seem to have had a base at Qumran, used a completely different calendar. Theirs was solar, so for them the day began at sunrise.[18] Two of the early Jewish texts found in several examples at Qumran, the Book of Jubilees and the Book of Enoch, both used a solar calendar, as did the sectarian Temple Scroll.

The Temple of Onias may also have conducted its religious year on the basis of a solar calendar: according to the Jewish philosopher and patrician cultural leader Philo of Alexandria, writing around the time of Jesus, the central candle of the seven-branched menorah in the Temple of Jerusalem represented the sun. However, according to Josephus, the Temple of Onias did not contain a seven-branched candlestick but instead had a "hanging lamp with one single flame which shed 'a brilliant light.'" This in all probability represented the sun,[19] suggesting that the Temple of Onias did indeed use a solar calendar.[20] If so, this would be sufficient proof to place it in the wider Zealot world.

It is now time to draw these complicated threads together and see why this temple engendered such hostility – and why it seems to remain so sensitive today. Although this may seem a minor point at first, it will prove to be as important as the many other seemingly minor facts we have already noted, such as Jesus's anointment with spikenard or the mysterious nocturnal visit of Joseph of Arimathea and Nicodemus to Jesus's tomb with medicinal ointments and spices. Once we become more familiar with the territory and can carry these details in our minds, we are able to watch as a completely different perspective on these events unfolds.

When Josephus was writing his histories, sitting in what was undoubtedly considerable luxury in the imperial palace in Rome and contemplating life after the destruction of the Temple in Jerusalem and the slaughter of many thousands of his compatriots, he had every reason to vilify the Zealots and all they stood for. After all, it was the least he could do for his new patrons, the Roman imperial family.

It was, we will remember, the Zealots whom he blamed for the outbreak of the destructive war that caused such loss. He cleverly handled his own past as a Zealot commander so as to absolve himself of any blame. Similarly, he was at pains to portray the Jewish nation as blameless: loyal subjects of their overlords, the Ptolemies in Egypt and the Romans in Judaea, they were led astray by hotheaded Zealot agitators and assassins. And here we have the crux of the matter: as we have seen, the priesthood of the Egyptian Jewish temple were Zadokite; the Zealots in Judaea and Galilee were also Zadokites; those who wrote the Dead Sea Scrolls were Zadokites and Zealots. The disastrous war had been caused and fought by Zadokites who were "zealous for the Law." Of course Josephus had to diminish the status of the Jewish temple in the Egyptian delta served by priests of the legitimate Zadokite lineage. He had no other options if he wanted to retain his privileged position in the heart of Rome's aristocracy.

Furthermore, we must remember that the Egyptian Jewish community, especially the huge Alexandrian urban population, similarly wished to avoid the troubles so recently visited upon their brethren in Israel. When fleeing Zealots arrived in Alexandria and began agitating there and murdering some prominent Jews who opposed them, the Jewish population quickly gave them up to the Romans, who just as quickly tortured them to death.[21] Clearly the Alexandrian Jews would have wanted as much distance placed between their community and the Zadokite movement as possible; Josephus was evidently very happy to oblige.

Also note that, despite the existence of the Jewish temple in the delta, the leading Alexandrian Jews were great supporters of the Temple in Jerusalem; the lack of a legitimate Zadokite priesthood was apparently of little concern to them – or at least, of little concern to the patrician Jews who held wealth and power. The financial controller of Egypt, the Jewish patrician Alexander Lysimachus, was a major donor to the Jerusalem temple. He had personally paid for the thick gold and silver plating on the fifty-foot-high double doors on the gate from the Court of the Women.[22] His son, General Tiberius Alexander, prefect of

Egypt from A.D. 46 to 48 and in A.D. 66, was, as we have already noted, a close friend of Titus's and chief of staff of the Roman army that destroyed the Temple in A.D. 70. Neither father nor son would have had any love for the Zealots – or, by extension, the Zadokites. And as we have also noted, General Tiberius Alexander was a close friend of Josephus's.

Alexander Lysimachus had a famous brother: the philosopher Philo of Alexandria. Philo attempted to draw together Platonic and Jewish philosophy, taking a mystical approach to Jewish thought. In those of his works that survive, he wrote about many of the Jewish religious groups he considered important. He tended to side personally with those groups of a mystical, even esoteric, nature – groups within Judaism that, to his mind, seemed to be the Jewish equivalents of the Greek philosophical traditions he admired most, such as the Platonists and the Pythagoreans. Yet, in all his surveys of the variations of Judaism, Philo never once mentioned the temple built by Onias in the delta.

This silence is curious, but we cannot read much into it except to conclude that he had, for whatever reasons, decided to ignore its existence. But this, in itself, is revealing. For one would expect that the most notable Jews in Alexandria would take pride in the existence of a Jewish temple that had so august an ancestry and that continued to work in Egypt. That they did not, and that they, like Philo's brother, continued to support the Temple in Jerusalem – a temple run by a priesthood vehemently opposed by the

Zealots – is perhaps significant. Was this silence on the part of Philo due to some knowledge of Zealot sympathies among the priesthood serving the temple in the delta? Could he have been aware of the Zealots' political ambitions and been opposed to them? It is a reasonable suggestion that does have the advantage of making sense of Philo's curious omission.

This temple was on the road from Judaea to Heliopolis, an important city in Egypt and the site of the present-day Cairo airport. Any overland travelers from Judaea into Egypt would have begun on the road to Heliopolis. While the road to the Greek cities of Naucratis and Alexandria branched off to the west, an undeviating journey down the road led to the temple and to Heliopolis, Memphis, and Upper Egypt. If Jesus and his parents had traveled to Egypt and, as good Zealots, had wished to avoid the strongly Greek-influenced Jewish communities, they would have moved south along this road that passed by Onias's temple. It would simply have been impossible to avoid it.

And it is highly unlikely that Jesus and his family, raised in a Zealot environment, one that hoped and prayed for a reinstatement of a Zadokite priesthood in the Temple of Jerusalem, would have just passed by this Egyptian Jewish temple. All of these observations lead naturally to the thought that the Temple of Onias served as the initial training site of Jesus. It was here perhaps that he received his introduction into the politically active world of the Zealots.

In a sense, we can see the temple as an overseas branch of

Galilee where Greek-speaking Zealots could learn their trade. It would have also been a good place for Jesus's family to bring him so that he could learn what it would mean to be the Messiah of Israel, for all the texts and commentaries on the role of the messiah would have been available there. So we do now have a good reason for the Holy Family to have traveled to Egypt, and a reason for Matthew's brief comment, disguised as a flight from the dangers posed by Herodian infanticide. In fact, it would seem not to have been a flight at all but rather a positive action undertaken in order to allow Jesus to grow, to study, and to teach away from the troubles in Judaea and Galilee.

Despite his training in the Zealot cause, Jesus, as we have seen, at some point secretly took another path – one revealed only after he had been anointed as messiah, when it was far too late for anybody to challenge him. That path was a more mystical path. Yet where in the Jewish world of Egypt could he have learned such a path? For the answer to this question, we need to look at one of the mystical groups of the time, one described by Philo of Alexandria.

Lake Maryut stretches away to the southwest of Alexandria. Between the lake and the sea is a low limestone hill that runs approximately eighteen kilometers from the city walls. During the time of Philo of Alexandria, on either side of this hill, was lower land that held individual dwellings, perhaps summer villas owned by the rich of Alexandria, and a number of villages and small towns. Because of its proximity to both the lake and the sea, this limestone spur was swept by breezes that kept the air fresh and cooler than the air in the city. On this hill lived a small community of Jewish philosophers who took advantage of the rural peacefulness, the relative security afforded by the nearby villas and towns, and the cool and healthy sea air to devote themselves to lives of contemplation.[23]

This community was given the name of Therapeutae, which, as Philo explains, carries both a sense of healing – not only of the body but also of the soul – and a sense of worship. Therapeutae worship centered on the "Self-Existent" – a belief in the One Divine Reality, never created but eternal.[24] This was a concept of divinity far beyond the capability of language to describe.

In one important way, the Therapeutae were very different from the other dedicated groups Philo describes, such as the Essenes. Among the Therapeutae, women were admitted as equal members and participated fully in the spiritual life of the community. By contrast, the Essenes, according to Philo, Josephus, and Pliny, were proud of the fact that they excluded women; women, they believed, were a distraction.[25] We should recall here the inclusive attitude of Jesus toward the women in his entourage and the criticism that this engendered among some of his male disciples in the Gospels, for there have been many questionable attempts to ally Jesus with the Essenes.

The Therapeutae were an elitist community made up apparently of well-educated and wealthy Alexandrians of

Philo's patrician class who had chosen to give up all their possessions and live lives of communal simplicity, dedicated to worship. It seems, from his comments, which have the character of personal experience, that Philo had visited this group and participated in some of their services.[26]

But this group was not alone: Philo describes other such groups dedicated to a type of meditative contemplation throughout all the regions of Egypt.[27] As Philo explains, noting that similar groups existed in other parts of the world within other religious traditions, the Therapeutae represented a Jewish version of a widespread mystical tradition that found expression in all lands.

The implication of the Therapeutae's inclusion of women, however, is that when a group is dedicated to the contemplation of the highest experience of the soul – to that sight of the soul "which alone gives a knowledge of truth and falsehood" – the gender of the worshiper is irrelevant. This may seem self-evident to us today, but in the world of Philo and Jesus this concept was truly revolutionary.

The Therapeutae were mystics and visionaries: "It is well," Philo writes, "that the Therapeutae, a people always taught from the first to use their sight, should desire the vision of the Existent and soar above the sun of our senses."[28]

Members of the Therapeutae wanted to have a direct vision of reality – or of the "Self-Existent," to use Philo's term – in order to experience what truly exists behind the rough-and-tumble world of this transitory life. This too was the aim of many groups operating in the classical world, especially in those great and secret cults called "the Mysteries." Here we appear to have a Jewish version, seeking the same end, but operating in a much simpler manner within the Jewish tradition.

The Therapeutae prayed at dawn and sunset. During the day they would read the holy texts, but rather than taking these as the history of the Jewish nation, they understood them as allegory. According to Philo, they considered the literal text a symbol of something hidden that they could find only if they looked for it.[29]

Every seven days they would gather together and hear a talk by one of the senior members; every fifty days they would have a major assembly where they would all put on white robes, eat a simple sacred meal, and form a choir, men and women together, to sing hymns with complex rhythms and vocal parts. This festival would continue all night until dawn, revealing the solar nature of their worship: "They stand with their faces and whole body turned to the east and when they see the sun rising they stretch their hands up to heaven and pray for bright days and knowledge of the truth."[30]

Clearly this is a very different type of Judaism, one that does not depend upon temple worship at all. In Therapeutae worship, which has a very Pythagorean tinge, there is no concern with the cult of Judaism, which was so important to the priests in the temples of Jerusalem and the Egyptian delta, or with the purity of the high priests serving that cult, which was of such concern to the Zealots, or with the coming of the Messiah of the Line of David. For both male and female members of the Therapeutae, there was simply the possibility of a visionary experience of Divinity.

Their kingdom was truly not of this world: Jesus would have approved.

There is one further implication of the Therapeutae's beliefs that warrants more discussion, and that is the practice of treating the entire Old Testament as symbolic. They would have read all the messianic predictions made by the prophets symbolically. There would have been no reason in their minds for an actual messiah to come to liberate Israel; there would have been no reason for Jesus to be the actual king and high priest; the oracular pronouncements of the messiah would have been simply symbolic of something deeper and more mysterious. We have seen before how the "Star" is a symbol of the messiah, but can we now take this concept a little further? Can we see the statement by Peter in the New Testament as reflecting this kind of speculation, albeit in a Christian context? Could the phrase "Let the Day Star rise in your hearts" (2 Peter 1:19) be interpreted as an encouragement to let the mystic light rise from within?

With such attitudes apparently widespread, perhaps even common, it is no wonder that Judaism in Egypt, and Christianity afterwards, had a distinctively mystical quality: it was in Egypt that Christian monasticism first began; it was in Egypt at Nag Hammadi that someone hid the Gnostic texts, that collection of Christian and classical mystical texts – including one by Plato and one from the texts of

Hermes Trismegistus, the *Asclepius* – that had been compiled and used by a desert monastery.

The Christian Church in Egypt had mystically minded figures even as late as the third century – theologians Clement of Alexandria and Origen, for example. We have Egyptian traditions leaking into Judaism from very early days – the times of Joseph and Moses – and in more recent times, as we see in the writings of Philo. In the midst of all this we have groups such as the Therapeutae working a mystical type of Judaism and the Temple of Onias maintaining the true Jewish Zadokite priesthood.

At this point one is tempted to ask, "What was it about Egypt that gave this mystical focus to Judaism and the Christianity born out of it? What kind of soil were these foreign faiths growing in?"

The irony of these questions is that it was not so much the land that nourished these faiths as it was the sun, which poured out its life-giving sustenance from above. A clue lies in the fact that both the Therapeutae and the Jewish Zadokites adopted the solar calendar from the Egyptians, whose major deity, Ra, was in fact an expression of the sun as the source of life, the source of all creation. Texts reveal that the pharaoh, at least, sought mystical union with Ra as the "deepest fulfilment of our human divine nature."[31]

The profound mysticism that lay at the very heart of the Egyptian experience of reality clearly influenced many of the other faiths that had established themselves there. This Egyptian mysticism, which employed secret readings of myth and private rituals, often played out in secluded underground chambers and temples, professed to connect this world with the next, to connect heaven and earth.

The approach of the Egyptians was not a kind of philosophy, a speculation on divine possibilities, or a faith built solely upon the hope for a better life after death. The Egyptians were not only mystical but intensely practical. They did not want to talk about heaven – they wanted to go there. And return. Just like Lazarus in fact.

It's time now to look at the hidden mysteries of Egypt.

9

The Mysteries of Egypt

In the beginning, according to the ancient Egyptians, everything was perfect. Any fall from this state of eternal harmony, called *Ma'at*, was due to mankind's imperfections, and the greatest of these human imperfections were those caused by greed.

It was the task of everyone, the great as well as the humble, to work toward maintaining this perfection and restoring any imbalance in it. But the ultimate responsibility lay with the pharaoh, aided by a network of temples that covered all of Egypt.

Every morning saw the same ritual of awakening the gods in the temples at the moment of sunrise, when the doors of the Inner Sanctum would be opened. The director of the Petrie Museum in London, Dr. Stephen Quirke, has likened the Egyptian temple, only half in jest, to "a machine for the preservation of the universe, a technical operation that requires technical staff or knowledge ... in order to ensure that the crucial task of survival is never impaired."[1]

At the same time the temple was a gateway to the Beyond: it was the place where the earth and the sky joined as they seem to do on the horizon, and for this reason many texts refer to the temple as a celestial horizon. The ancient word for "horizon," *akhet*, had a number of significant meanings: it referred not only to the joining of the sky and the earth but also to a specific part of the horizon where the sun god rose from the Far-World, the *Duat*, every morning and returned to it every evening.[2] Clearly, for the Egyptians, the horizon marked a portal into the Far-World.

Pyramids too were imbued with this quality: the Great Pyramid of the pharaoh Khufu at Giza was termed the "akhet of Khufu." Furthermore, the root of the word *akhet* means "to blaze, to be radiant."[3] On one level this term referred to the blaze of light at sunset or sunrise, but it also had a much more secret meaning, which we will discover.

The primary role of the pharaoh was to serve as the guarantor of Ma'at. The only – and greatest – thing asked of human beings was to live in Ma'at, bringing the cosmos and the physical world into harmony. This perfectly balanced state was personified by the goddess Ma'at, who was depicted with an ostrich feather in her hair. She brought truth and justice, the fruits of harmony, into the world.

Coexisting within this universal perfection were two

worlds: the physical world, which we are born into and within which we live, and the other world to which we travel when we die, the Duat, or the Far-World.[4] The Far-World was not seen as separate, as some heaven or hell far away from or unconnected with mundane existence. Rather, the Far-World was ever-present. It was believed to exist simultaneously with the physical world, intertwining with it like the two snakes around the caduceus of Hermes. It was with us all the time even though we could not normally see it or travel to it until we died.

These two worlds occupied the same space, in some mysterious and unexplained manner, except that the physical world remained within time whereas the Far-World existed beyond time. Time began with creation, but the Far-World was seen as eternal, not in the sense of being an infinite stretch of time reaching forever into the future and stretching from a past forever distant, but rather eternal in that it was *outside* of time. The ruler of the Far-World was the god Osiris, and the guide for the dead was Thoth, who led them up to the kingdom of the gods.

A further aspect of the Far-World is that it was understood to be the eternal background to everything in the visible universe. It was considered the divine source of all things, the source of all power and all vitality. Life itself was believed to come from the Far-World, which seeped into the physical world and revealed itself in all the forms we see about us.

For the ancient Egyptians, the world of the dead was always very close to the world of the living – there was an intimacy between the two. Paradoxically, the world of the dead was the source for the world of life. Indeed, the dead were believed to be the truly living ones.

A tomb inscription dating from the New Kingdom (around 1550–1070 B.C.) reminds us that "a trifle only of life is this world, [but] eternity is in the realm of the dead."⁵ An earlier Middle Kingdom (around 2040–1650 B.C.) tomb of the priest Neferhotep in Thebes – now Luxor – contains several "Harper's Songs," the second of which ends:

> As for a lifetime done on earth, it is a moment of a dream. It is said: "Welcome, safe and sound" to the one who reaches the West.⁶

The "West" for the Egyptians was the land of the dead. Tombs and pyramids were always built on the west bank of the Nile, where it was thought that the sun vanished at night into the Far-World.

To understand this, it is useful to look at the ancient Egyptian concept of time: they understood that two types of time were operating simultaneously. There was the kind of time they called *neheh*, the cyclical time involved in natural patterns – the seasons, the movement of the stars, and so forth. The other was known as *djet*, which was no time at all – a state of being outside of time entirely. Only in neheh did time move; djet represented time in suspension.⁷ While neheh might be infinite, only djet was eternal; one inscription reads: "The things of djet-eternity do not die."⁸

This dual perspective is very different from our modern concept of time in which we are ever tumbling onwards into a future that we can only hope will be perfect – a hope that for many religions rests upon the fulfillment of a promise that a messiah will someday appear to win the final battle against the forces of evil and in so doing will usher in a perfect world. Our political philosophy too is very dependent upon linear time, on a trajectory stretching from the past into the future where, if we manage our legislation correctly, we will achieve satisfaction for all citizens, as if legislation is something that does more than plaster over cracks.

And yet, those of our culture who have stepped out of time – the mystics – report, like the ancient Egyptians, that the world of the dead is indeed a world of the living, that it is ever-present and very close. Making allowances for the great differences in culture and language, we can see this same sense of proximity to the divine world stressed in the reports of the great sixteenth-century mystic Saint Teresa of Ávila, who often fell into a mystical "rapture" wherein she was utterly "dissolved" into the divine kingdom. Speaking of God she stressed:

> There was one thing that I was ignorant of at the beginning. I did not really know that God is present in all things; and when He seemed to me so near, I thought that it was impossible.[9]

The main aid of those who would preserve Ma'at was the great god Tehuti – called Thoth by the Greeks and identified with Hermes. He knew the deepest secrets of Ma'at and could initiate both the dead and the living into its wisdom. Thoth knew "the secrets of the night."[10] The Far-World was where perfection reigned, and with Thoth's aid – that is, with an education in the correct techniques – humans could visit there. They could visit *and* return from the kingdom of the gods.

Since the earliest records began, we can see that all the temple rituals were designed to maintain universal harmony. And in these temples both men and women were initiated into its secrets. But they were also told that they had to keep silent about what they saw. In fact, everything about the temple secrets was guarded. Among the many texts carved on the walls of the Temple of Horus at Edfu is the blunt warning: "Do not reveal what you have seen in the mysteries of the temples."[11]

So how can we find out what occurred in these "mysteries"? Did anyone ever break cover and reveal their secrets?

One of the problems we face when seeking to understand the early religious practices of the wide variety of ancient cultures is that until writing was not only invented but sufficiently developed to record ideas and beliefs, we do not know what our ancestors believed. Although a symbolic recording system for commercial transactions using small clay tokens began around 8000 B.C., it did not develop into writing until around 3000 B.C.[12]

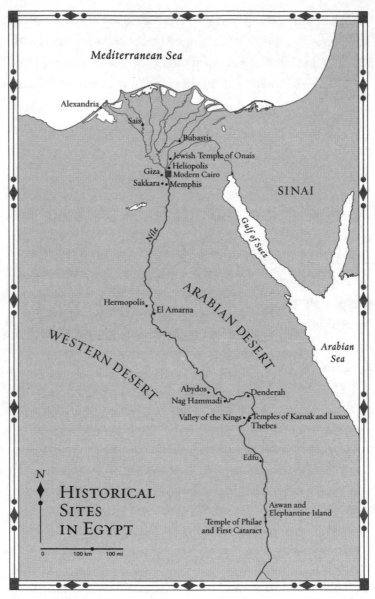

Key places to visit in Egypt today

An example of this problem is seen with the excavation of the great ziggurat at Eridu, once a prominent Sumerian city in what is now Iraq. The ziggurat itself could be dated to 2100 B.C., and texts have revealed that it was dedicated to the deity of the city, Enki, god of wisdom, learning, and the subterranean waters. However, careful excavation revealed the remains of twenty-three earlier temples lying beneath the ziggurat in successively deeper occupation levels, the earliest being a simple chapel built upon an ancient sand dune and dating back to at least 5000 B.C. Eighteen levels were revealed from the so-called Ubaid period, which preceded the appearance of writing.[13]

The ziggurat was devoted to Enki, but what can be made of the previous occupation levels? Can we say that since it was the same temple, the cult of Enki must have existed right back to the beginning? Of course we can't. An invader, for example, might easily have imposed one cult upon an earlier one; in fact, this happened quite frequently. Or a cult might have departed to another site, leaving an empty temple to be filled by something quite different. There are certainly examples of temples being put to different uses from those of the original cult they were built to serve. We have already seen the case of Onias's temple in the Egyptian delta, which began as a temple for the worship of Bubastis but, when derelict, was converted to one serving the Jewish faith. The physical building is proof only of the existence of an organized cult; it cannot tell us much, if anything, about which cult it hosted.

Even the existence of symbolism does not necessarily help. Without texts, we cannot understand what the symbols meant to those who used them. The bare stone walls of the strange inner rooms of the Great Pyramid, for example, so different from the others on the Giza Plateau, leave us with no idea of the primary use of the structure. Conversely, the town of Chatel Hüyük in southern Turkey, the largest Neolithic town known in the Near East, dates from almost eight thousand years ago and has over forty shrines filled with symbolism distributed through a number of occupation levels. The interiors of some are decorated with painting; one has rows of horns of the extinct wild bull, the *auroch*, on benches; another has plaster relief work of bull heads and horns; one combines women's breasts and bull horns; and painted geometric patterns abound. Each shrine is different; apart from an obsession with bull horns, any consistency in this bewildering range of symbolic decoration is hard to discern. And beyond the shrines can be found small statues of a female goddess.[14] Why are there none within the shrines? The area is rich in symbolism, yet without texts we have no clue to their meaning.

We can, however, glean some idea of general trends: we can see that there was a deep concern with the relationship of this world with the "other" world, the Far-World. When literature began to appear, one of the earliest texts was so important that it was written down many times over: in the great Epic of Gilgamesh, a king of Uruk travels to the Far-World seeking immortality. He fails at his task because he cannot stay "awake" and so returns to tell the story of his spiritual journey.

This epic is unlikely to have been created simply to take advantage of the development of writing. We can be sure that the ancient oral tradition of Mesopotamia was concerned with the relationship of the Far-World with the physical world. Even this is a remarkable conclusion. But we can go back to much earlier times for evidence of this concept's origins: it seems likely that from the first time humans began observing ritual ceremonies at the burial of the dead, a distinction between this world and the "other" was established – that the existence of the two was acknowledged and that a ceremony was deemed appropriate for the final passing from one to the other.

The earliest known example of a deliberate ceremonial burial was conducted by Neanderthals: one hundred thousand years ago a young man was buried in central Asia. Russian archaeologists discovered his remains surrounded by pairs of goat horns. Another Neanderthal skeleton was excavated at Le Moustier in France, a site dated to some seventy-five thousand years ago. This burial had also been subject to funeral ritual. The dead man was covered with red ochre, his head lay on a mound of flints, and the burned bones of cattle were spread around him. Later burials dating from approximately sixty thousand years ago were found in a large cave at Shanidar in Iraq. One individual had been laid down upon a layer of flowers, all with medicinal possibilities.[15] Some thirty-six other ceremonial burials have been found in Europe and Asia over the succeeding millennia. We can be reasonably confident that the Far-World has been of concern for tens of thousands of years – at the very least. And further, implicit in this concern is the question of the source of life itself and the existence of human self-consciousness.

But we are still left grappling with the challenge posed by the fact that there are no texts whatsoever inside either the Great Pyramid or the others on the Giza Plateau. They were all built by Fourth Dynasty pharaohs around 2500 B.C. The earliest texts appear at the end of the Fifth Dynasty and during the Sixth – around 2300 B.C. The very first is inscribed on the walls of the subterranean chambers of the Pyramid of Unas, the last pharaoh of the Fifth Dynasty. Then, during the next two hundred years or so, another five pyramids were similarly inscribed with texts. Called, for obvious reasons, the Pyramid Texts, they have provided us with valuable information, but they have also ushered us into a mystery. It seems that they have been well translated but badly understood.

It's not surprising that misunderstandings have occurred because it is about now that archaeologists begin edging their way out of the room. They feel uncomfortable; they know that things are about to start becoming distinctly weird. But no one ever said that they wouldn't.

In truth, it was just a matter of time.

Because texts were found in certain pyramids that are assumed to have been solely concerned with death and burial, the texts too have been assumed to be concerned only with

the dead. Such a view would seem supported by one utterance carved on the wall in the subterranean chambers of
these pyramids: "The spirit is bound for the sky, the corpse
is bound for the earth."[16]

But there are some curiosities that need looking at: "O
king, you have not departed dead, you have departed alive,"
reads one utterance in the Pyramid Texts.[17] Certainly this is
ambiguous: it could be read as meaning that since the king
has died he is moving into eternal life, and so in that sense
he is alive to the heavenly world, but it could equally be read
as meaning that while the king will depart to the Far-World
when he dies, on this occasion he is traveling there while
still alive.

If so, this means that he would have expected to return
after his journey. Or are we reading too much into this? Can
such an idea even be supported by the texts?

Another line in the Pyramid Texts reads: "I have gone
and returned... I go forth today in the real form of a living
spirit."[18] It is hard not to see this as lending direct support
to the idea of the living visiting the Far-World.

There are also many illustrations of the soul of the dead
– or as it was called in ancient Egypt, the *Ba* – in the funerary literature found in tombs and coffins. There the Ba is
depicted as a bird, but with the head and face of the deceased
person. In its claws this bird is often shown holding the *shen*
sign, a symbol of eternity – revealing the gift it brings from
the world it inhabits.

While *Ba* is usually translated as "soul," it implies much

more. It reveals that it is an inner yet hidden aspect of the person who has died, that it is as mobile as the vehicle by which that person's inner spirit moves independently of the dead body and flies back to its divine source.

But it implies even more than this: first, the Ba always exists; it does not simply come into existence upon death. According to the Egyptian priests, it is an integral part of every human being. If this is true, there would appear to be no reason why a person could not experience his or her Ba form *before* death.

Dr. Jeremy Naydler, who has made a study of the deeper mysteries expressed in the Egyptian texts, stresses that we must never allow ourselves to forget the experiential nature of these ancient religious writings. He makes the important point that "the *ba* could be defined as an individual in an out-of-body state." He explains that at the point of death this state "occurred spontaneously," but during life "this out-of-body awareness had to be induced."[19] It had to be induced, in other words, by ritual or some other specific method of initiation. Implicit in Naydler's analysis is the suggestion that the ancient Egyptians practiced some extraordinary techniques of initiation that led to knowledge of the Far-World and thus allowed individuals to visit there and to return.

There is indeed a very curious feature of certain Egyptian temple rituals that scholars do not fully understand: according to texts we have found, the officiating priest would sit in a quiet place and use specific techniques to enter a state described in hieroglyphs as *qed*. Under usual circumstances, this state would translate as "sleep," but in this specific ritual context, it indicates something more akin to a state of trance or meditation. Its main use, scholars think, was during the animation rite for sacred statues called "the Opening of the Mouth," when divine power was called down to reside in the statue, which was thereby rendered sacred. This same rite also formed part of the funerary practices. It is evident, in the latter case at least, that while in this ritual state the priest somehow moved into the world of the dead, the Far-World, and that on his return he was able to describe what he had experienced as a dead person.[20] We need to take this seriously, because these texts record something that not only happened but seems to have happened regularly during these rituals.

We can be confident, I would suggest, that this ritual journey was not just an intellectual invention or some kind of priestly drama, a "pious fraud" that provided smoke and noise enough to impress but little true fire. Around the late third to early fourth centuries A.D., the philosopher Iamblichus of Apamea, one of the most prominent Platonic scholars of his era, was teaching in what is now Lebanon. His teaching was centered upon what he called *theurgy*, which we have already briefly touched on – that is, "working with" the gods. He contrasted this with *theology* – "talking about" the gods. He was interested in practical effects rather than intellectual argument; he wanted his students to *know*, not just to believe.

Iamblichus had become familiar with the secret teachings

of Egypt. One of his major works was entitled *On the Mysteries of the Egyptians*; in it he reveals much of the heart of the inner knowledge of the temples. He is quite open about the abilities of the priests to separate their consciousness from their bodies and move into the Far-World. He reports that the priests' souls were drawn upwards by the gods' "accustoming them, while they are yet in body, to be separated from bodies" in order to be guided to their eternal source.[21]

Iamblichus states explicitly later in the same work that the priests did not gain their knowledge of the divine realms "by mere reason alone" — which, incidentally, was a direct and deliberate challenge to the popular approach of Aristotle — but rather, by means of a priestly theurgy, "they announce that they are able to ascend to more elevated and universal [realities]."[22]

Iamblichus is not speaking of possibilities or fantasies. He is stating a simple fact of the Egyptian priesthood. He is confirming that they knew how to travel to the Far-World. The real questions are: Why should we be surprised? And have we gained or lost something as a result of our modern suspicion and skepticism?

Around the second millennium B.C., texts began appearing on the inside of wooden coffins. These texts were derived from the earlier Pyramid Texts, but they reveal more about the spiritual concepts involved. Their focus is given in spell number 76, which is entitled "Ascending to the sky ... and becoming an *Akh*."

The *Akh* is "the shining one," a "being of light," and is the root of the word *akhet*, or "horizon." It describes the end sought by the Ba: to convert into pure spiritual radiance. In terms of the dead, it reveals that the person after death, following a period when he is free of his body in his Ba form, eventually ascends to enter a state of transcendence and merges with the radiant Source of all. Stephen Quirke explains that "the akh is the transfigured spirit that has become one with the light."[23] The word used in the texts for this process is *sakhu* – meaning "to make [the deceased] an Akh ... a being of light."[24]

A further development of these texts in the midfifteenth century B.C. gave us what is known as "The Book of the Dead." But this is not the original name of this collection of texts, which was called "The Book of Coming Forth by Day" – which perhaps would be better rendered as "Instructions for Coming Forth into the Light." A late second-millennium B.C. form of the title includes the word *sakhu*, "transfigurations," which implies that these are texts to be used for the transformation of "a person into an *akh*."[25]

This concept can be shown to go back earlier: the collections of Pyramid Texts and Coffin Texts preserved in the library of the Temple of Osiris in Abydos were copied – or recopied – onto papyri in the fourth century B.C., following the same order in which they were written some fifteen hundred years earlier. These too were given the title "Transfigurations."[26] The temple priests knew what they were about even if modern translators do not.

Plutarch, a Greek historian and author, was in his early twenties and probably still a student in Athens when the Temple of Jerusalem finally fell to the Roman forces in A.D. 70. He was initiated into the mysteries of Delphi and from late in the first century A.D. served as a priest of these mysteries; thus, he knew a thing or two about the hidden side of religion. Because of the demand for secrecy among the Egyptian priests, these mysteries do not appear to have been chronicled. In fact, Plutarch's account of the story of Isis and Osiris is the only fully detailed text known. In that account, he makes an intriguing comment: speaking of the chambers and corridors of the Egyptian temples, he writes: "And in another portion [the temples] have secret vesting-rooms in the darkness under ground, like cells or chapels."[27]

But he does not add any further information, nor does he pursue this tantalizing idea further. Certainly most Egyptian temples have underground rooms or galleries. Denderah, for example, has ten of them – single rooms, corridors, and long galleries, some on three levels.[28] At the Temple of Horus in Edfu, an entrance in the wall of the chapel of Osiris, Lord of the Far-World, leads into a tunnel within the wall itself that gives access to two underground chambers. I have been in them several times to meditate quietly in the darkness and utter silence. The tunnel is now closed by a padlocked door.

Archaeologists often claim that these secret rooms were used for the storage of ritual objects or for items of high value. But Plutarch is revealing something important that hints at a greater mystery behind their existence. At Denderah, for example, the hidden spaces are carved with hieroglyphs and symbolic images – hardly the mark of a storage facility.

Heliodorus of Emesa, writing in the third century A.D., adds some information regarding these rites in the mysteries of Isis and Osiris: he states that the story of these two gods contains secrets that were not made clear to profane people and that those who were skilled in the secrets of nature "instruct those who wish to know these private matters in their chapels by candle light."[29]

Few Egyptologists pursue these matters. Apprehensive about mystical matters, most scholars want to keep their archaeology "scientific," and this means sticking with apparently rational explanations of everything they find, even when doing so is rather like trying to stuff an inflatable toy back into its original packaging.[30]

There are a few scholars, however, who have the courage and confidence to speak out about the hidden side of Egyptian cults: Professor Claas Bleeker, a specialist in the history of religion at the University of Amsterdam, readily conceded that "obviously there existed in Ancient Egypt certain cultic mysteries which were only known to the initiated." In fact, he reported, one participant in these secret rites proclaimed proudly that "I am therein initiated ... but I do not tell it to anybody."[31]

Egyptologist Walter Federn also realized the esoteric cultic background to Egyptian religious writings and explained that certain of the spells found in the Pyramid and Coffin

Texts "were also available to the living" and, he adds, "developing, in some cases, into initiation texts."[32]

There is one extraordinary text that we have not yet looked at: the Amduat – "The Book of What Is in the Far-World," the earliest copies of which date to around 1470 B.C. and carry the original title of "Treatise of the Hidden Chambers." It records the journey, in twelve hours, of the sun god Ra in his celestial boat through the Far-World each night, and it gives instructions for passing through all the dangers and difficulties. It is ostensibly written for the instruction of the deceased pharaoh to aid his own journey after his death. But what is significant about this text is that it states, explicitly, that it is also useful for those still living: "It is good for the dead to have this knowledge, but also for a person on earth."[33]

This relevance to the physical world is regularly stressed throughout the text. There is little doubt that this journey through the Far-World concerns both the dead and the living. Indeed, the book ends with the unambiguous statement that "whoever knows these mysterious images is a well-provided Akh-spirit. Always [this person] can enter and leave the netherworld. Always speaking to the living ones. Proven to be true, a million times."[34] It couldn't be put any clearer than that. This journey has to do with experience. It concerns initiation.

This point has not escaped scholars: an Egyptologist at the University of Chicago, Professor Edward Wente, has

concluded that certain texts, including the Amduat and another called "The Book of Gates," "may have originally been
composed for use in this world and were not designed solely
for funerary use in tombs."[35] He explains that such works
are examples of "practical theology" in that living people
identified themselves "with beings in various states and
stages who dwell in the netherworld" and that it was not
necessary to await the time of death to receive the benefits.[36]
Such identification means ritual. Wente adds:

> It seems much simpler, in my opinion, to assume that
> the Book of Amduat, as well as the Book of Gates were
> originally designed for use upon earth as well as in the
> other world and were only secondarily adapted as
> specifically royal funerary literature.[37]

The Amduat itself says that it was to be considered secret;
only a few were allowed to view its contents. Wente
concludes:

> One might view these two great compositions as com-
> plementing each other in providing different means,
> or possibly "two ways" for entering the netherworld
> and participating in the process of death and renewal.[38]

We can be very sure that there were some deeply esoteric
and secret practices regularly conducted in the secluded
rooms and chapels of the Egyptian temples, and that men

– and undoubtedly women as well, the priestesses of Isis for one – were initiated into the secrets of the kingdom of the gods and taught how to journey safely through the eternal night, avoiding all the sudden dangers, until they became illuminated like a star.

For the last few years I have guided groups of twenty or thirty people through Egypt. Normally on such tours the visitors are herded in groups around the various temples and, while fighting for space, filled with the history of invasions, battles, and architectural features, all punctuated by a blur of pharaohs. What is not usually given is information about the purpose of these temples, the rituals that occurred in them, and the meaning of these rituals to the ancient Egyptians. Another crucial feature of such tours is that the crowds and the relentless schedules – which seem to revolve around restaurants owned by brothers or cousins – leave little opportunity to try to actually *feel* the sites.

It does not really matter to me who built the temples. What is more important is what was done in them. In our groups, we try to experience the sites themselves, and in doing so something important often occurs – some eruption of unexpected emotion that is as deep as the past is far, but as immediate as the past is ever-present. In fact, we learn to expect these moments as part of the experience that the land offers and to take them as proof that somewhere deep within ourselves rests an ancient memory just waiting for the right moment to break free. It is common for one of our group to suddenly find himself or herself in a flood of tears, or to simply feel "spaced out." I well remember one person wandering, as if in a dream, around the Osireion at Abydos muttering to himself, as if it were all he could manage to articulate, "This is the *real* thing. This is the *real* thing."

He was, of course, quite right. I had to make sure that he was on the bus when we left.

I remember too the occasion following one visit to Abu Simbal in the extreme south of Egypt. As we were leaving, our cruise ship slowly pirouetted on Lake Nasser before the two temples: that of Ramses II, distinctive with its four huge, seated figures at the entrance, and the more modest one of his daughter, Nefertari. As the ship swung slowly about, selections from the operas *Aïda* and *Nabucco* soared into the light breeze from speakers placed on the upper deck; we were all caught by surprise.

What could have been overtheatrical, even gauche, was a delight. I found the music and the graceful dance of the ship before the temples and the ancient deities so unbelievably moving that it sent shivers up my spine. I stood, overcome and immobilized by the profound stillness that had quietly but effectively taken hold. I wanted the moment to last forever. In its own way, perhaps it did. Members of my group told me afterwards that they had felt moved to tears – on what was otherwise a sunny Tuesday morning.

I remember well the first time I took my stepdaughter to the Valley of the Kings. She is the style editor for a major English fashion magazine aimed at the under-thirties. Her life generally revolves around contemporary fashion, travel, and design; she is not one to spend too much time dwelling upon the past. It was early morning, and the temperature was just rising as our bus turned the corner into the narrow valley entrance where we confronted, for the first time, the sun-bleached dry rock valley with its tomb entrances and high hills stretching ahead of us. She suddenly burst into torrents of tears. She cried uncontrollably. Something powerful had erupted from within her and taken her over. "I felt as though I had been here before" was all she could say. It was enough.

And it is not just personal memories that can arise; there are some other memories that linger and, on certain occasions, present themselves. Memories seemingly held by the stones and the sites themselves. It is as if the past is separated by a thin veneer of time that occasionally peels off to reveal what lies beneath. I like to talk with the guards who patrol the sites at night, who sleep there and know the quiet places and the quiet moments. I also like to talk to the Egyptologists who immerse themselves in the sites and also know the still places. I have heard stories of sudden visions of ancient rituals, of priests gathered at the sacred lakes, of gods walking through the corridors and chambers. I have been taken to small chapels in remote parts of large sites where, I can say, something very special is present – and something special which can be experienced.

But some of these places should always be kept discreet, visited only by those who understand how to approach them with the reverence they deserve and who can receive their gifts. It is extraordinary that probably every day in Egypt there are small groups of visitors – pilgrims – who are seeking and having these experiences. They are learning to know the living past of this amazing country.

To all of us "pilgrims," it is evident that the Pyramids are more than just the extravagant tombs we have been led to believe they are. Stephen Quirke states bluntly that the Pyramids, along with many other buildings that disintegrated over time, formed part of an ornate complex dedicated to the cult of the pharaoh as a divinity, adding that "they are only secondarily tombs."[39] The Pyramid of Djoser and other buildings in the complex at Saqqara, he explains, provide "unambiguous evidence" for their ritual use – in this case, for the *sed* festival, a great festival held every thirty years or so that aimed to renew the power of the pharaoh.[40]

The most significant study of the cult of the pharaoh has recently been completed by Dr. Jeremy Naydler and presented in his book *Shamanic Wisdom in the Pyramid Texts*. He explains that the sed festival was conducted to allow the pharaoh to bring the physical world and the Far-World into harmony, a balancing that would benefit all of Egypt. The "central rite" of the sed festival "involved the king crossing the threshold between worlds," with the aim of bringing himself into a "direct relationship to the normally hidden spiritual powers." To allow this to happen, during the most secret parts of the ritual ceremony it appears that the king had "an ecstatic visionary experience."[41] This experience was deliberately induced by those conducting the rites, who well understood the linkage between the two worlds and the importance of the pharaoh as a point of contact between the two.

Naydler is blunt: his conclusion from his study of the Pyramid Texts is that "far from being funerary texts, [these texts] were primarily concerned with mystical experiences of a type similar to those that the living king had during the 'secret rites' of the Sed festival, for they can clearly be seen to belong to a genre of archetypal human experiences at the crossing point between this world and the spirit world."[42]

Of course, most scholars would dispute this experiential approach to the texts and rites. It is assumed that the huge amount of ancient Egyptian literature describing the Far-World is not really knowledge, in the sense of being true, but the result of millennia of imaginative speculation by generations of priests who may have believed what they were writing but who were nonetheless trying to describe something that was impossible to know. "But," Naydler points out, "it could equally well be maintained that this knowledge was the outcome of the type of mystical experience that involved crossing the threshold of death while still alive."[43]

It is here that I am reminded again of the unique term "*ahket* of Khufu" applied to the Great Pyramid of the pharaoh Khufu at Giza, which I referred to at the beginning of the chapter. Could this name, meaning "to blaze, to be radiant," and indicating the point of entry into the Far-World on the horizon, possibly suggest that the pyramid was the place from which Khufu passed into the Far-World? And the place from which he returned?

With the responsibility of maintaining Ma'at upon him, could it be that Khufu sought answers from the spiritual beings in the realm beyond on how to ensure harmony in this world? And if he did indeed cross the threshold into the kingdom of gods, how did he do it? What specific techniques were known to the Egyptian priests who assisted Khufu and other Egyptians before and after him?

A close look at the rites of initiation revealed elsewhere in the ancient world will surely aid in our study, and so that is the next stage on our journey.

Initiation

Some places are simply mysterious. They may appear to have a logic about their construction, but parts of them steadfastly defy explanation, refusing to submit to any obvious rules of purpose. During my many years of research, of all the ancient and enigmatic crypts and galleries and tombs I've explored, one of the most utterly strange places I have ever been is located in Italy, in the northwest corner of the Bay of Naples, above the small port of Baia. Its narrow entrance is cleverly concealed among crumbling Roman ruins spread on terraces along the hillside.

I clambered cautiously over a stone wall, found the metal ladder, and descended approximately fifteen feet to the base of a narrow passage that had been carved out of volcanic rock perhaps 2,600 years ago. Waiting at the bottom was a friend of mine, the writer and academic Robert Temple, an expert on ancient technology. After many years of requests, the Italian archaeological authorities had granted permission for Robert to enter the site; he had asked me along owing to my experience in subterranean exploration and photography. It was Thursday, 24 May 2001.

Ahead of us a narrow doorway carved into the cliff face lent access to the enigmatic underground complex. For us, the moment was significant, for there is no one alive today who had entered this place before us. We adjusted our hard hats, switched on the lights, and walked from the blazing sun into the abruptly pungent darkness. The sudden change was unsettling.

In fact, we were a bit hesitant at first to continue, for we had absolutely no idea what the conditions farther inside would be like. Conjecture about what lay ahead had all been quite negative. The Italian authorities had long insisted that the underground passages were filled with dangerously poisonous gases, and so they had required us to sign an agreement before entering, absolving them of all responsibility should we be fatally overcome.

The entrance tunnel was approximately six feet tall but only twenty-one inches wide — there was room enough for just one person to pass down it at a time. On either side we saw, at regular intervals, small niches clearly designed to hold lamps. Much to our puzzlement, this tunnel ran directly east to west while slowly descending. Behind us the brightly lit entrance quickly faded from view, leaving us in the fetid silence.

It was hot, although not excessively so but it was very humid; our clothing soon became soaked with perspiration. The tunnel was filled with thousands of large mosquitoes that fortunately proved to be more curious than belligerent. We wore dust-masks with chemical filters just in case the noxious vapors should prove a reality. Our lights shone ahead: the tunnel continued in a straight line, its path steadily declining. It rapidly began to feel lonely, and very, very strange. Nevertheless, we just kept walking.

After we had traveled approximately four hundred feet, the tunnel changed. We passed a curious construction on the left side that looked like a bricked-up doorway; at the same time the tunnel forked to the right and began to descend even more steeply. We followed it down into the rock. After another one hundred and fifty feet, we suddenly came to a halt: facing us was a body of water. The tunnel disappeared down into its depths as though it had been drowned by a rising subterranean river. But this underground waterway was artificially constructed, just like the tunnel. Several shallow steps led out into the water, but the level had evidently risen considerably since ancient times and the roof, which became lower ahead of us, progressively sloped down until it touched the clear water. It was impassable.

Just before we reached this underground waterway we had seen a hole in the right wall of the tunnel; we returned and crawled through it on our hands and knees. Shortly

The final image of the Stations of the Cross in the church at Rennes le Château in the south of France. It is from a standard series produced for churches in the nineteenth century by a firm in Toulouse. They would normally be left unpainted, but this image is adorned in an eccentric and enigmatic manner: the moon is shown as having risen, night has fallen, the Passover has begun. No one of the Jewish faith would be handling a dead body at this time. This image then is depicting Jesus, still living, being carried *out* of his tomb rather than into it. What great secret was the priest of this church, the Abbé Béranger Saunière, revealing?

The village of Rennes le Château on its hill above the Aude river valley in the foothills of the Pyrenees, southern France. Fifteen hundred years ago it was a substantial fortified community and traces of the stone walls can still be seen.

The small medieval castle that now stands at Rennes le Château and is still a private residence although partially ruined.

The "Tour Magdala" in Rennes le Château built by the priest, the Abbé Béranger Saunière, to house his library.

The secretive priest of Rennes le Château, Béranger Saunière, who was resident during the late nineteenth and early twentieth century until his death in 1917. Local tradition has it that he was refused the last rites by a priest.

The Rev. Dr. Douglas Bartlett interviewed at his home in Oxfordshire, England, in 1982. He had told us the extraordinary story of the manuscript providing proof that Jesus survived the crucifixion and was still alive in 45 A.D.

The church at Rennes le Château was decorated in an explosion of color and images on the instructions of Saunière. The altar, in particular, is a prime example of his eccentric and extravagant symbolism.

The pulpit in the church at Rennes le Château.

An enigmatic painted relief at the base of the altar within the church of Rennes le Château depicting Mary Magdalene in the empty sepulchre of Christ, her hands clasped curiously together, weeping before a sprouting sapling in the form of a cross that has a skull placed at its foot. This is hardly an orthodox image to be placed upon the altar before which the Catholic mass was performed.

Painted relief on the west wall of the church at Rennes le Château depicting Christ at the summit of a hill strewn with flowers calling to him all who are suffering. A mysterious bag with a hole torn in it lies at the foot of the hill apparently unconnected with any of the figures. This is yet another enigmatic element of the priest's designs.

The site of the ancient Jewish city of Gamala (now Gamla) in the Golan Heights where, during the Jewish War of 66–73 A.D., many thousands of the zealot occupants – men, women, and children – chose to commit suicide by jumping into the ravines below rather than be captured by the Romans. They believed that if they died together, in ritual purity, they would be resurrected together. Capture by the Romans meant losing that purity and so losing the chance of resurrection.

The ruins of the Herodian fortress of Hyrcania in the desert above the Dead Sea on the route from Bethlehem and Wadi Kidron.

The northern edge of the fortress of Masada showing the remains of Herod's luxurious palace and many of the numerous caves and tunnel entrances in the hill.

The ruins of the Herodian fortress of Masada near the Dead Sea, Israel, showing the remains of the huge causeway built by the Romans. It was taken by the zealots in 66 A.D. and held until their mass suicide in 73 A.D. after the Romans attacked crossing the causeway and breaking through their defenses. Some 900 zealots and their families died.

PHOTO BY MICHAEL BAIGENT

The castle of Montségur on its precipitous rocky mountain, the last headquarters of the heretical Gnostic Cathar movement in the south of France during the thirteenth century. On March 16, 1244, 220 Cathars were taken from the castle by the invading army and burned alive in a field below.

PHOTO BY MICHAEL BAIGENT

Between the wall of the castle and the cliffs are the remains of a small village for the leading Cathar teachers, the "Perfects," both men and women, who taught what they insisted was the original message of Jesus. They were relentlessly hunted down by the Inquisition and many hundreds were burned alive.

The remains of the large Jewish town on Elephantine Island in the Nile at Aswan, southern Egypt. This was once the frontier of the Pharaohs where there was a large Jewish military garrison and a temple to Yahweh. The town was destroyed sometime around the year 400 B.C. It is being methodically excavated by members of the German School of Archaeology in Cairo.

An overview of the remains of houses and streets in the Jewish settlement on Elephantine Island.

The Goddess *Ma'at* as depicted in a crypt in the temple of Hathor,
Denderah. *Ma'at* was defined as the state of harmony, balance, truth,
justice, and completion that linked the physical world with the divine
world. The wide network of temples in ancient Egypt, their daily rituals,
and the Pharaoh himself, existed primarily to maintain this state of
Ma'at for Egypt.

PHOTO COURTESY OF THE BRITISH MUSEUM

The Egyptians considered that every person had a *Ba*, a spirit body that was released by the death of the body and could move independently toward its divine goal. It was depicted as a bird with the head of the deceased. This example is from the Papyrus Book of the Dead of the Royal Scribe Ani around 1250 B.C. It is considered that this spirit body could also be released before physical death by initiation into the secrets of the "Far World," the *Duat*, world of the dead.

PHOTO BY MICHAEL BAIGENT

Two of a number of *Ba* images carved around the antechamber to the chapel of Osiris, Lord of the *Duat*, on the roof of the temple of Hathor, Denderah.

Enigmatic image in one of the secret underground crypts beneath the temple of Hathor at Denderah, a crypt that only initiates would have access to. The raised hands represent the *Ka*, the vital living energy of a person and in this case they are attached to the *djed* column, the backbone – and thus the strength – of Osiris. The snake the *Ka* holds up normally represents time. Is this communicating some secret that links Osiris and his vital energy with maintaining the existence of time?

The temple of Hathor at Denderah, well preserved because for two thousand years it was almost completely covered by sand.

The entrance to a tunnel running inside the walls from the chapel of Osiris, Lord of the "Far World," in the temple of Horus, Edfu. This entrance was undoubtedly originally covered by a carved stone insert that disguised its existence.

Tunnel running through the wall behind the chapel of Osiris in the temple of Horus. Ahead some shallow steps can be seen.

Beyond the steps lies the entrance to an underground room beneath the temple of Horus at Edfu. The room is oriented due east-west and is most likely one of those places described by ancient writers as a place of secret initiations into the secrets of the "Far World."

Seth and Horus giving life to the Pharaoh in a ritual action that would have been performed by priests wearing the appropriate masks. The fact that the participants are not wearing any shoes indicates that this ritual is being performed in a sacred place.

Thoth (*Tehuti*), the God of Initiation and guide to the "Far World," giving eternal life to the Pharaoh Seti I. In the temple of Seti I at Abydos, Egypt.

The anointment of Pharaoh Seti I from the wall of a chapel in his temple at Abydos.

The "Porta Rosa," one of the ancient city gates still standing in the ruined city of Velia, southern Italy. In the 5th century B.C. an ancient Greek philosopher-priest here established a tradition using a special technique called "incubation," which involved the candidate withdrawing into silence, darkness, and stillness in an underground room or cave where they would have a Divine vision. Archaeological evidence has revealed that this line of priests continued for at least 446 years, into the age of Jesus and his teaching.

One of the inscriptions found at Velia in 1958, reading "Oulis (priest of Apollo), son of Ariston, Iatros (healer), Pholarchos (Lord of the Lair, Master of incubation techniques), in the 280th year." The latest of these series of inscriptions is dated "the 446th year" but others, even later, may have vanished. It is evident that these initiation techniques were known and available at the beginning of the Christian era.

ABOVE LEFT: Professor Gichon, an expert on Simon bar Kochba, the Jewish leader who led the revolt against the Roman domination in 132 A.D. Initially the revolt was successful and expelled all the Roman armies from Israel but it was defeated in 135 A.D. and bar Kochba killed.

ABOVE RIGHT: Remains of a bar Kochba fortress near Emmaus, Israel. When it was taken by the Romans the defenders found refuge in tunnels beneath the structure.

LEFT: Professor Robert Eisenman beside one of the wells within the fortress. Their bulbous shape beneath the ground allowed those hiding in the tunnels beneath to draw water without the Romans' knowing.

PHOTO BY MICHAEL BAIGENT

Beneath the stone platform of the bar Kochba fortress were many crude tunnels where the defenders lived until their discovery by the Romans.

PHOTO BY MICHAEL BAIGENT

Professor Robert Eisenman in front of the sealed entrance to the tunnel leading deeper into the hill. Beyond this sealed door lie the bodies of the defenders of the fortress who retired down this tunnel to avoid being captured by the Romans.

Michael Baigent in the deep trench leading to the narrow entrance to the mysterious six-hundred-foot-long tunnel to the underground ritual complex "the Oracle of the Dead" at Baia, near Naples, Italy. This entrance had long been sealed by the Italian authorities and was opened especially for this investigation.

Writer and university professor Robert Temple above the trench leading to the entrance of the underground complex. It was due to his persistent requests that the Italian authorities opened the site after forty years.

The tunnel into the cliff at Baia. It runs due west, steadily downward, to end at an underground waterway and gives access to another series of tunnels together with what appears to be an underground temple completely filled with rubble since the time of the Romans two thousand years ago.

The sealed entrance to the underground temple at Baia with a fresh green offering placed in the small niche at the lower right. Whatever rituals this "Oracle of the Dead" involved would have been carried out in this sealed sanctuary. Something about this site and these rituals so frightened the Romans that they wished to prevent it from ever being used again and so filled it with rubble. It has not yet been excavated.

The rubble has settled over the last two thousand years allowing a small space to crawl down. One hundred and twenty feet along one such tunnel it mysteriously divides into two and then ends. Only excavation will be able to reveal why this is.

PHOTO BY MICHAEL BAIGENT

Michael Baigent within the humid tunnel complex of Baia.

The waterway at the end of the entrance tunnel to the Baia complex, considered a possible inspiration for Virgil's description of the Styx, the river that divided this world from the next. Steps at the far end of it make it clear that in ancient times the ritual involved being rowed along this waterway in a small boat.

PHOTO BY MICHAEL BAIGENT

A walled-up entrance to the underground temple at Baia.

PHOTO BY MICHAEL BAIGENT

The tunnel through the cliff at Cuma to the underground rooms of the prophetic Sybil. This mysterious complex is only a few miles from Baia.

PHOTO COURTESY OF THE LIBRARY AND
MUSEUM OF UNITED GRAND LODGE OF ENGLAND

Jacob's Ladder as depicted in the "Tracing Board" of the First Degree in Freemasonry. This symbol is a powerful expression of the concept that earth and heaven are intimately linked, that communication is possible between the two, and that a sacred place is that from which it is possible to pass from one world to the other, to go, and to return.

PHOTO BY PAINET INC.

The monastery of Mar Saba in the Wadi Kidron below Bethlehem. It was here in 1958 that professor Morton Smith discovered a letter speaking of a secret understanding of the teaching of Jesus.

The Assyrian sacred tree, understood only by initiates and the source for the later "Tree of Life" used in the mystical Jewish practice of Kabbalah.

The desert monastery of St. George on the west bank of the Nile near Aswan, southern Egypt. It was desert communities such as this that preserved texts long considered heretical such as the Gnostic Gospels found in the Nag Hammadi codices.

Members of the California State University, Long Beach team, during the extensive survey of the caves, population, and agricultural evidence in the precipitous cliffs alongside the Dead Sea south of Qumran where the Dead Sea Scrolls were found.

Excavation of Cave 37, around six hundred feet high in the cliffs to the south of the ruins of Qumran. Two occupation layers were found as well as two iron-age graves.

Sieving all the spoil extracted from Cave 37 during the excavation. In this manner many small objects, otherwise missed, might be found.

A small advance lookout position serving the zealot garrison at Masada above the Herodian stone wharf at Khirbet Mazin at the end of Wadi Kidron. From here the number of troops being landed by the Romans could be observed. Although we discovered this site for the first time, it was not excavated for some years.

Tony Wood and Greg Mills, experts in the operation of the ground radar system, during the survey of the ruins of Qumran near the Dead Sea, near where the Dead Sea Scrolls were found. The aim was to check the earlier archaeology and to seek the existence of any further caves that might contain ancient texts.

The difficult process of drawing the ground radar transducers down the cliff face at a constant speed in order to get a profile of the interior of the cliff. Any caves would show up as a void in the printouts.

Wadi Qumran, showing the ruins of the settlement and the caves in the cliff beneath, within which large numbers of fragments of texts were found.

The exit of the tunnel that brought water from the Wadi to the settlement at Qumran.

Following a heavy rain in Jerusalem, water pours from the Wadi above the ruins of Qumran. It was water from such occasional rains that was collected by the resident community.

The remains of the water channel from the tunnel to the settlement of Qumran.

Operating the sensitive transducer for the ground radar system at the ruins of Qumran.

thereafter we found ourselves in another side tunnel, which turned sharply to the left and then led upwards at a steep angle; evidently there had once been steps there, but now the incline was covered in loose rubble. With some difficulty, we managed to crawl up it.

After climbing roughly twenty feet, we found ourselves before something quite extraordinary: the bricked-up entrance to an underground room or gallery – a sanctuary perhaps, or a small temple or some special pillared hall. Tunnels led off to both the left and right. We veered to the right. After approximately twenty feet, the tunnel became blocked with close-packed rubble, but we knew, from the original investigations, that this tunnel joined the far end of the underground waterway.

We then crawled back to the sealed entrance of the sanctuary and moved along the left tunnel. This led us into two further tunnels, at least one of which appeared to lead back in the direction from which we had first entered the complex but at a higher level, thereby avoiding the waterway.

This tunnel too had once been packed with rubble, but over the two thousand years or more since it had been sealed the filling had settled, leaving roughly eighteen inches between the top of the rubble and its roof. It stretched ahead in the distance for as far as our lights could shine. Then it disappeared into the darkness beyond. I was determined to explore it.

To say that the situation was claustrophobic was something of an understatement. However, I had spent some time in the past exploring caves and tunnels at archaeological sites throughout the Middle East and knew that I could deal with the occasional panic that erupts whenever one is alone in a deep enclosed space that occasionally feels like a living grave.

As I prepared to explore this passageway, Robert declined to join me. The two Italian archaeological workers, Gino and Pepe, also began to look the other way, fiddling with their backpacks and ropes. They did, however, decide that I should tie a rope around one leg. I suppose their reasoning was that if I should have a heart attack and die while up in the tunnel, they could readily pull me out. This hope seemed forlorn to me at the time, and it very quickly proved impossible as well.

The roof of the tunnel was so close that with my hard hat on to protect me from the rough stone above, I had to slide along on my stomach, pushing with my feet and pulling with my hands. I was unable to raise my head to see much of where I was going. I was also unable to turn around, since the tunnel remained at the same width of roughly twenty-one inches. I simply hoped that it would all lead to somewhere – and that when I arrived I would be able to turn around to get out again. Otherwise, I would have to retrace my crawl, backwards. A laborious prospect, it is true, but possible, so I was not too worried about it. I set off, crawling with my face near the earth, my dust-mask justifying its price. I had to push my bag of cameras on ahead of me as I went along since there was no space to wear it on my back.

I continued wriggling through the tunnel as fast as I could while simultaneously keeping a rough measurement of the distance I was covering. I stopped occasionally to blow a whistle and was reassured by the whistles I heard coming back down the passage that my friends were still within reach of me. But soon, deeper into the tunnel, I could no longer hear any response. Then, even farther in, the rope came to an end. I untied it from my foot and continued along without it.

The roof and walls were bearing close upon me. I was alone. All was silent. A couple of times I had to pause. Despite my attempts to avoid such thoughts, I became aware of the huge weight of rock pushing down onto the roof of the tunnel from above. My head scraped the roof, my elbows scraped the sides, my body was prone upon the two-thousand-year-old rubble. Behind me was a long tunnel; what lay in front of me was a complete mystery. The whole task suddenly seemed completely mad, even foolhardy.

If the roof had collapsed at this very moment, no one would have come to get me: claustrophobic panic began mounting in my mind. Despite the physical heat, a chill swept up my back and I stiffened; in an uncontrolled performance of internal amateur dramatics, I began to feel as though I were already in my grave just waiting for the moment when I would be covered with earth. I had to calm down; the tunnel had been there a long time and was not about to suddenly collapse just because I had happened along.

I took several slow deep breaths, and the feeling finally subsided. I pushed my camera bag ahead and slithered forward. Soon I passed what I estimated to be the hundred-foot point, and still the tunnel was running flat into the solid volcanic rock.

Near to the one-hundred-and-twenty-foot point, the tunnel changed once more: its roof became a little higher, and its width doubled. It began to drop approximately one foot every three feet. I was relieved; if necessary I could turn around here. But ahead of me I could see that the tunnel inexplicably turned into two tunnels. Dual dark entrances gazed at me like the twin barrels of a shotgun. I chose to enter the right tunnel first and crawled in on my hands and knees.

But this tunnel ran for only a short distance; curiously, it ended abruptly at approximately one hundred and fifty feet from the entrance. This made no sense at all. Had it been sealed up? A cursory examination failed to reveal any evidence that this was the case. To my left was a hole in the rock. It dropped down into another tunnel, so I crawled through. Oddly enough, I found myself at the end of the left tunnel. This eccentric complexity seemed utterly pointless. Why would anyone construct two tunnels ending in the same place? And directly ahead of me I saw the remains of a space – a doorway of some sort had been sealed with stone blocks securely cemented into place. To the left of this was another wall with a hole battered into it. I put my head through. It revealed yet another tunnel, but it too was sealed with rubble after a few feet. I kicked at the rubble-covered floor, and the strange resulting ring seemed to indicate that there was another, deeper tunnel running beneath me. I always carried a trowel in my bag, but this was not the time to start excavating.

Nevertheless, I took it out and repeatedly banged upon the stonework of the sealed doorway while simultaneously yelling as loud as I could. I heard nothing, but as it turns out Robert Temple could hear me. I had been standing on the other side of the bricked-up portion of wall we had passed on our way in just before the main tunnel led off down to the right.

It appeared as if originally this tunnel had also afforded an entrance to the "sanctuary" or "temple" deep underground, providing a route that was higher than the other tunnel and bypassed the artificially constructed waterway beneath. I now had some insight into the logic of the place: this odd construction was indeed as Robert Temple had suspected – a place where people came to be introduced to the divine secrets of the Far-World. These initiates, as they were called, would enter, take the right-hand path – which was always recommended in the ancient texts – and be rowed along an artificial river to reach the inner sanctuary, which served as the doorway or portal into the netherworld they sought and the kingdom of the gods. To return, the initiates could pass back across the river. In the meantime, the alternative tunnel provided the priests of the site direct access to the sanctuary, where they would wait for the initiates to arrive.

It was all rather reminiscent of the visits to the under-world that classical writers had described. They began with accounts of visitors to the infernal regions being rowed across the River Styx by the silent boatman Charon. Then, after entry into the sacred kingdom, the traveler experienced, as Vergil describes it, "places of delight, to green park land, Where souls take ease amid the Blessed Groves."[1]

I returned to my camera bag and with some difficulty in the confined space extracted one of my beloved Leica cameras, several lenses, and a flash and began to comprehensively photograph everything I could see. From long experience of the vicissitudes of exploration, I always operate as though I may never be able to return. "Get it in the can" is the guiding principle, and it is a good one. And as it happened in this case, a prescient one.

An hour or so later I returned down the tunnel, where I found Gino and Pepe sitting, waiting, rather nervously. They had not been able to hear me move about for some time. Neither had I responded to any of their calls. When the rope went slack, they had pulled it back, but I had not been attached. They must have reported their fears to the authorities, because on every future occasion that I visited the complex I was prevented from reentering this tunnel. Not in any obvious way, of course – nothing was ever said, but one of them always kept very close to me, and when I neared the entrance to the deep narrow tunnel, they would arrange to sit between me and it. They had clearly been given their orders: it was considered too dangerous. So the color photographs I took that first time are, for the moment, the only ones that exist.

No one knows who built this subterranean structure. It could have been excavated by the Greeks as early as the seventh century B.C. No one yet can say with certainty what it was used for. Neither does anyone know when it was sealed up or why its existence was hidden. The best suggestion is that Marcus Vipsanius Agrippa, a prominent Roman general and admiral in the time of Augustus Caesar and the grandfather of the emperor Nero, for reasons that we cannot now know, decided that the place was so dangerous that it had to be eradicated from the face of the earth and so ordered it to be filled with rubble, probably some time around 37 – 36 B.C., when his nearby fleet was being built and his sailors were training in Lake Avernus and Lake Lucrina prior to their last and victorious sea battle in the Sicilian war.[2]

Whoever was responsible was certainly focused upon the task: the destruction of the underground complex took enormous effort – estimates suggest thirty thousand man-journeys – testifying to a strong, if not obsessive, determination to shut the site down forever.[3] If Agrippa was responsible, what had frightened him? And if not Agrippa, who else could have done it, and why?

That was roughly two thousand years ago. The outer doorway to the complex was rediscovered during archaeological excavations in 1958, but the tunnel was entered for only a short distance at that time. The full complexity of the site was not to be found until 1962, when it was explored but not excavated by a retired chemical engineer named Robert Paget. After Paget's efforts, the Italian government swept in and sealed the doorway, keeping its very existence secret. No one had entered it again until Robert Temple and I – along with Gino and Pepe – ventured to do so nearly forty years later. For all intents and purposes, the site had quietly faded from the archaeological horizon. Anyone who asked after it was informed that it was just another uninteresting tunnel leading to a source of hot water, one that had been built during Roman times to serve their thermal baths. Most scholars lost interest. Only Robert Temple took the site seriously.

On 21 September 1962, Robert Paget and a colleague had first entered the site.[4] No one else had done so for two thousand years. What exactly did he discover that made the Italian government respond the way it did?

Paget had long been intrigued by the possibility that an oracle of the dead existed in the area. He believed that Vergil's account of Aeneas visiting the underworld was based upon the experience of a real visit to this famous oracle. Crucially, Vergil makes it clear that the Oracle of the Sibyl at Cuma – of whose actual existence there is no doubt – was different from the oracle of the dead said to be somewhere in the area of Lake Avernus,[5] which is a water-filled volcanic crater about a mile from Cuma and a mile or two to the north of Baia (formerly Baiae).

In Vergil's *Aeneid*, Aeneas visits the Sibyl of Cuma and asks for directions to the underworld. She replies, "The way downward is easy from Avernus."[6] In other words, Vergil is stating that the entrance to the underworld is nearby – within a mile or so, as we have seen.

Was this merely a literary creation, or had Vergil first-hand knowledge and experience of a real place? Paget believed the latter was true. This possibility cannot be discounted, for it is known that Vergil was a resident in the area for a time.[7] Paget was certain that this oracle, like that of Cuma, had really existed. And there is no doubt that he was correct about this: when Hannibal had sacked the area in 209 B.C., he had made a point of sacrificing at an important sacred site, meaning the oracle, which was also said to be near Lake Avernus.[8] Of course, skeptics could say that this was the source for Vergil's text and so there was no need for Vergil to have ever seen the oracle himself.

To prove his theory, Paget and his wife moved to Baia in 1960. Along with Keith Jones, a fellow archaeological enthusiast who had been serving with the U.S. Navy at the NATO base in Naples, they resolved to begin a methodical exploration in a determined attempt to find the remains of the oracle.

They began searching at the ancient Greek city of Cuma, roughly two miles northwest of Baia. They explored all the many tunnels and caves in the area, including that of the famous Oracle of the Sibyl, which was rediscovered in 1932 and subsequently excavated. But they were unable to find anything resembling an oracle of the dead.

Paget and Jones then turned their attention to Lake Avernus, where many traditions placed the oracle. They found considerable evidence of Agrippa's shipyards and his military constructions, including two large tunnels; one of them was a mile long and ten feet square and led underground from Lake Avernus all the way to Cuma. They again explored many tunnels and caves, but still could find nothing that matched the idea of an oracle of the dead. So again they moved.

Along the coast, roughly two miles south of Lake Avernus, lies the ancient city of Baiae, much of which is now under the sea owing to the unstable geology of the region. It had once been a very important Roman town. The Roman geographer and historian Strabo – who died around A.D. 24, a few years before Jesus was baptized – described Baiae and its hot springs as "a fashionable watering-place ... for the cure of diseases."[9] It was a chic seaside resort where the elite of Rome spent their holidays. It was also where the emperor and the other patricians maintained large villas, the ruins of which can still be seen on the hillsides or under the sea, for the land has fallen and most of the ruins can be seen today under the water stretching for a mile or so around the Gulf of Pozzuoli from a glass-bottomed boat. Still on the hillside of Baia among the ruins of the hot spa baths are the remains of three temples: those of Diana, Mercury, and Venus. Modern-day Baia is now only a small fishing port, with a center of small but fine restaurants – the kind of discreet place Italian businessmen contentedly take their pretty companions for lunch.

The excavation of Baia's hillside ruins from 1956 to 1958 had revealed a complex of Roman bathhouses, but everything was in chaos owing to numerous rebuilding efforts, perhaps following damage from the frequent earthquakes in the area. In fact, a huge earthquake in A.D. 63 had caused landslides, which covered many of the original buildings.

Paget and Jones began searching all the tunnels in this area, as they had done at Cuma and Avernus. They estimated that they had entered at least one hundred tunnels in their work up until this point in time. Here they were drawn to a specific part of the site: a platform supporting the remains of an ancient Greek temple that was estimated to date from at least the fifth century B.C.[10] Beneath this platform were many tunnels and underground rooms.

Paget concluded that he had found the dwellings of the priests of the oracle of the dead, who were said by Ephorus to have never seen the light but to have communicated by means of underground tunnels.[11] The director of the Baiae site told Paget and Jones that beneath the temple itself was another tunnel they had not seen. He claimed that the lower tunnel was dangerous because of its "foul air." The excavators who discovered it had moved only a short distance inside before withdrawing. In fact, Paget reported, "The Inspector of Antiquities had given orders, that no one was to risk further exploration."[12] They decided to leave this tunnel until last.

Meanwhile, they searched all the other tunnels. In one of them, they crawled along for one hundred and fifty feet before realizing that there was nowhere to turn. Ultimately they had to retrace their steps backwards. Finally the time came to look at the tunnel that was said to be too dangerous. A volunteer from Paget's group was tied to the end of a twenty-five-foot rope. The procedure was pure military: "The idea was that he marched forward to the limit of the rope. If he stood up we assumed the air to be good ... if he fell down we hoped we should be able to pull him back to safety."[13] He didn't fall.

Paget and Jones decided to enter the tunnel themselves to explore it. They moved through the entrance cautiously:

> In the dust on the floor we could see the footprints of the excavators who had entered the tunnel in 1958. These ceased ... and we saw in front of us, the clean virgin dust of the floor stretching away into the darkness of the tunnel.[14]

As they continued, they became increasingly fearful, and after four hundred feet, with the temperature still rising, they decided they had done enough and quickly returned to the surface and to fresh air. They decided to say nothing about what they had done to the Italian authorities, who still believed the site to be filled with dangerously poisonous fumes.

Soon afterwards Paget and Jones entered the tunnel again and this time moved five hundred and fifty feet down until they were stopped by an underground repository of water. It seemed to them that this was the end of the tunnel. It was extremely humid and hot in the tunnel, and they complained about a lack of oxygen. They could stay at the water's edge for only fifteen minutes at a time, and so they took many color photographs on transparency film so that they could project them on a screen later for study. It was on the screen that they discovered the existence of a tile set into the roof above the waterway.

When they next returned, they pushed at the tile. It moved. They were able to slide it to the side far enough for Keith Jones to squeeze through the small opening. Once on the other side, Jones found himself in a tunnel that sloped steeply upwards. It led directly to the sealed doorway of the underground "sanctuary," which they later calculated was six hundred feet in from the cliff face and one hundred and forty feet below the surface of the earth above. They had entered a most mysterious underground complex that they would go on to explore in great detail.[15]

Paget reported that the temperature of the tunnel was 120 degrees Fahrenheit and the water was 85 degrees. In May 1965, a U.S. Army diver, Colonel David Lewis, and his son explored under the waterway; together they discovered that at the other end of the waterway – about eighty feet long – was a landing giving access to a tunnel that led straight to the underground sanctuary. Almost thirty feet deeper, Lewis found two artificially cut chambers containing very hot springs releasing water over 120 degrees Fahrenheit. Farther on, the water became so hot that he had to abandon further exploration.[16] Since that time, the temperature, at least in the accessible part of the waterway, has dropped considerably. When we explored the site, we found that the water was now 83 degrees Fahrenheit, and the tunnel itself was one degree lower.

As it turns out, Robert Paget and Robert Temple had many interests in common. In 1984 Robert Temple wrote a fascinating book called *Conversations with Eternity*, which explored oracles and divination in the ancient world. In the book, he mentions this curious underground complex at Baia and describes it. I bought the book when it first came out and was struck by the extraordinary nature of the place, and this fascination stayed with me. In particular, I was taken by the precision of the engineering that was revealed: the long entrance tunnel is oriented exactly toward the point of sunrise on the summer solstice, and the underground sanctuary is oriented toward the sunset on the same day.[17]

Another profound mystery was raised by these descriptions: just how did the builders know that there was an underground river or water source six hundred feet down the tunnel and one hundred and forty feet below the surface of the hill? As was noted:

There are no traces of exploration or random passages, or of false starts. The solid tufa rock into which this is

all cut does not have natural caverns, tunnels or chan-
nels, which would allow exploratory access or naturally
occurring streams of water.[18]

When asked about this oddity, Robert Paget had allowed
himself simply the deadpan observation that "there are several engineering problems that call for a little discussion."[19]
Deeply curious, I resolved, sometime, to take a look at it.

Then I met Robert and Olivia Temple in a taxi in Cairo in
1998. We were among a number of writers on a tour of
Egypt that had been organized by fellow writer and friend
Robert Bauval, author, along with Graham Hancock, of a
book delving into Egyptian mysteries, *Keeper of Genesis*. We
were going to give some talks to his group.

My very first question to Temple was, "How can I go and
see that strange underground sanctuary you wrote about?"
He looked pleased that I had picked up on the book he had
written fourteen years earlier, but he also looked embar-
rassed. He explained that even he had not been inside because it had been sealed up by the Italian government with
stones and rubble in the 1970s. Now no one was allowed to
enter. "But," he said, "I am trying to get permission from
them to reopen it." He had been trying for almost twenty
years, however, without success. Even the British School at
Rome reported to him that the tunnel was "absolutely not
accessible for safety reasons," and the Italian authorities said
that the passages were "full of poisonous gas."[20]

It was three years later, in 2001, that Robert Temple, whom I had seen regularly since our first encounter, rang me and gave me the exciting news: the Italian authorities had given him permission to enter the Baia complex – would I like to come and use my experience in photography to compile a comprehensive record of the site? I considered it for only a nanosecond before agreeing. That May, my wife, Jane, and I traveled with Robert and his wife, Olivia, to Naples, where we hired a car and drove to Baia. We had organized the rental of an apartment above a restaurant on the quayside for the duration of our stay.

On the afternoon of our first entry into the site, following a fine lunch, Robert and I were working deep inside the complex, seeking out traces of doorposts in the tunnel, when we heard the echo of voices – women's voices. Had the ancient oracle come back to life, we wondered? As it turned out, it was our wives, courageously making their way down the tunnel to the waterway. For two women of severely claustrophobic nature, it was something of a feat. Clearly no one wanted to miss the day's discoveries. Now standing at the foot of the river leading to the "underworld" is a memory that we all share.

On that day we also gained an understanding of the Italian authorities' attitude toward the site. The archaeologist in charge, Dr. Paola Miniero, was of the opinion that the tunnel simply supplied hot air to the Roman thermal baths. The area was famous for such baths, and a number of other tunnels in the hillside were constructed for this purpose.

But those tunnels were simple and rough; ours was straight and smoothly cut. Nevertheless, that was the official view. So the delays may have been occasioned, we realized, less by aversion than by disinterest.

To try to change Dr. Miniero's thinking on this matter, we took her down into the site. She was astounded at its complexity and admitted that the tunnel did not fit the usual pattern of access tunnels to hot-water sources. She said that she was going to have to think about what it all meant.[21] Moreover, we could see by the change in her attitude that she now understood why we were interested in it.

In the meantime, it had become clear to Robert and me that we needed to organize a systematic excavation of the site. We felt too that since someone had been sufficiently upset by the place to order it to be filled with rubble, it was unlikely that those who had done so would have taken anything out of the sanctuary. It seemed most probable that they would have broken up or hammered flat everything they found inside and then simply covered the space with rubble. To take something out would have left them vulnerable to a superstitious dread of angry spirits following after them. This line of reasoning opened the possibility that all the cultic objects once used here still lay within the site.

We applied to the Italian authorities for permission to excavate, and while we were waiting, we also gave two short papers to a conference of academic experts on early Greek cults in Italy that was held at Cuma in June 2002.[22] While we were there, we took several of the visiting experts down into the tunnels to see it for themselves; they were convinced of its importance. At the conference, Robert spoke about Baia and its apparent links to classical works on the oracles. I then gave a short presentation that focused solely upon the internal logic of the architectural features of the site: I wished to present evidence indicating that it was not simply a water tunnel but a cultic construction worthy of archaeological excavation.

I stressed that this tunnel was precisely, skillfully, and purposefully constructed and that if it were merely a water tunnel, it was eccentrically overengineered. The main tunnel ran due east-west, a familiar direction found in religious sanctuaries; it ended at an underground room of unknown size and linked up with a number of complicated tunnels. The logic, I argued, implied a journey, one involving a number of features that were all consistent with mythological motifs found in classical literature describing places of initiation and entrance to the world of the dead. The point of traveling through this tunnel, it seemed, was to inculcate a certain experience within the person making the journey. I concluded that the site was sufficiently enigmatic to make it important now to excavate and seek further understanding. The feedback we received convinced us that we had made our point, and indeed, a number of the experts present promised to help us in any way they could to organize an excavation to learn more.

Although permission to work on the site has not yet been

granted by the Italian authorities, we are hopeful: we have at least entered into discussion with these authorities regarding the costing and the length of time an initial excavation would take. In fact, Robert and I hope to have the funds and the permissions in place before too long. In the meantime, Robert wrote about our explorations at Baia in his latest book on the subject of oracles and divination, *Netherworld*, published in 2002, and he has also printed a number of the photographs taken inside the complex.

There is one last mystery: Vergil wrote of the underworld in his *Aeneid*: Aeneas descends and crosses the River Styx, but before he can enter the "Blessed Groves," he must leave an offering of a bough of mistletoe at the gate. Aeneas stops at the entrance, "and on the sill before him fixed the bough."[23] It is such an incidental episode in the saga, yet when we were looking at the bricked-up entrance to the underground sanctuary at Baia, we were struck by an almost insignificant feature. To the lower right-hand side of the door was a small curved niche with a flat base, one that would hold an offering. The implications of this are significant: that Vergil's description of the journey to the underworld was not a literary fantasy but was indeed based upon a real event and a real place – the underground complex at Baia.

Robert Paget, who knew his Vergil and had noted the niche, was convinced that this was so and named the underground waterway "the Styx." It was clear that at least part of the journey involved riding along this waterway in a boat, for steps were found at the other end that gave passage to a tunnel leading to the underground sanctuary. Robert Temple, who also knows his Vergil, concurs.

The very notion of crossing to the realm of the dead has had a long tradition in the Greek world. The earliest report of such a journey appears in the famous book XI of Homer's great epic, *The Odyssey*. Odysseus, on his complicated journey back to his home after the battles at Troy, is required by a witch, Circe, to descend into Hades, where Persephone is queen, in order to seek advice from the soul of a famous but dead Theban. Homer describes Odysseus sailing to a "fogbound" place called the "City of perpetual mist," a place where the sun never breaks through the heavily veiled skies.[24] It is there that Odysseus descends into the world of the dead.

Strabo reports an ancient belief that the misted and "fogbound" place of dread mentioned by Homer was the region of ancient Baia; it had once, he informs us, been "covered with wild forests, gigantic and impenetrable ... imparting a feeling of superstitious awe" and it was "full of sulphur, fire, and hot springs" – frightening and dangerous volcanic activity that ultimately depended upon the same tectonic forces as Mount Vesuvius roughly fifteen miles away.[25]

Strabo relates details given by an earlier historian, Ephorus, who lived in the fourth century B.C. Ephorus told of an underground oracle site near ancient Baia. He spoke of the specialist priests who served the oracle, lived beneath the ground, and never emerged into the sunlight, communicating by means of subterranean tunnels down which they took seekers to an oracle center "built far below the surface of the earth."[26] Strabo, while repeating this story, considers it a fable.

Some modern scholars think that this oracle was located on the edge of nearby Lake Avernus.[27] Others, acknowledging the importance of the oracle, realize the imprecision of the early sources and acknowledge the likelihood that references to Avernus are pointing to ancient Baia.[28] But those who have actually entered the tunnels and seen the evidence for themselves have little doubt. This great underground center at ancient Baia, run by priests who never saw the light of day – if Ephorus can be believed – was the famous oracle of the dead. There are no other candidates in the area.

Oracles, which were widespread all over the ancient world, were places where kings and leaders went to gain political advice. They were also places to which anyone – or at least those who could pay the required fees – might come for answers to questions regarding important decisions they were about to make. But certain of these oracle centers were special – those that won renown as "oracles of the dead."

There were four major sites where communications with the dead were encouraged: the one under discussion here at ancient Baia (Baiae), also still sometimes called Avernus, in the northwestern part of the Bay of Naples, Italy; another at Acheron near ancient Ephyra in Thesprotia in northwest

Greece; a third at Heracleia in Pontus in northern Turkey
on the shore of the Black Sea; and the last at Tainaron in
Lakonia, on the southernmost tip of the Greek mainland.
There are no traces left of the last two sites; the ruins at
Acheron were excavated from the late 1950s, having been
discovered lying beneath a Christian church built over the
site. Even so, these ruins are disputed; some say that the remains are of a fortified farmhouse and that the oracle of the
dead has yet to be discovered, if any of it even exists today.[29]
In other words, at present, Baia – if the identification is correct – is the only oracle of the dead to survive from antiquity, and this alone makes the site one of great importance.

While all the oracle centers of the ancient world were
mysterious, there was a special quality about oracles of the
dead: they were entry points to the underworld and to a
meeting with the gods. For this reason, some at least must
have involved initiation as well – initiation into the secrets
of what we have been referring to as the Far-World.

Dr. Peter Kingsley points out in his book *Ancient Philosophy, Mystery, and Magic* that very early concepts of travel to the
Far-World have survived in nonliterate societies by means
of shamans, who consistently teach that it is impossible to
reach "heaven" without first having gone to "hell" and that
these ancient journeys into the world of the gods begin with
a descent into the infernal regions by means of a "death,"
following which the seeker arrives at a place that gives immediate access to both the upper and lower worlds.[30] We
see this in the report of the second-century Greek writer

resident in Rome, Lucius Apuleius. He famously and enig-
matically described his initiation into the Isis cult:

> I approached the frontier of death, I set foot on the
> threshold of Persephone, I journeyed through all the
> elements and came back, I saw at midnight the sun,
> sparkling in white light, I came close to the gods of the
> upper and the nether world and adored them from
> near at hand.[31]

While it is difficult to deny that oracles of the dead and initiation held something in common, we lack specific evidence of the relationship. Very suggestive in this respect is
that the oracle of the dead at Baia and the oracle center of
Apollo at Claros, near Colophon in Turkey, have many
similarities; in addition, the evidence is compelling that the
oracle at Claros was also considered an initiation site.[32]
There is no need to suggest any dramatic machinery and
noises; it is enough that the seeker descended to Hades –
the Greek term for the world of the dead, the Far-World –
met with the gods, and was then initiated into their secrets,
the secrets of Divinity, just like Apuleius.

For the ancient Greeks, initiation and death were intimately entwined. It is implicit in their language: *telos* means
the end, perfection, completion. Its plural form, *telea*, "was
the standard word for initiatory rites – which offer fullness
or completion, but at the same time involve a termination
or death."[33] The word, in many variations, is found all

through the rites of initiation: *teleín* is "to initiate"; a *teleste-rion* is the hall in which initiations take place; the *telestes* is the initiation priest; the *telete* is the initiation ceremony itself; and finally, the *teloumenoi* are those who have been initiated.[34]

When the Greek philosopher Socrates was condemned to death because he lacked respect for the Athenian gods, he was required to commit suicide by drinking poison. Plato, in his *Phaedo*, constructs a record of the discussions of Socrates on the day he died, a record that is not supposed to be journalistic reportage but rather an imagined dialogue based upon what Plato knew of Socrates and his beliefs.

Naturally talk turns toward death and the philosopher's attitude about it. Plato, putting words into the mouth of Socrates, explains that while the general public may not be aware of it, those who are involved in following philosophy correctly "are practising nothing other than dying and being dead."[35] He stresses soon afterwards that the true occupation of philosophers is to allow the soul to be released from the body and run free. "Truly then," says Socrates, "those who practise philosophy aright are cultivating dying."[36]

A description attributed to Themistius (but probably actually by Plutarch[37]) in his treatise "On the Soul" gives the secret teaching that to be initiated is to experience the same knowledge as one obtains upon one's death – though, of course, with initiation the seeker returns to this world.

At the point of death, Themistius informs us, "[the soul]

has the same experience as those who are being initiated into great mysteries."

This definitive assertion can be taken as a true expression of one who had himself been through the great mysteries. This is not just an intellectual belief but something learned from participating in such a journey to the Far-World.

Themistius continues:

At first one wanders and wearily hurries to and fro, and journeys with suspicion through the dark as one uninitiated: then come all the terrors before the final initiation, shuddering, trembling, sweating, amazement: then one is struck with a marvellous light, one is received into pure regions and meadows, with voices and dances and the majesty of holy sounds and shapes: among these he who has fulfilled initiation wanders free, and released and bearing his crown joins in the divine communion, and consorts with pure and holy men.

He then describes the lowly and degraded situation of those who never seek initiation: the seeker can see "those who live here uninitiated ... abiding in their miseries through fear of death and mistrust of the blessings there."[38]

Seneca, the first-century A.D. Roman statesman and intellectual, understood the importance and point of initiation. "There are [wisdoms], initiatory rites, by means of which are revealed, not the mysteries of a municipal temple, but of the world itself, the vast temple of all the gods."[39] Plato states that "to die is to be initiated."[40] Mircea Eliade, professor of religious history at the University of Chicago for many years, explains that, in essence, an initiation is an encounter with the sacred.[41]

In a similar manner to that which we have seen in ancient Egypt, in the ancient Greek world initiation lay at the very heart of their culture's earliest recorded spiritual life, yet this has been both forgotten and deliberately excised.

After Homer but before Plato is a very mysterious period in ancient Greek history. It is a period when the philosophers did not just sit around talking and arguing over jugs of wine, but when they were active: they healed, they taught, they sang, they chanted, they wrote and recited rhythmic incantatory poetry, they used sacred ritual, they meditated, they used any technique they knew in order to carry the seeker to the very deepest divine sources of reality. Above all, they sought to enter the silence and the stillness. Rather than talk about their philosophy, they experienced it; they lived in the real world rather than in the idealized world of a secluded intellectual elite. We now call these early religious teachers the Presocratic philosophers, but this is just a name, a modern nonsense born of our obsession with classification.

Some of the names of these teachers have survived: Parmenides, Empedocles, Heraclitus, and Pythagoras were all of this group. Plato studied them and lived for a time in communities of their followers in Sicily and Italy. He took over their work and converted it into argument by filtering out all the experiential qualities. Plato's student Aristotle completed the process of deifying the human intellect, stating that all we can know we can find out only by means of our reason and that truth is to be found by discussion and logical argument. Although he advocated learning by experience, he limited the experiences considered acceptable sources of learning. The Presocratics would have laughed in his face.

As must we. For truth, as we have seen, is something to be experienced directly rather than sought intellectually. As we have already pointed out, a fire's flames can be believed to cause pain, but until one's hand is pushed into them, the pain cannot be known. It goes without saying that to know is always greater than to believe.

These matters are not well known because of politics, both ancient and modern. Plato and Aristotle were Athenians; Parmenides, Pythagoras, and the others were residents of the Greek cities that had been founded in southern Italy and Sicily, and these cities were often at war with Athens. They also had close contacts with the mystical and shamanistic currents coming across Asia Minor to the Aegean. And above all, these cities had close contact with the ancient Egyptians, and their leading philosophers often studied in the Egyptian temples. Pythagoras himself, at age twenty-two, went to study in Egypt, where he stayed for approximately thirteen years in the temples before being taken to Babylon by the invading Persians.[42]

Modern universities are Athenocentric in their approach to ancient history and philosophy – that is, their orientation is toward the politics and thought that arose from ancient Athens. These ideas have been given a status far beyond their worth, and yet, because of our modern confidence in reason and intellectual ability, this artificially exalted status of Athens and Athenian philosophy is held to be self-evident and beyond dispute. To criticize it is to be considered radical, even subversive. Yet the truth is that in ancient times, as Peter Kingsley, an expert on the Presocratic philosophers, explains, "many Greek centres of culture preferred to side with the Persians rather than with Athens. They considered them more civilized."[43]

"Certainly," he adds, "Plato and Aristotle were neither the be-all and end-all of ancient philosophy; and all roads did not necessarily pass through Athens."[44]

I remember with considerable amusement a talk delivered by Kingsley to a group of about twenty university dons – all experts in classical philosophy – at All Souls College in Oxford. Kingsley was speaking on the subject of Parmenides: "You cannot ignore," he said to his politely attentive audience, "the experiential in the work of Parmenides." Then he slammed his fist down onto the table, making it and his audience jump in unison: "How *dare* you ignore the experiential in the work of Parmenides," he roared, directly challenging all that his audience had learned and taught. Their mouths dropped, and they gaped at him; such a thing should never happen in an Oxford college.

But Kingsley's point was important: Parmenides was not simply an early "philosopher," as the Athenians would have deigned to acknowledge, in a condescending manner that has been continued in modern times; he was no mere fore-runner of the intellectual games they termed philosophy.

Parmenides was important because he had personally traveled to the Far-World and returned. And he had writ-ten about it, in an incantatory poem.

Kingsley explains: "In Parmenides' writings it is clear that he is given the wisdom he has by going into the world of the dead. He can only do this by dying before he dies; driven by his own longing."[45]

Parmenides begins his poem: "The mares that carry me as far as longing can reach..." We should note the spiritual importance that Parmenides gives to "longing" – meaning that innate need to return to our true home.

Parmenides continues: the mares, he says, "rode on, once they had come and fetched me onto the legendary road of the divinity that carries the man who knows through the vast and dark unknown."[46]

Parmenides was on his way into the Far-World.

In 1879 an Italian archaeologist conducting a survey noted a large number of graves near the site of the ancient city of Thurii, which had been founded by Greek colonists in Italy around 444 B.C. Four of the graves were particularly large, and so he explored them. Two contained some thin gold plates near the body of the dead person. These had been folded up into a small package similar to the amulets that have been found elsewhere in the classical world. When they were unrolled, they proved to contain a text in ancient Greek.

What is curious is that not only were these texts designed to help the dead person on the journey through the underworld, but some were so closely parallel to the Egyptian "Book of the Dead" and other texts advising on the journey to the Far-World that it seemed impossible to avoid seeing a direct connection between the two. It appeared that the early Greek cults that had written these texts, especially those active in Italy, were in some way derived from or using material derived from the ancient Egyptian temple cults.[47]

"O fortunate and blessed one, you are a god, no longer mortal," reads one plate from Thurii, dating from the fourth or third century B.C., addressing the dead person.[48] This is almost identical to some of the utterances in the Pyramid Texts from two thousand years earlier.

From Petelia in southern Italy comes another gold plate, of the same date, bearing a text that is quite poignant. Speaking of some guardians before a sacred spring who will apparently demand to know who the Far-World traveler is, the text advises:

> Say, "I am a child of Earth and starry Heaven;
> But my race is of Heaven [alone]."[49]

A gold plate found more recently in a grave at Pelinna in Thessaly, Greece, mentions a celebration or ritual performance by the "blessed ones" taking place underground: "And you go beneath the earth, performing the rite which also the other blessed ones [are performing]."[50] Mention of the "blessed ones" is suggestive: the Greek playwright Aristophanes, whose career stretched from the fifth to the fourth century B.C., in his play *The Frogs*, depicts Herakles speaking of visiting the Underworld and describing the great feasts of the "Blest." Dionysius asks him, "Who are they?" Herakles answers, "The Holy Ones, who understand the mysteries."[51] Meaning, it is evident, those who had been initiated.

We cannot avoid it: we are forced to take seriously the idea of initiation in underground chambers, and of initiates sharing with the dead secret rites and knowledge. This is a strange claim for a modern person to take seriously, but we must view the ancients in their own terms: this is how they explained what happens, and there seems to have been little ambiguity or doubt involved. Simply because we find it hard to believe is no reason to think that they misunderstood what was occurring, or worse, that they made it up as part of a "pious fraud." All the evidence at our disposal leads to the conclusion that those who passed through the initiation ceremonies felt that they had been well served. There are no reports of disgruntled initiates demanding their money back.

Perhaps it is time now to look at how the priests did it — that is, how they helped initiates actually leave their bodies and travel to the Far-World.

These matters may seem far too arcane to have any relevance whatsoever to our story, which, after all, concerns Jesus and the source of his teachings. Yet Jesus, as we shall soon see, also took an experiential approach to his mysticism. Could men like Parmenides have transmitted ideas to the classical world of the time of Jesus? Could they have added to the fertile mix of techniques that found a center in the great city of Alexandria and a Jewish expression in the Pythagorean-influenced group of Therapeutae whom Philo described living in a community outside the city?

Archaeologists made an astonishing discovery in Italy in 1958: while excavating the ruins of ancient Velia, the home of the Presocratic philosopher Parmenides, they discovered what had once been a hidden gallery in an ancient building. There they recovered the stone bases of three statues. Of course, the statues had long since vanished, but each base held an inscription. They were evidence that a long succession of the healer-priests of Apollo had survived at Velia, the first being none other than Parmenides himself. The latest date inscribed was 446 years after the death of Parmenides – indicating a time somewhere around the beginning of the Christian period. And there could have easily been later priests, for there is no way of telling whether this stone base represented the last.

These healer-priests were important: one of their titles was *Pholarchos* – "Lord of the Lair." This is revealing, as these priests were specialists in an initiatory technique once well known in the ancient world as the technique of incubation.[52]

In antiquity the best way of actually making contact with divinities of the underworld was through the practice of "incubation" – of awaiting a dream or vision while sleeping, as a rule, either on or even inside the earth.[53]

The ritual practice of incubation involves lying down in complete stillness and silence in an underground room, or perhaps a cave, in order to have a prophetic dream or to fall into a state of consciousness that is neither waking nor sleeping. It was here in the enclosed dark spaces that the seekers might have experienced passing across to the Farworld, where they could receive a vision from the Divine, the Source of all. The god of incubation was Apollo.[54]

The god of the sacred groves around the area of Lake Avernus, which were cut down by General Agrippa to use in his ships, was also Apollo; we would therefore expect incubation to have been conducted somewhere in the area. Which brings us back to the underground tunnels of Baia.

The sacred journey was undertaken for healing or for a revelatory experience. These healer-priests of Apollo were experts in incubation and, as Kingsley explains, "used incantations to enter other states of consciousness."[55]

We can see here that the practices of ancient Greece, using such sites as found at Baia or the deep caves or underground sites that must have existed in Velia, were not so different from the uses made of the crypts beneath the temples in ancient Egypt. Such dark secluded places were chosen by seekers who, after dutiful preparation and appropriate ritual and incantation, lay in the stillness and entered another state of consciousness. We are left with little alternative but to seriously consider that they did indeed leave their bodies in their *Ba* form (according to the Egyptians) or in their *psyche*, or soul (according to the Greeks), and travel to the Far-World.

We can also see that by the time of Jesus the two traditions were drawing ever closer together. In fact, during the Greek and Roman domination of their country, the Egyptians despaired of their secrets surviving; the first- or second-century A.D. Hermetic text the *Asclepius* laments:

> A time will come when it will appear that the Egyptians paid respect to divinity with faithful mind and painstaking reverence – to no purpose. All their holy worship will be disappointed and perish without effect, for divinity will return from earth to heaven, and Egypt will be abandoned... When foreigners occupy the land ... a prohibition under penalty prescribed by law (so-called) will be enacted against reverence, fidelity and divine worship. Then this most holy land, seat of shrines and temples, will be filled completely with tombs and corpses... Only words cut in stone will survive to tell your faithful works.[56]

The Egyptians evidently took steps to maintain their secrets: the philosopher Iamblichus informs us that Egyptian priests learned to express themselves in Greek philosophical words, giving rise to a whole collection of wisdom texts that, as we have already noted, "circulated under the name of Hermes" and drew their essentials from Egyptian tradition.[57] And amazingly, this collection distills the secrets of even the most ancient texts, such as the Pyramid Texts, the Coffin Texts, and the Book of the Dead, and the often inconsistent cosmology of the ancient Egyptians.[58]

This collection of literature was attributed to the ancient Egyptian god Thoth – who in the late classical world was known as Hermes Trismegistus, meaning thrice-greatest Hermes. There are quite a number of these texts, but the first – and in many ways the archetypal – text is one called "The Divine Pymander," or, originally, *Poimandres*.

Even the title betrays its Egyptian source: "Poimandres" is a Greek play on words from the ancient Egyptian *P-eime nte-re*, meaning "the knowledge of Ra," the sun god of ancient Egypt.[59] The account of creation given in this text can also be shown to derive from Egyptian originals.[60] The Egyptian custom of magically animating statues and other representations of the gods also finds its way into the Hermetic texts.[61] Above all, and of most relevance to our investigation, the Hermetic concept of man is "as a cosmic rather than a terrestrial being."[62] The Greek gold plate put it well: "My race is of Heaven [alone]."[63]

A particular value of this Hermetic literature is that, despite its late production, it comes from the very source of the mysteries of the ancients and so can be used as a lens through which to view the earlier texts, allowing us to gain a deeper understanding of their true concerns.[64] Significantly, at the very heart of the Hermetic texts is the concept of mystical initiation: "Then he [Poimandres] sent me forth, empowered and instructed on the nature of the universe and on the supreme vision."

It is still more curious that the production of these books of Hermes began about the time of Jesus and paralleled the rise of Christianity. At the end of the second century A.D., Clement, the Christian bishop of Alexandria, referred to them as "containing the whole philosophy of the Egyptians."[65] The pagan philosopher Iamblichus, writing a little later, was also aware of their importance: "Our ancestors dedicated the inventions of their wisdom to this deity, inscribing all their own writings with the name of Hermes."[66]

This collection of texts attributed to Hermes Trismegistus has had an enormous and incalculable effect upon the Western mind. It is fair to say that the Western world would not have developed as it did without them. Science itself might never have evolved without the impetus given by men and women enamored of these works. For they were rediscovered in the Renaissance and translated by Marsilio Ficino about 1463 at the behest of the wealthy Florentine banker Cosimo de Medici. When Cosimo obtained a manuscript of these texts, he was determined to read them before he died. He called Ficino and told him to drop every other work of translation and to concentrate upon the works of Hermes. Such was their reputation.

Though the texts found in the Renaissance were only partial, we have since discovered a number of additions to them, as well as new texts. We have also discovered that these Renaissance texts were censored – much of the magic and ritual were extracted to make them more "philosophical." But it doesn't really matter too much – the kernel of them has survived. And there is much we can learn from them.

In fact, one of the most significant revelations at the beginning of the *Poimandres* is that the seeker is first taken through a vision of what is true, and then he sees himself as part of a group of initiates compared to whom most people are asleep or drunk. At the end of the text the task that confronts them all is unveiled. Theirs is the task of "sanctification": bringing the spirit back into the world to teach others the way to the Far-World.

As we shall now see, this is precisely the task that Jesus set for himself.

Experiencing the Source

I love to travel to sacred sites and to feel them, to seek to understand them. I am constantly surprised – even after all these years – that places where I didn't expect to feel much turn out to be filled with a peace and stillness of the most sacred kind: the top of Mount Sinai; a certain Roman Catholic reliquary lying preciously in its darkened chapel; ruined churches and temples; a group of ancient weathered rocks jutting out above a landscape that has felt too often the tide of blood ebb and flow upon its shores and whose earth, darkly fertile, still gives up its broken pots.

Are such places intrinsically sacred, or do we make them so? Perhaps both. Sacred sites demand participation from the visitor, an entering into a relationship with them, an experience. And there lies the difference between a pilgrim and a tourist.

No one individual, no culture, no civilization, has a monopoly on truth. For this reason, we should not make the mistake of thinking that the techniques of entering the Far-World were known only to the Egyptians or the Greeks. The gates to the Far-World have always been open to those whose world-weary longing draws them across the divide.

And there were few more world-weary than those who came to be baptized in the River Jordan by John the Baptist, a unique event that even Catholic editors of the Jerusalem Bible consider to be an initiation.[1] Was this perhaps the true meaning of John's statement, "The kingdom of heaven is close at hand?" (Matthew 3:2).

Although it is evident that Jesus learned his skills among the mystical Jewish groups in Egypt, the teachings and techniques available to him there had long been imbued with the mysticism of several earlier traditions. One prime example can be found in the story of Jacob's ladder in the Old Testament.

Jacob sets out from Beersheba on a journey to Harran. At sunset he stops to spend the night. He takes up some of the stones he finds there and uses them for a pillow. Then he has a dream: he sees a great ladder with one end set on the earth and the top of it reaching up to heaven. On the ladder he can see "the angels of God ascending and descending." And above it stands God, who promises Jacob and his descendants the land upon which he sleeps. Then Jacob wakes up and, realizing that he is in a sacred place, says, "This is none other but the house of God, and this is the gate of heaven." He rises early in the morning, takes the stone that he has used as a pillow, and sets it up like a pillar, pouring oil over the top of it. He names the place Beth-el, or "the house of God" (Genesis 28:10 – 19).

Such Old Testament stories are not history, of course, but "hero tales" that have been subjected to greater or lesser degrees of mythological reworking – like the story we have already seen of Gilgamesh, King of Uruk, who crosses over to the world of the dead.

What is important is not the historical accuracy of these stories but what they tell us about the deeper concerns and beliefs of the cultures that produced them. It does not matter whether Gilgamesh ever existed or not; what matters is that people at the time believed in the possibility of traveling to the Far-World in order to gain insights into human existence. Understanding our history is not simply a matter of collecting and collating facts; we also need to understand the beliefs that motivated our ancestors. For these beliefs all too often created the historical events that we find recorded.

In this story about Jacob, it is certainly possible that Bethel is in fact located among the sacred stones of some hilltop Canaanite shrine – such shrines were traditionally built in "high places." This would have been an ideal spot to have a prophetic dream in the tradition of incubation. The fact that Jacob reportedly set up one of the stones afterwards and ritually anointed it further suggests that a shrine, a "dwelling place of God," already existed there. Although it is downplayed in the text, it is evident that, in some way,

Jacob clearly felt that the stone had contributed to his vision and contained some sacred magical quality. Obviously this story was written for an audience who would have immediately understood the implications of Jacob's action. After all, the early Israelites were no strangers to the Canaanite religion. It is only we modern folk who miss the point.

More significantly, Jacob's "dream" is better understood as a vision, and one that teaches us a number of important things. Perhaps the most crucial lesson lies in the report of angels "ascending and descending." This is clearly a symbolic demonstration that the link between heaven and earth is dynamic, that the divine qualities are constantly flowing to and fro. This expresses the idea we have already seen in Egypt that the Far-World and the terrestrial world are intimately – and dynamically – interlinked. This is proof, should we need it, that Jacob's vision emerged from a living tradition of which this Old Testament report is just a fragment, a glimpse of the lush landscape of the promised land.

We can be sure that beneath the Old Testament's apparent obsession with family descent, adultery, sin, violence, and the number of deaths in obscure battles, lies an ancient teaching concerning the link between the terrestrial and divine worlds. But in this tradition – as it has been packaged for us by unknown early scribes – the link between the two worlds is portrayed as broken: angelic beings with flaming swords block the entrance to the Garden of Eden; Jacob is not encouraged to climb the ladder to heaven. Religious administrators had apparently taken over the tradition and

restricted its message about the pathway to the Far-World
– much as Vatican strongmen did later with regard to the
teachings of Jesus.

As we can see, truly understanding the Old Testament is
not a matter of digging into the ground to find physical proof
of events, as so many archaeologists over the last two
centuries have done, but rather of reading its stories symbolically – which is what the Egyptian Jewish group, the
Therapeutae, evidently did. Philo reports that they "read the
Holy Scriptures and seek wisdom from their ancestral philosophy by taking it as an allegory, since they think that the
words of the literal text are symbols of something whose hidden nature is revealed by studying the underlying meaning."[2]

Jacob's ladder set upon the ground in a sacred place also
symbolizes another concept we have seen: the notion that
there are specific places where the Far-World and the terrestrial world are linked – places that serve as the perfect
conduit between the two worlds.

It is truly a pity that the story does not depict Jacob climbing the ladder, crossing from this world to the other, in order to return with what he can learn. Had it done so, the
history of the Middle East might have developed in a very
different manner given the profound effect these stories
have had over the region and its people for the last two and
a half millennia.

To see further into the earlier traditions that left their
mystical mark on Judaism, we need to look at two of the

strongest influences upon its development. The first derives from Egypt, as expressed in the stories of Joseph and
Moses and from the hundreds of years during which Jewish
soldiers, traders, farmers, and administrators were resident
there. The second comes from Mesopotamia as a result of
the sixth-century B.C. "Babylonian exile": the king of Babylon Nabu-kudurri-usur – known to us as Nebuchadnezzar
– besieged and captured Jerusalem in 587 B.C. and deported
the Jewish king, along with thousands of his people. Many
others fled into exile in Egypt.

We can see, for example, the Babylonian rite of baptism
as the origin of the Jewish practice of purification before
rituals, the aim being to separate the person from the terrestrial world while at the same time establishing a pure relationship with the divine world.[3] The Jewish calendar also
derives from a system used by the later Babylonians. Even
the traditional incantation bowls used by Jewish rabbis were
of Babylonian origin. The Babylonian Talmud too has
medical information from earlier Babylonian lore, and
Babylonian astrological texts have been found to have
been used by Jewish groups as well.[4] Even the belief in one
god, which carried over into Christianity and Islam, has
been seen by some scholars as deriving from ancient
Mesopotamia: the name of the god of the Assyrians, Ashur
(*Assur*), means the "One," the "Only," the "Universal God."[5]

Mesopotamian influence can also be seen in some of the
mystical images found in the books of the prophets, particularly in Ezekiel's. At the beginning of his account, Ezekiel

(1:26–27) describes a vision of God saying that he saw the Divine in human form sitting on a throne of sapphire surrounded and illuminated by amber. In fact, the throne was not made of sapphire. This was a mistranslation: it was made of lapis lazuli, greatly prized by the Babylonians.[6] But the important point is that this is a very specific image and would seem to emanate from an existing tradition.

Ezekiel lived in Babylonia and had this vision in 593 B.C. while beside the Grand Canal linking the Rivers Tigris and Euphrates, very near Babylon. It is clear that Ezekiel's vision, as written down, derived from an ancient Babylonian text that described the great Babylonian god Marduk sitting on a throne of lapis lazuli illuminated by glistening amber.[7] This is significant, for it reveals that Ezekiel must have been involved with esoteric mysteries in Babylonia as an initiate. We know this because the Babylonian text ends with the stern warning: "Secret of the great gods: let the initiate reveal it to the initiate, but do not let the uninitiated see it."[8]

This text not only points to a connection between the Babylonian and Jewish priesthoods but also indicates that these links were closer and more profound than has previously been supposed.[9] It seems apparent that Jewish priests were able to be initiated into the deepest secrets of the Babylonian cult.

Kingsley explains that, "in the rabbinic tradition of Judaism the central details of Ezekiel's vision remained as esoteric, as strongly guarded a secret, as they had been in the Babylonian priestly tradition which preceded him." In other words, there was no simple borrowing of symbolism or concepts across the two cultures but rather a living connection "between the heart of one tradition and the heart of another." From this we can see that "Ezekiel stands close to the fountain-head of Jewish mysticism. And yet he also occupies a place alongside a much larger channel of mystical and cosmological doctrine which stretches back through the centuries before him."[10]

Mesopotamian influence can also be detected in the origin of the Tree of Life, now the backbone of the mystical Jewish practice known as the Kabbalah. The great Finnish scholar Professor Simo Parpola, who has done so much to translate the esoteric texts of the Assyrian and Babylonian empires, became intrigued with a perplexing aspect of the carved images found in ancient Assyrian and Babylonian palaces: the hundreds of representations of a mysterious sacred tree attended by strangely attired priests, some wearing a fish skin, some with wings, others with the head of an eagle, but all of them carrying a water bucket in one hand and a pinecone in the other. These images are never discussed in the clay tablets on which the ancient writings were inscribed and so have long remained enigmatic.

Parpola points out that the inner doctrines of the sacred tree were not permitted to be written down but remained the preserve of a small and select group of initiates. Indeed, archaeologists have known for many years that there was a large body of secret teachings in the Mesopotamian empires at least as long ago as the second millennium B.C.[11]

However, Parpola believes that the secret teachings were much older than that. In his opinion, those concerning the sacred tree, for example, could easily have reached back to the third millennium B.C., "if not earlier," he adds provocatively, although utilizing the small print of a footnote.[12]

This speculation raises the possibility that we are confronting material that could easily predate the invention of writing and may even have been part of the secret oral teaching of early humans for millennia. It is difficult to avoid seeing the sacred Tree of Life as related to the very earliest mythology of culture – that is, to the "Tree of Knowledge of Good and Evil" that stood in the Garden of Eden. The point implicit in the story is that an understanding of the sacred tree is as old as humans themselves.

We are here touching the edges of the beliefs that were running through the ancient cultures we have already mentioned, those that were first expressed with ritualized burials. I think it unwise to ignore the possibility that in the teachings of the sacred tree we have some residues – however disguised they might be – of the knowledge possessed by those Neanderthals who stood around the grave of one of their own over sixty thousand years ago in a cave at Shanidar, just to the northeast of the lands that later became part of the Mesopotamian empires.

The basic understanding of the tree symbol was that it depicts "the divine world order maintained by the Assyrian king," with the king himself placed in this order as the "Perfect Man."[13] A comparison of the imagery and numerical symbolism of the Assyrian sacred tree and that of the Tree of Life of the Kabbalah shows extraordinary correspondences. Parpola concludes that the Kabbalistic tree is certainly based upon the Assyrian original.[14]

The tree in Kabbalah symbolizes the manner in which the One Divinity is manifested in all the multiplicity of creation. The creative power is visualized as a divine flash of light that emerges from the unformed One and, streaking to the earth, brings all form into being. The tree is made up of ten *Sefirot*, which are symbols of the emanated divine principles. The tree has three pillars formed by the central trunk and the vertical alignment of Sefirot on either side; the two side pillars represent the opposites found in the terrestrial world, such as severity and mercy, discipline and tolerance, theory and practice, feminine and masculine; the central trunk provides a balanced path between them as expressed in its names – the pillar of holiness, the Way of Knowledge.[15]

The tree also symbolizes a means by which humans can journey from the terrestrial world back to that of the divine – it provides the map and method of a spiritual "Way." In this respect, it serves as a similar image to that of Jacob's ladder.

The examples of prior mystical tradition influencing Judaism keep on coming: in 1768 the Scottish explorer James Bruce traveled up the Nile in an attempt to discover its source. His travel was difficult and maintained only by his ability to produce gold when necessary and to use his blunderbusses and pistols. Travel was a dangerous business, even without the diseases that often resulted from bad water and rotten food. After two years he reached Ethiopia, which was in the grip of a civil war. He survived and returned to Europe bearing some treasures, among which were three copies of an Ethiopian edition of an ancient Jewish text called "The Book of Enoch."

This text had been accepted by the second- and third-century church fathers such as Clement of Alexandria and Tertullian. But even then its inclusion on the official list of Jewish sacred texts was not certain; Tertullian mentioned that some rabbis would not accept it.[16] However, Christians at that time had few qualms. They considered the text canonical since parts of it could be read as predicting the coming of Jesus and since it was mentioned in the New Testament in the Letter of Jude (14). But following the Council of Nicaea in A.D. 325, the Book of Enoch became sidelined and was eventually banned by late-fourth- and early-fifth-century theologians such as Jerome and Augustine.

Although the Book of Enoch is presented as one composition, it is immediately apparent that it was not written by a single author. It is actually a mixture of pieces by a number of writers brought together under the name of Enoch. Yet despite its internal inconsistency, it is an extraordinary work.

It uses many of the motifs that are now familiar to us: Enoch has a visionary dream (13:8); he asks for an explanation of the Tree of Life (25:1 – 3); he mentions three eastern portals through which stars pass on the eastern horizon

(36:3), in accordance with the Babylonian and Assyrian astrolabes, which date from around 1100 B.C.; and he also speaks of the actions of men as being weighed in the balance, like the Egyptian concept of afterlife judgement (41:1).[17]

We are once again on familiar ground: we have esoteric matters taught to a seeker by means of dream visions of the Far-World – and in a Jewish context. As we have seen, these dream visions occur as part of an initiation, and the dreamer goes to a quiet, dark place, such as a cave or a temple crypt, and uses the techniques he or she has been taught to enter the stillness from which the Far-World is accessible. So we would expect, somewhere in the Book of Enoch, to find a reference to the experiential, the initiatory. We are not disappointed.

"And it came to pass," the text explains, "that my spirit was translated and it ascended into the heavens: and I saw the holy sons of God" (Enoch 71:1).[18] This report has all the appearance of being an account of something that truly occurred to the writer – a mystical experience that could be induced by someone seeking initiation into the esoteric tradition of Judaism.

Enoch was taken up "from amongst those who dwell on the earth ... he was raised aloft on the chariots of the spirit" (Enoch 70:2).[19] This image seems to be a Judaic equivalent of the Egyptian winged Ba. But there is no doubt that this event concerned an initiation, since the text explains what happened to Enoch after he had been raised to heaven but before his spirit became transfigured:

> And the angel Michael seized me by my right hand,
> and lifted me up and led me forth into all the secrets,
> and he showed me all the secrets of righteousness. And
> he showed me all the secrets of the ends of the heaven.
> (Enoch 71:3–4)[20]

The anonymous ancient writer continues, describing what then occurred: "And I fell on my face," he recounts, "and my whole body became relaxed, and my spirit was transfigured" (71:11).[21]

This is precisely the type of experience that we would expect to find among the Therapeutae, for example. And crucially, just in case we have failed to spot it, the text makes a point of explaining that this ascent into the heavens occurred while Enoch was still living – as the text puts it, "during his lifetime." This is virtually identical to the explanation in the Egyptian Pyramid Texts that the king has "not departed dead" but has "departed alive."[22] It is hard not to see the two statements as describing an essentially similar experience, an experience deriving from an initiation into the mysteries of the Far-World.

These visionary texts cannot be any other than records of initiations – records gathered together under the name of Enoch in much the same way as in Egypt those attributed to Hermes Trismegistus were collected together in the Books of Hermes.

Given the visionary nature of this text, it is, at first sight, curious to discover that seven pieces of the Book of Enoch form part of the Dead Sea Scrolls.[23] All were found in 1952 in the Qumran cave in the marl cliff face near the ruins of the community, now called Cave 4. So, on the face of it, it seems as though the Zealot group that produced the Dead Sea Scrolls and was so important a part of Jesus's political milieu and the messianic Jewish group that gave rise to Christianity were both well aware of the Book of Enoch. But an analysis of it reveals an interesting fact.

The Book of Enoch, as we have said, is a compilation of texts from different authors. In fact, scholars have separated the text into five sections, each distinctive and different from the others.[24] The section that contains the report of the mystical ascent and transfiguration is the second section, which is also known as "the Parables." *This mystical, initiatory section is completely absent from the texts found at Qumran.*

The Dead Sea Scroll texts contain fragments, written in Aramaic, from sections one, four, and five only of the Book of Enoch. Not only is the mystical section missing, but so too is the following section on astronomical and calendar matters – in particular, the section providing the basis of the solar calendar, which, we will remember, was evidently used in the Jewish Temple of Onias in the Egyptian delta.

We can see here the same clash of traditions that we find expressed in the story of Jesus when he rejects the Zealot position on the payment of taxes to the emperor. Jesus took a mystical approach; the Zealots took a worldly approach. The Zealot Book of Enoch clearly rejects this mystical approach. This stands in further evidence that – as we have said before – Jesus could not have learned his skills among the Zealots of Galilee.

Mystical texts like the Book of Enoch, texts that would have been very dear to the Therapeutae, would also have been very dear to those who taught Jesus. With the Book of Enoch, we finally have a text that appears to issue directly from the Jewish milieu within which Jesus was nurtured and from a group concerned with initiation into secret teachings, with an ascent to heaven, and with an experience of the Divine Light. Of this there can be no doubt, for according to the Book of Enoch (96:3), "A bright light shall enlighten you."[25]

We have now journeyed far enough; while we have not gathered everything, we have gathered all that we can carry.

It is time to return to Judaea and Egypt and to the man we remember as Jesus the *meshiha* – the Christ.

12

The Kingdom of Heaven

There were always secrets in Judaism and the Christianity that developed out of it; secrets which we hinted at – sometimes even explicitly mentioned – but never written down in the memoirs and letters that became the texts of the Christian New Testament we have today. Those secrets were carried by an oral tradition. The early church fathers knew this clandestine teaching well; even if they had not been exposed to it themselves, they recognized its existence in the Gospels.

One Sabbath day before the execution of John the Baptist, Jesus was teaching by the side of the Sea of Galilee; such were the crowds who had come to hear him that he had to sit in a boat and speak from there. He taught those watching and listening by means of parables – simple stories that conveyed insights into the way of life he sought for them. Later, when he was alone with his disciples, they asked him why he always spoke in this manner. He gave them a surprising explanation: parables are designed for the masses, he said bluntly, but for his disciples he had a deeper truth. He explained, "It is given unto you to know the mystery of the kingdom of heaven" (Matthew 13:11; Mark 4:11; Luke 8:9–10).

We can understand from Jesus's plain-spoken answer that there were two levels of expression: the inner secrets given to his close companions and the outer teaching given to the public. This inner teaching concerned the "mystery of the kingdom of heaven."

The Gospel of Mark, describing the same conversation, uses a slightly different terminology, speaking of "the kingdom of God." Luke does the same, as does John, who uses this phrase in another context. The concept of the "kingdom" is also found in certain other texts that never made it into the New Testament, such as the Gospel of Thomas. Throughout these texts we can note slight differences in wording – "the kingdom," "the kingdom of Heaven," "the kingdom of God," "the kingdom of the Father" – but we need not doubt that all these terms mean the same thing.

What exactly might this kingdom of heaven be?

The New Testament, apart from stating that this kingdom is concerned with something secret that is not given to the public, provides little further explanation; no clues are provided on how the kingdom might be reached, or how we might know it should it arrive. Indeed, the impression given by commentators is that it refers to some kind of future ideal kingdom that, with the return of the Messiah, will bring heaven on earth, as in some messianic thousand-year Reich. But first there is the difficult matter of Armageddon – at least according to the Book of Revelation, a tricky text if ever there was one.

However, there are hints in the New Testament that we, now knowledgeable in the ways of the Mystery traditions of Egypt and Greece, can recognize as motifs we've encountered before.

Not only is the pathway to the kingdom of heaven meant to be revealed only to the initiated, but there seems to be a sense in which, once discovered, this "kingdom" is always present. It is not something we need to look forward to in an uncertain future, but rather something that seems to have more in common with what the Egyptians called *djet* – the time that is the stepping outside of time. Furthermore, there is an assurance of immanence; we have already noted John the Baptist's statement that "the kingdom of God is at hand" (Mark 1:15). We can understand this as meaning that it is *immediately accessible* – not due to come in a month, a year, or a decade, or to be manifested in the arrival of Jesus's preaching mission in Israel, which seems to be the most common interpretation of this statement. Rather, *it is already available to those who know the way*.

Furthermore, courage is needed: gaining access to the kingdom of heaven demands a true focus, steady nerves, and complete commitment. "No man, having put his hand to the plough, and looking back, is fit for the kingdom of God," said Jesus (Luke 9:62). He also revealed little patience with those who professed spirituality yet did not allow the gates of heaven to be opened to those who sought them; Jesus complained about the "scribes and Pharisees," whom he described as "you who shut up the kingdom of heaven in men's faces, neither going in yourselves nor allowing others to go in who want to" (Matthew 23:13).

This is not a description of a teaching mission in Judaea or even a future thousand-year rule. Jesus is wanting us to understand that the kingdom of heaven is a place we can travel to, a place we can enter.

This is beginning to sound rather familiar.

Luke adds a little more: Jesus was asked by the Pharisees when the kingdom of God was going to come. They were evidently intent upon seeing it as taking form on earth, rather like the self-ruled state envisaged by the Zealots when they first hatched their plans for Jesus to be the high priest and king who would physically rule over an independent Judaea, the role he so dramatically rejected when he held up the coin bearing the image of the emperor and stated that the tax should be paid. In a similarly direct manner that must also have been shocking to the Pharisees, who seem to have asked their question more in sarcasm than in a spirit of genuine inquiry, Jesus replied:

The kingdom of God cometh not with observation: Neither shall they say, Lo here! Or lo there! For, behold, the kingdom of God is within you. (Luke 17:20–21)

We cannot see the kingdom – we cannot find it by reason and physical observation. Yet Jesus has already stated that it is accessible, that it can be traveled to. Here he is letting us know that it resides "within." And how does one travel within? This much we now know: by entering the silence. Jesus has returned us to the concept of incubation and the still, dark, silent underground crypts and caves where a seeker can be initiated into the world where the dead live – the Far-World.

Is the "kingdom of heaven" Jesus's name for the Far-World? It seems very likely. But we should look at some further data.

In January 1941, with English cities being pounded by the Luftwaffe, the Second World War seemingly going Hitler's way (he had not yet invaded Russia), and the United States remaining officially neutral (Pearl Harbor was still eleven months away), a young American doctoral student named Morton Smith was studying in Jerusalem.[1]

Smith was living in a Greek hostel next to the Church of the Holy Sepulchre in the Old City of Jerusalem. Also in the hostel was one of the top officials of the Greek Orthodox Church in Israel, Father Kyriakos Spyridonides. He and Smith became friends. After Christmas, Father Kyriakos invited Smith to accompany him for a few days to the desert monastery of Mar Saba, one of the oldest monasteries still working. Its towers and thick walls nestled deep into a wadi that linked Jerusalem with the Dead Sea, Mar Saba had been in existence for almost fifteen hundred years.

The Greek Orthodox religious services began six hours before dawn, and Smith found them fascinating but difficult: the services "were not long – they were eternal."[2] The rituals served the Divine in a manner rather similar to that of the daily services in the Holy of Holies in the Egyptian temples. For Smith, it was a genuine revelation: "The service was not moving toward its end, it was simply going on, as it had from eternity and would forever. As one ceased to be in time, one ceased also to be in a definite space."[3]

As he looked up toward the roof of the church, the small candles above seemed like stars to him, the huge church walls seemed set back in the remote distance, and the frescoes of saints and monks seemed "present in this realm among the stars, above space and time, the unchanging kingdom of the heavens, where the eternal service was offered to eternal God."[4]

Smith was obviously deeply moved by what he experienced at Mar Saba. But while participating in the liturgy, he realized that it was not for him; he appreciated the service as an expression of great beauty, whereas for the monks it was first and foremost a spiritual duty. The liturgy had to be performed using particular words and particular actions; it was, Smith realized, essentially magical ritual. This insight was to lead him to investigate the magical and mystical techniques used by Judaism and early Christianity.

He left the monastery after six weeks, but before his departure he found time to look at the caves that had been the first refuges for the monks who had lived there fifteen hundred years earlier and subsequently had been incorporated into the monastic building. The first church was in the largest of these caves. He saw also many icons, although the best had been destroyed in a disastrous fire during the eighteenth century. This fire had also destroyed or badly damaged many ancient manuscripts; the majority of those that survived had been taken to the Patriarchal Library in Jerusalem for safekeeping. Despite this removal, a large number of books still remained in two libraries: the main library in the new church, and a smaller one located in a room within the great tower, where a jumble of books sat on dusty shelves. This library was to be the site of a significant discovery that, it is fair to say, later dominated Smith's life.

Smith finished his doctoral thesis in Jerusalem and returned to Harvard – where, scholar that he was, he began a second doctorate. He remained in contact with Father Kyriakos, finished his doctorate, and began his illustrious teaching and research career as a professor of religion at Columbia University in New York. In 1958, needing a break, he decided to return to the peace and silence of Mar Saba. He chose to occupy himself making a catalog of all the old manuscripts and books haphazardly stuffed into bookcases or piled on the floor in the tower library. Every morning around dawn he would climb the twelve or more stories of stairs into the tower room, where he would gather a few books or manuscripts and take them back to his monastic cell for examination and recording.

He discovered that many of the books also contained long handwritten passages, copies from earlier texts that were squeezed into every space and blank page; even the margins sometimes had been used. These handwritten additions dated from the eighteenth and nineteenth centuries and revealed how difficult it had been back then to obtain paper. He also discovered parts of old manuscripts that had been used in the binding process, material of interest to classical scholars. But among the books and papers of this dusty library Smith was to find a true treasure.

One afternoon, sitting in his room reading through the group of books he had brought back that day, he found a handwritten text on previously blank pages within a seventeenth-century edition of the letters of Saint Ignatius.

It was a copy of a letter from Clement, Bishop of Alexandria, in the late second century. Smith knew that Clement had written many letters, although none were known to have survived; his discovery was therefore unique and important. He photographed the text so that he would have some copies with which to prepare a translation and some to show other scholars. This translation proved to be extraordinary.

Around A.D. 195 Clement wrote to Theodore, one of his canons, on a very sensitive subject. It concerned a *secret* Gospel of Mark: Clement explained that a licentious heretical group called the Carpocratians had come upon the secret gospel through deceitful means and that the text was not to be considered accurate.

Essentially Clement was confirming that this secret gospel existed, but he was also asserting that neither he nor Theodore could possibly admit this publicly without granting this heretical sect some measure of credibility.

Clement was asking Theodore to lie in the service of the truth — to deny that the gospel was by Mark, even under oath.

Clement explained that Mark spent some time in Rome with Peter and there began writing the account of Jesus's actions that later became his Gospel. Peter too was scribbling in the service of posterity. After Peter's death, Mark moved to Alexandria, bringing both his and Peter's writings with him. There he wrote his Gospel but held back certain stories that he included only in a special "secret" gospel that he gave to the Church in Alexandria, where, in Clement's day, it was still carefully preserved, "being read only to those who are being initiated into the great mysteries."[5]

The "great mysteries"? In Christianity? What *is* Clement talking about?

Clement certainly knew about initiation and the mysteries. He had been very well educated in classical philosophy. His writings are filled with quotes from Plato, Parmenides, Empedocles, Heraclitus, Pythagoras, Homer, and dozens of other monumental figures of the classical heritage. He had obviously fully explored and critically examined all the philosophies of his time before converting to Christianity sometime in the latter part of the second century. Furthermore, he was aware that the Egyptians hid secret knowledge in the symbolism within their writing and images, he knew of the Hermetic texts, he knew the mystical meanings conveyed by number and proportion, and like the mystical Therapeutae of the century before him, he knew of the hidden meanings conveyed by the stories of the Old Testament.[6] Clement, we can be sure, was no fool.

His use of these words illustrates the variety and complexity of the world of Christianity in Alexandria. We would expect it to include some such ritual practices, and we mustn't forget that the earliest Gnostic teachers, such as Basilides and Valentinus, emerged out of Alexandria. Gnosticism itself maintained and developed much from the secret traditions known to early Christianity.[7] The early third-century theologian Hippolytus preserved a Gnostic psalm that ended with the claim that,

> *The secrets of the holy way*
> *Called Gnosis, I will hand down.*[8]

The Gnostics held that they were the custodians of the true Christianity: at the heart of their system lay an initiation into true knowledge of Divinity.

Clement argued at length against the Gnostics, even though he held a certain sympathy for their teachings. Mysteries and initiation were a strong feature of Alexandrian Christianity of whatever persuasion, but in general these teachings were not written down. Rather, they were maintained within the oral tradition. Clement addresses this directly at the beginning of his book *The Miscellanies*: "But secret things are entrusted to speech, not to writing."[9]

After urging Theodore to maintain silence, Clement made a remarkable admission of the secret gospel by proceeding to provide its complete text. There are two extracts; the crucial one slides neatly into the Gospel of Mark, within chapter 10, between verses 34 and 35. The second and smaller addition fits into verse 46, where the current text has been mutilated.

The central point of the text of Mark's secret gospel is that a youth was ritually initiated by Jesus into the "kingdom of God"!

As it turns out, this incident occurred at Bethany, the same place where the "raising of Lazarus" took place (John 11:1 – 44). Could it be that the two events are in fact the same? And after all we have now seen, we must wonder what was really meant by the raising of Lazarus "from the dead." Was he literally brought back from the world of the dead? Or from the Far-World after an initiation in the darkness and silence – in a cave with its entrance covered by a stone as the Gospel depicts (John 11:38)? Was he, as Jesus perhaps would say, returning from a visit to the kingdom of heaven?

And does this text relate to another very mysterious event in the Gospel of Mark that remains steadfastly anomalous? When Jesus is arrested in the Garden of Gethsemane, after a brief fight in which one of the high priest's men has his ear cut off, Jesus's disciples flee. Mark then describes a young man fitting the same description as the one Jesus is said in the secret Gospel of Mark to have initiated. No one has ever found an explanation for this event. But it seems inconceivable that the two are somehow not related.

But as Smith points out, "Plausibility is not proof." Nevertheless, he adds, "history ... is by definition the search for the most probable explanations of preserved phenomena."[10]

Having found the letter, Smith first had to prove that it was what it claimed to be: it could have been a complete forgery created any time since 1646, the publication date of the edition of Ignatius's letters into which it was copied. Or it could have been an honest copy of an early letter that was itself a forgery. Or it could have been authentic in every respect. He had to know.

It was known that a collection of at least twenty-one letters written by Clement of Alexandria were in the possession of the monastery of Mar Saba as late as the eighth century because three extracts from them were quoted by John of Damascus while he was in residence during this time.[11] This is the only known collection of Clement's letters. Smith thinks it likely that this collection of letters was mostly destroyed in the fire that caused so much damage in the eighteenth century; one of the surviving letters was found afterwards and copied by hand into the edition of Ignatius's letters. This would make sense as a primitive means of filing – copying a manuscript letter into a printed edition of letters.

The first thing Smith did was to show the photographs of the text to leading scholars in the field. Of the fourteen he approached, only two felt that the letter could not be by Clement. Smith decided to take as "a working hypothesis" that the letter was indeed what it claimed to be.[12] Next he spent years making a detailed and exhaustive analysis of the writing style, comparing it to other texts by Clement and comparing the secret Gospel extract to the text of canonical Mark. Both of these exercises supported the hypothesis.

Unfortunately, Smith was never able to produce the hand-written copy of Clement's letter for other scholars to study and for forensic examination, and for this he has drawn much criticism. That omission has been seen as very sloppy for a scholar normally so precise. Unfortunately, I know only too well that not every manuscript one sees can later be retrieved for scholars to test and work on — however much one may want this to be done. And this is especially true for those manuscripts with a commercial value, those that are hidden away, or those considered too controversial or embarrassing to the group holding them.

However, it must be recorded that despite Smith's in-ability to produce the original text, other scholars have seen the original letter. Two Hebrew University scholars, Guy Stroumsa, a professor of comparative religion, and David Flusser, a professor of early Judaism and Christian origins, have both seen it. In 1976 these scholars visited the library at Mar Saba especially to take a look at the text.

A few minutes' search was all it took to find the book still sitting on a shelf where it had been put by Smith. They obtained permission to take the book back to Jerusalem to the library of the Greek Orthodox Patriarchate. Their intention was to arrange for a chemical analysis of the ink in order to date the writing. But once the book was in Jerusalem, they discovered that the only people who could carry out this kind of testing were the Israeli police. The Greek Orthodox authorities refused to hand the book over to the police, and so no further analysis was possible.[13]

Stroumsa later found out that the letter had been removed from the book and separately stored in a secure place. It is safe to assume that no other scholars will see it again soon.

If the extract is indeed authentic, then what is the "kingdom of heaven"? And how might we go there? Even without the letter there is quite a bit of information available to us, if we can but recognize it.

Jesus explains in the Gospel of Luke (11:34): "When thine eye is single, thy whole body ... is full of light." This is a statement of the purest mysticism worthy of any Buddhist or Taoist from the East. What does Jesus mean by it? In essence, he is saying that if our vision is of the One, then the divine light will embrace us. We will become absorbed into "God," just as the sixteenth-century Catholic mystic Saint Teresa of Ávila tells us.

Saint Teresa frequently experienced what she termed "rapture" – a state in which a spiritual desire "permeates the whole soul in a moment, [and] it begins to become so weary that it rises far above itself and above all creation."[14] And the soul rises to become absorbed in "God" for a short time. During this time the senses cannot know what is occurring. But when the soul reaches the state of rapture, "the soul is utterly blinded, absorbed." She explains that "when it looks on this divine Sun, it is dazzled by the brightness."[15]

Also realizing the similarity between such profound experiences and death, Saint Teresa wrote:

> I lost almost all my fear of death, which had always terrified me. Now it seems to me a very easy thing for a servant of God that in a single moment the soul should find itself freed from this prison and at rest. This moment in which God raises and transports the soul to show it things of such a sublime excellence seems to me like that in which the soul leaves the body.[16]

So why haven't we been taught all of this from the beginning? The answer is, in part, because of the Church's dislike of the freedom unloosed by mysticism.

Saint Teresa, for instance, lived in constant fear of transgressing and being dragged away to the dark prisons of the Inquisition. She came from a family that, on her grandfather's side, had been Jewish but had converted to Catholicism. Unfortunately, these *conversos* were the very people of whom the Inquisition was most suspicious. She sought counsel, and though she had ventured into very dubious paths doctrinally and was regarded suspiciously by some of those she confided in, she survived because of her honesty, her humility, her obviously deep spirituality, and, importantly, a good relationship with her Jesuit confessor. Others were not so lucky; for them, there was only prison and the flames.

So great is the Church's distaste for mysticism that it has distorted Luke's mystical statement by forcing a nonmystical interpretation upon it; truly the Church has castrated its spirit. The official Catholic commentary on this text removes all sense of achievement, commitment, and mystical adventure as it explains these lines:

> Here they imply that undistorted vision is required to see the light of Jesus... Its meaning would seem to be: "When a man, through the *inner* light of sound eyes is full of light and has no trace of darkness (evil), then and only then will the light *from without*, the God-enkindled light of Jesus, enlighten him wholly."[17]

In other words, even the *New Catholic Commentary* is not sure what it means; it has to be satisfied with what it *seems* to mean.

But by now we know better than this. We can be certain of what it means: it represents an uncompromising mystical stance and advice on how to experience the Divine Source of all – how to travel to the kingdom of heaven.

More about the kingdom of heaven can be found, of course, in the Gospel of Thomas. Harvard's Professor Helmut Koester feels strongly that this gospel should be included in the canon of the New Testament, and many other scholars agree with him. It was a product of Egyptian Christianity from the second century, which was an immensely productive period.

At Easter in A.D. 367, Athanasius, Bishop of Alexandria, declared that all noncanonical books in Egypt should be destroyed. Few texts survived. It is probable that the monks in a monastery near Nag Hammadi decided to hide their sacred texts rather than burn them, so they placed them in a large jar that they buried in the desert near the Nile. In December 1945 the jar was uncovered by a worker digging for fertilizer. Inside he found twelve papyrus codices plus eight pages of a thirteenth codex – in all, the jar contained forty-six different texts. Some of the pages were burned, but the codices were eventually sold to the Coptic Museum in Cairo, where they are all now kept.

Eventually scholars got their hands on them. Some were published early, but until UNESCO organized an international team of scholars to translate them, a small group of scholars kept them to themselves. Professor James Robinson, the leader of the UNESCO team, speaking of the inordinate delays in publication and the difficulties in allowing other scholars access, not only with this collection but also with the Dead Sea Scrolls, reflected sadly, "Manuscript discoveries bring out the worst instincts in otherwise normal scholars."[18]

This collection of codices found at Nag Hammadi is now popularly termed the Gnostic Gospels, and Princeton's Elaine Pagels is probably the most well-known commentator on them. An interesting aspect of this collection is the wide range of texts that were considered to be spiritual – not only the Gnostic texts of varying factions, but works of Plato and the Hermetic texts. It shows the nonsectarian approach to spirituality of those times. The monastery that originally held them may have been Christian, but it was prepared to recognize the spirituality in these texts wherever they came from. It appears that it was the message of the texts that was important, not the religious or philosophical tradition from which they might have emerged. The monks' focus was upon the kingdom of heaven rather than upon sectarian point-scoring.

The Gospel of Thomas was among the texts found at Nag Hammadi. It is clear that its information comes from a hidden tradition that was passed only to a special few; as its opening sentence states, "These are the secret sayings which the living Jesus spoke and which Didymus Judas Thomas wrote down."

This gospel is, in some ways, perhaps the closest to the canonical Gospels. Unlike the other Gnostic texts, it contains a number of stories and parables in parallel with the New Testament Gospels. But it also contains more. It gives fresh information about the "kingdom" – or "the Kingdom of the Father." Jesus's disciples ask, "When will the new world come?" Jesus replies, "What you look forward to has already come, but you do not recognize it."[19] And the gospel describes where this "Kingdom of Heaven" is to be found: "The Kingdom is inside you and it is outside you."[20]

It is reality, not the reflection of reality in the visible world. "The Kingdom of the Father is spread out upon the earth," the gospel states, "and men do not see it."[21]

And how might we approach it? In answer, we are presented with imagery parallel to the quote of Jesus we have already noted – that "thine eye" should be single. "Jesus said, 'When you make the two one, you will become the sons of man.'"[22]

To see through the multiplicity of the world to the One of reality is his advice:

Jesus said to them, "When you make the two one, and when you make the inside like the outside and the outside like the inside, and the above like the below, and when you make the male and the female one and the same ... then will you enter [the Kingdom]."[23]

And in a further statement similar to one in the Gospel of Matthew, Jesus explains, "The Pharisees and the scribes have taken the keys of Knowledge and hidden them. They themselves have not entered, nor have they allowed to enter those who wish to."[24]

Paul, for all the orthodoxy that is nailed to his every word and nuance, was not beyond the circle of those who knew that far more was going on in the new faith than could be written down: "We speak wisdom among them that are perfect," Paul writes. "We speak the wisdom of God in a mystery, even the hidden wisdom" (1 Corinthians 2, 6–7).

The description "hidden wisdom" is a translation of the original Greek *sophian en musterio*, meaning "a wisdom in mystery" – a wisdom that is secret. This, Paul states, is given only to the *teleiois*, "the perfect ones," which relates to the *telete*, the ceremony of initiation, and the *telestes*, the priests who conduct initiations into the mysteries. Paul is using the terminology of the classical mystery tradition.

But Paul never knew Jesus. He never even met him. And he didn't get on with the messianic Jewish community in Jerusalem. This is hardly surprising, given his previous leading role in the forces of persecution. The Jerusalem community didn't trust Paul. The Book of Acts coyly, but firmly, explains that he was quickly dispatched to Tarsus in southern Turkey. It suggests that this was for his own protection, though it is less clear about who exactly he needed protection from (Acts 9:30). The point is that Paul was removed from Judaea.[25] The Zealots wanted him out of the way. In fact, there were plenty who would have happily arranged for Paul to be out of the way permanently.

Yet his knowledge joins plenty of other evidence for the existence of an esoteric and mystical teaching being passed on secretly within Christianity.[26] Sometime late in the second century, however, this teaching was relegated to the background. It was degraded and its validity rejected until it faded away. Stroumsa suggests two main reasons for this: first, since the heretical teachers adopted the esoteric teachings when the heresies were condemned, so too were the secret teachings condemned. Second, there was a realization that to increase the universal appeal of Christianity it had to shed any doctrines that were kept away from the mass of believers.[27] And at the same time, with the rise of written gospels, the oral tradition, which was the main vehicle for carrying these secret traditions, lost its importance.

There is one further text we should note, for it brings together a number of strands that have become shaken loose during our off-road journey.

In 1896 a fifth-century codex written in Coptic on papyrus was discovered in Cairo. It contained four new texts – one of which was later to be found also at Nag Hammadi – and all of them were very early texts. One of the texts, never seen before and known only to the Egyptian church, was called the Gospel of Mary of Magdala. It was dated to early in the second century A.D.[28] So, like the Gospel of Thomas, it has as much claim to validity as the Gospels in the New Testament. While two further fragments of the gospel have been found, only half of the original remains. Despite this, it is revealing.

Like the texts we have looked at earlier, the Gospel of Mary of Magdala carries a warning from Jesus against looking for physical evidence of the kingdom of heaven. The words used in this gospel are slightly different from those we are used to.

The translator, Professor Karen King of the Harvard University Divinity School, has used a nonstandard expression to replace "Son of Man" — she uses "child of true Humanity," which is probably a better phrase, avoiding, as it does, the sectarian and dogmatic baggage; for similar reasons, she replaces "kingdom" with "Realm."

"Be on your guard," says Jesus, "so that no one deceives you by saying, 'Look over here!' or 'Look over there!' For the child of true Humanity exists within you. Follow it! Those who search for it will find it. Go then, preach the good news about the Realm."[29]

Yet there is a twist in this gospel: with the disciples depicted debating about what Jesus means, Peter says to Mary Magdalene:

> Sister, we know that the Savior loved you more than all
> other women. Tell us the words of the Savior that you
> remember, the things which you know that we don't
> because we haven't heard them.[30]

Mary Magdalene, it transpires, has received some secret teaching from Jesus that the others have not. She replies to Peter, "I will teach you about what is hidden from you."[31]

Several of the disciples are irritated by Mary's knowledge and dispute whether Jesus ever said what she claims, or they protest that he spoke to a woman before them, a fact that they find hard to believe. Peter demands to know: "Did he, then, speak with a woman in private without our knowing about it? Are we to turn around and listen to her? Did he choose her over us?"[32]

But a disciple by the name of Levi defends Mary Magdalene: "Assuredly the Savior's knowledge of her is completely reliable. That is why he loved her more than us."[33]

We can be confident – on the basis not only of the Gospel of Mary, the Gospel of Thomas, and Smith's extract from the secret Gospel of Mark, but also by virtue of the statements in the New Testament itself – that Jesus taught secret doctrines that concerned the passing over to the kingdom of heaven – a metaphor, as I have noted, for the concept described by the ancient Egyptians as the Far-World, or by the Greeks variously as the land of the Blessed or the Netherworld. All depict the divine world. The disciple of Jesus who understood his teaching the best was Mary Magdalene, the disciple he loved above all others, and the one whom, according to the Gospel of Philip, he kissed often.[34]

Are we closer then to understanding why, when Jesus was anointed in Bethany – anointed as messiah, as I have proposed – the ceremony was performed by a woman, Mary of Bethany, the sister of Lazarus, who was "raised from the dead" in what appears to be a garbled account of an initiation into the secrets of the Far-World (John 11:2)?

I have also proposed that we should accept the old traditions and see Mary of Bethany as the same woman as Mary Magdalene: Jesus's confidante and, arguably, his wife. She was the companion of Jesus; there was no male exclusivity on Jesus's path to the kingdom of heaven.

It was Mary who understood better than anyone the secrets of the kingdom of heaven, who had stood upon the
verdant pastures of the promised land, who possessed all
the keys to traveling through the Far-World. *Of course* Mary
would be the one who anointed Jesus into his role as messiah. An important component of such a ritual anointing is
that it be done by someone who understands what is being
done, and by one who can participate in recognizing the
messiah – for the anointment is just the final act of a longer
process, the details of which have not been recorded in
the Gospels.

No wonder the power brokers of Rome wanted to exclude knowledge of this sacred path as well as knowledge of
these additional gospels. Unfortunately – for them – they
could do nothing about the Gospels that later became the
New Testament except to control the interpretation of
them – to control the "spin." The conceit, of course, is that
some theologians with attitude presume to understand
hundreds, perhaps a thousand or two years later, what the
writers meant better than they did themselves. Why ever
have we believed this for so long?

Although there were always scholars and commentators
who saw through the spin, it is only in recent times that the
manipulation and error have come so much to the fore
in public. But so far, particularly in the ornate halls of the
Vatican, nothing has changed. Power prefers spin to truth.

13

The Jesus Papers

Kibbutz Kalia was hot and sleepy that January afternoon, and January was supposed to be the coolest month. For some years this agricultural kibbutz, located on the edges of the Dead Sea, had become our base for an annual expedition mounted by the California State University at Long Beach under Professor Robert Eisenman, chairman of the Religious Studies Department. Our long-term aim was to discover further Dead Sea Scrolls. But first we had to methodically check all the caves along miles of almost vertical cliffs reaching up to twelve hundred feet above the flat seashore.

We stayed in a group of motel units that the kibbutz had built to take advantage of the constant stream of tourists drawn to the ancient stone ruins of Qumran, which sat on a nearby escarpment – ruins that had been made famous by the discovery of the Dead Sea Scrolls in 1947. Members of Kalia looked after the site and ran the restaurant and bookshop at the entrance; its air conditioning was a welcome refuge that inevitably attracted every visitor.

Our days began early and work would finish at noon, for the temperature after that became uncomfortably hot even at this time of year. We would return to the kibbutz and eat together with all the permanent members in the large communal dining hall. Afterwards we retired to our row of motel units to analyze the morning's findings, clean and prepare equipment, or, after the heat had passed, wander until sunset in the silence of the desert where stone remains, potsherds, and small animals and birds provided a leisurely fascination. After sunset, however, security considerations encouraged a return to the protective fences and armed patrols of the kibbutz. We were on the border after all. Each season we would experience at least one security emergency. During this particular visit, we were engaged in a lecture when a guard burst into the room ordering, in a tight whisper, "Turn all the lights off. Lie down on the floor" – some intruders had been detected. Evidence remained of a small boat having crossed the Dead Sea. The day before a member of a neighboring kibbutz had lost a leg to a mine.

But this particular afternoon, 17 January 1992, the leader of the expedition, Robert Eisenman, had driven to Jerusalem – about forty minutes away – to meet with an Israeli archaeologist. I was sitting on a low wall talking with a

biblical expert, James Tabor, who was an associate professor of the New Testament at the University of North Carolina at Charlotte, and with a Californian postgraduate
student on the team, Dennis Walker. Other members of the
team were either resting or talking quietly in small groups.
Into this bucolic scene intruded two well-dressed Israelis
exuding the barely controlled self-importance of official-
dom. They also carried a file of papers. My suspicions were
immediately aroused. In Israel, paranoia is a rational, life-
affirming trait. Sheaves of official papers always mean trouble. I overheard a brief conversation.

"Is Professor Eisenman around?"

"No," was the reply, "he is not."

"When will he return?"

"Later," was the cautious response.

Problems? Why?

We had all thought that the monopoly over the Dead Sea
Scrolls, maintained for almost forty years, had finally been
broken two months earlier when the Huntington Library in
California had decided to make the complete set of photographs of the Dead Sea Scrolls, which it had held, available
to scholars; Eisenman had been the first to consult with them
that first day. But it was clear from the surface events that
powerful, vested interests were still moving at every chance
to claim rights over the Dead Sea Scroll materials, two-
thousand-year-old documents that reveal a long hidden reality, embarrassing to both Judaism and Christianity, a reality
that had long been manipulated by a small group of scholars.

The Dead Sea Scrolls were first discovered early in 1947. The story has never been fully established because the young Bedouin shepherd who found them, Mohammad adh-Dhib, may have been engaged in more than a simple shepherd's tasks – there is some sensitivity surrounding the events that led him to the area of Qumran. But, as we have already noted, the story he told afterwards was very simple. He was searching for a lost goat among the cliffs and wadis when he noticed a small entrance to a cave. He threw a stone into it, hoping to hear the sound of a bleating goat. Instead, he heard the sound of shattered pottery. He crawled into the cave to see what was there.

He found a group of sealed pottery jars, each about two feet tall, some of which were broken. It is thought that at least eight of these jars were inside the cave, although no one can now be certain. Inside each jar were leather scrolls covered in an ancient text. The Bedouin admitted retrieving at least seven scrolls. While we know that there are others that have never been passed on to the authorities, we simply have no idea how many there were originally. Archaeologists have estimated that there were enough pieces of broken pottery in the cave to account for forty jars. But we cannot now be certain whether they were broken in antiquity or more recently, or even if they contained scrolls that might have been destroyed or hidden away for future sale.

From this initial find – called Cave 1 in the Dead Seas Scroll inventory – came seven scrolls that were more or less complete, along with pieces representing twenty-one others.

Why some scrolls were broken up while others remained intact is unknown. Of course, the explanation could be as simple as the jars being broken by roof-fallen stone and wild animals scattering the exposed scrolls about. I have been into hundreds of caves in the area and can attest to the fact that roof-falls are common and that predatory animals such as jackals abound.

The Bedouin shepherd passed the scrolls to Khalil Iskander Shahin, also known as "Kando," a Christian dealer in antiques who had a shop in Bethlehem. He was an experienced blackmarket dealer, and there are rumors that Kando and a colleague soon afterwards went to the cave themselves and removed further texts or parts of texts. In April 1947 one of the scrolls was taken to the metropolitan of the Syrian Jacobite Church based at St. Mark's Monastery in Jerusalem. The metropolitan was unable to read it, but he recognized its antiquity and importance. While three were sold elsewhere, the metropolitan was able to purchase the four other scrolls.

He took them to a scholar at the Department of Antiquities and then to another at the Dominican-run École Biblique et Archéologique in Jerusalem, which since 1945 had been under the direction of Father Roland de Vaux. While both seemed to think that the scrolls were recently written, another expert at the École warned the metropolitan about the great number of forgeries that were around in the hands of so-called antique dealers.

Professor Eleazar Sukenik, head of the Department of

Archaeology at Jerusalem's Hebrew University, heard about the scrolls soon afterward and was able to view them. After several unsuccessful attempts to purchase them all, Sukenik eventually managed to buy the three scrolls that the metropolitan did not possess. It was late in 1947 when Sukenik bought the Isaiah Scroll, the War Scroll, and the Hymns Scroll. But the four in the hands of the metropolitan – another Isaiah text, the commentary of Habakkuk, the Manual of Discipline, and an Aramaic Genesis Apocryphon – proved impossible to obtain. The three scrolls Sukenik purchased would be published by the Israelis in 1955–56.

The metropolitan had also contacted the American School of Archaeology in Jerusalem, and in early 1948 he offered his scrolls to this institution. In addition, he gave the American School permission to photograph three of the scrolls for a facsimile publication in the hope that this would increase their value. This photography was completed in March 1948.

In 1949 Israel emerged from its first war, and by the terms of the ceasefire Qumran was now part of Palestine. On 24 April 1950, Palestine was formally incorporated into Jordan. The main authority for any further exploration lay in the hands of the Jordanian Department of Antiquities and its director, Gerald Lankester Harding. But the metropolitan had already taken the scrolls to the United States, where they were exhibited in late 1949. At the same time, they were put up for sale.

Eventually, in 1954, these scrolls were purchased by the Israeli government through the efforts of Yigael Yadin, Sukenik's son. Today they are on display, along with an eighth text, the Temple Scroll (obtained in 1967), in the Shrine of the Book in Jerusalem.

At first scholars were not very impressed with the scrolls. Apart from the accusations of forgery and fraud, other prominent experts saw them as very late productions. In 1949 one prominent Oxford scholar, Professor Godfrey Driver, dated them to the sixth or seventh century A.D.; the next year he modified this to A.D. 200–500 – still later than the Judeo-Christian period. Another scholar from Manchester University saw them as much later, judging them to be a product of the eleventh century A.D. Others leaned the other way; Father Roland de Vaux, director of the École Biblique, initially saw them as much older than the Christian period. He dated the jars, and thus the scrolls found in them, to the Hellenistic period prior to the Roman domination of Egypt and Judaea – that is, to the early first century B.C.[1]

At the end of January 1949, two Jordanian military officers found the cave from which the scrolls had come. On 5 March of that same year, Roland de Vaux and Gerald Lankester Harding excavated it. They found pieces of linen, broken pots, and small pieces of written texts from twenty-one different works. Events were progressing slowly; the excavation was exciting, yet little if anything had been found to worry the Church. But all of this was about to change.

By the end of 1949, all the scrolls were either in the hands of the Israelis or in the United States. But events had their own momentum, and they soon began slipping out of control. In early 1950, the first volume of the publications by the American School of Oriental Research appeared. It was entitled *The Dead Sea Scrolls of St. Mark's Monastery*. This book contained photographs and transcriptions of the Isaiah manuscript and the commentary on Habbakuk – now known as the Habbakuk *pesher*. A *pesher* is the name commonly used in the Dead Sea Scrolls to refer to an ancient text that was interpreted by the Qumran group to serve its concerns, particularly its concern with the "last days" when the enemy would be defeated and Israel would be ruled by a Davidic king.

By noting how this group interpreted the Old Testament texts, scholars could gain valuable insights into their ideology and thinking. Scholars around the world began looking at the contents, especially those of the peshers; they also began drawing their own conclusions about the beliefs of those who had written these texts and about the implications of their contents. Inevitably parallels were drawn with Christianity.

The first shock came on 26 May 1950, when André Dupont-Sommer, professor of Semitic language and civilization at the Sorbonne University in Paris, gave a public lecture on the Habbakuk pesher at the Académie des Inscriptions et Belles Lettres. It caused an absolute furor. Dupont-Sommer had moved right to the heart of forbidden territory: he had openly and publicly linked the scrolls with Christianity. Many were disconcerted at what they felt was a challenge to their faith; others were utterly outraged and quick to express their offense.

Dupont-Sommer's hypotheses were that the Habbakuk pesher was written during the early Christian period; that the scrolls were hidden during the war of A.D. 66 – 70; that the community living at Qumran – who were concerned with holding to a "new covenant" in the pesher[2] – were the Essenes described by Josephus; and that the leader of the scroll community, a figure who was never named and was known only by his title as "the Teacher of Righteousness," was believed to be divine, then put to death by his enemies and expected to rise from the dead. Dupont-Sommer was particularly struck by the parallels between Jesus and the Teacher of Righteousness, whom he saw as some kind of original model for Jesus.

Alarmingly, he seemed to be attacking, head-on, the uniqueness of Jesus. Summarizing his conclusions in a book published the same year, Dupont-Sommer wrote:

> It is now certain – and this is one of the most important revelations of the Dead Sea discoveries – that Judaism in the first century B.C. saw a whole theology of the suffering Messiah, of a Messiah who should be the redeemer of the world, developing around the person of the [Teacher of Righteousness].[3]

Not only was the uniqueness of Jesus at stake, but Dupont-Sommer was proposing that he and Christianity had emerged out of a preexisting Judaic milieu:

> The documents from Qumran make it plain that the primitive Christian Church was rooted in the Jewish sect of the New Covenant, the Essene sect, to a degree none would have suspected, and that it borrowed from it a large part of its organization, rites, doctrines, "patterns of thought" and its mystical and ethical ideals.[4]

Every indication is that the Vatican was alarmed; certainly it began moving its forces into action. And these forces were powerful, to say the least. Although the Inquisition no longer burned people at the stake, the Holy Office still existed to protect, at all costs, the dogma of the Church.

As mentioned earlier, in 1902 Pope Leo XIII had created the Pontifical Biblical Commission to monitor and direct Catholic theological scholarship. In particular it opposed modernism, the work of those scholars we saw clustered about the Seminary of Saint Sulpice in Paris before such teaching was condemned late in the nineteenth century. The Pontifical Biblical Commission provided experts – "consultants" – to the Holy Office. It was the first line of defense against attacks on the faith. One of its major roles was – and still is – establishing and decreeing "the right way to teach ... scripture."[5] It is, in effect, the Vatican's "spin central."

Although the Holy Office and the Commission were

perceived as two separate organizations, this was in fact an illusion; there had always been considerable mutual membership in their leadership. The closeness between the two was formalized in 1971 when the Pontifical Biblical Commission was placed under the head of the Inquisition – now known by its sanitized title of the Congregation for the Doctrine of the Faith. Both organizations operate from the same building in Rome. In 1981 Cardinal Ratzinger became the cardinal in charge, the "Grand Inquisitor"; in 2005, as we all know, he became the pope.

In 1951 the opposition to those who linked the Dead Sea Scrolls with Christianity was hardening: too much was at stake for those who needed to maintain the uniqueness and divinity of Jesus. In February of that year, a prominent Jesuit scholar wrote an attack in *Études*, a Jesuit academic journal. His position was obvious to other scholars: he was seen as "alarmed by what seemed a threat to the uniqueness of Jesus."[6] Around the same time, another blow fell to worry Catholic scholars even more. Pieces of linen had been found in Cave 1 when Gerald Lankester Harding and Father de Vaux excavated it. One piece was sent to the United States to be carbon-dated: the result was a date of A.D. 33, plus or minus two hundred years – a period of production from second century B.C. to the early third century A.D.[7] This then meant that the scrolls could well have been produced in the Christian period. This was data the Church was going to have to live with *and* deal with.

Then in March 1951, Father de Vaux, who was maneuvering himself into a position of control over the scrolls, published a very negative review of Dupont-Sommer's talk and book in *Revue biblique* – which he himself edited. De Vaux didn't stint on his sarcasm: "His thesis is presented in a very seductive manner with an alluring enthusiasm. There is plenty of science and even more ingenuity."[8]

But Father de Vaux was prone to errors, and he made a major one in this review. One of his "proofs" against Dupont-Sommer's thesis was the "fact" that "the jars which contained these manuscripts are dated to the end of the Hellenistic period, before the Roman period in Palestine, by the competent archaeologists who have seen them." In this, as in many other assertions, Father de Vaux was wrong and was later forced to retract his statements. But he had managed to score an early point in the skirmishes that ultimately led to a major battle.

Late in 1951 Father de Vaux and Gerald Lankester Harding began to excavate the ruins at Qumran. It was then that another blow fell upon them: all the identifiable coins they found dated from the beginning of the Christian period to the end of the Jewish war in A.D. 70.[9] They also found, set into the floor of one room, a jar identical to those that had held the scrolls in Cave 1.[10] This strongly indicated that both Qumran and the scrolls were in use during the Christian period.

Then, in September 1952, the Bedouin appeared with cardboard boxes filled with fragments of scrolls. The

Bedouin had found Cave 4. This was to provide thousands of pieces of up to eight hundred different scrolls. But all these pieces were small, some very small. No complete scrolls were found there. So many fragments needed to be pieced together and translated that no one scholar could cope with it all. There was a need to form a specialized group of scholars to work on them in order to reassemble, translate, and publish the material. This provided Father de Vaux with an opportunity to regain some measure of control over the texts.

In 1953 a small international team of seven scholars was formed to "own" the scrolls and work on them. This team was under the charge of Father de Vaux, and it was dominated by the École Biblique. Of the team, after the early departure of a German scholar, four were Catholic priests; one, Monsignor Patrick Skehan, a professor at Catholic University of America in Washington, later became director of the American School of Oriental Research and a member of the Pontifical Biblical Commission. He was quoted as saying that "a proper part of the duty of every Old Testament scholar is to trace in sacred history the development of the readiness to be aware of Christ when he would come."[11] He was clearly no strong advocate of objective scholarship.

The scrolls were physically kept at the Palestine Archaeological Museum, later renamed the Rockefeller Museum. On the board of the Rockefeller was Father Roland de Vaux.

Father de Vaux became a member of the Pontifical

Biblical Commission in 1955. Also, as head of the École Biblique, he was at the forefront of biblical archaeology. In fact, from his time onwards, every subsequent director of the École Biblique was also a member of the Pontifical Biblical Commission.

Father de Vaux edited the École's journal, *Revue biblique*, dedicated to academic and archaeological investigation into biblical matters. The *Revue* also dominated a new magazine dedicated to the Dead Sea Scrolls, the *Revue de Qumran*. And when the new Catholic translation of the Bible was produced in 1956, later called "La Bible de Jérusalem," Father de Vaux was the general editor. He also produced a major work on the history of ancient Israel and on the Dead Sea Scrolls and his excavations of Qumran. Father de Vaux was indeed a very influential man in the field.

The chosen scholars held the scrolls very close: no one else but them or those they "licensed" academically were allowed access to them. But a scandal developed: while some scholars, notably John Allegro, published their texts relatively quickly, others took much longer. Forty years passed, and still some important scrolls remained unpublished. There was a growing suspicion that the Catholic scholars were holding back material detrimental to the uniqueness of Jesus.

The English member of the team, John Allegro, had his own suspicions. Hearing that Father de Vaux and other members of the international team were about to write a public letter to *The Times* of London condemning his interpretation of the scrolls – an outrageous action – Allegro wrote to Father de Vaux in March 1956, warning,

> At every lecture on the Scrolls I give, the same old question pops up: is it true that the Church is scared ... and can we be sure that *everything* will be published... I need hardly add what effect the signatures of three Roman priests on the bottom of this proposed letter will have.[12]

But Father de Vaux and the others ignored this warning and went ahead with their action to discredit Allegro. They were not going to let him get away with his independent action. Control was everything in the field of the Dead Sea Scrolls.

And from their perspective, this was wise. We only have to look at the "Son of God" text to see that.

One hot afternoon in July 1958, a new piece of text was purchased; it was in Aramaic and had originally come from Cave 4.

One of the experts present at the time, the Jesuit father Joseph Fitzmyer, now professor of biblical studies at Catholic University of America and a consultant for the Pontifical Biblical Commission, told me that they had managed to read the text by the next morning. We need to get this right: by 10 July 1958, the experts on the international team knew that they had a piece of text that referred to a figure who "will be called son of God."[13] Now, there are still arguments over whether this figure was a supporter of or in opposition to the Qumran Zadokite priesthood, but this doesn't matter: the important thing is that the title "son of God," previously thought to be exclusively used by Jesus in the world of Judaism, was now seen to be a preexisting usage.

Naturally this was controversial. The Catholic scholars were determined to keep as much distance between the scrolls and Christianity as they could; to release this text would show the vacuity of their arguments. So they did what they could: they sat on the text for many years. Its existence was kept secret. Finally, the scholar whose responsibility it was – Father Joseph Milik – mentioned it in a lecture in 1972. In 1990 the text was leaked to a popular journal, the *Biblical Archaeology Review*, which published it. But this was thirty-two years after the text had been obtained and translated. In the absence of a permanent solution, such as the destruction of the text, playing for time was the next best thing.

Of course, all such delaying tactics came to an end in 1991 with the release of the complete set of Dead Sea Scroll photographs by the Huntington Library in California, which was soon followed by other institutions around the world making public the photographs they also had been given for safekeeping. Those wishing still to control the Dead Sea Scrolls, despite having lost physical control over the raw material, were forced now to shift their focus to attempts to control the interpretation of the scrolls. This struggle continues to this day.

Make no mistake: the Vatican *cares*. It is no small thing to deny the uniqueness and divinity of Jesus.

Indirectly, the Vatican's earlier strong hold on these documents encouraged others of us to seek understanding elsewhere. But first we had to disprove some of de Vaux's clearly erroneous conclusions. For instance, at one point during his monopoly over the texts he had become convinced that Qumran was some kind of monastic foundation that contained a "refectory" where members ate and a "scriptorium" where the Essenes, the writers of the scrolls, worked. This monastic model guided all his subsequent interpretations – and his excavations. More recent studies, however, have cast grave doubts on the notion that the scrolls were written at Qumran at all. It seems increasingly likely that they were brought down from Jerusalem and hidden in the caves.

In fact, since Father de Vaux never prepared a final report on the site, archaeologists working from his notes concluded that far from being an isolated monastery, Qumran was more likely the center of a commercial farm, perhaps one producing perfume oils. It appears that Father de Vaux proclaimed vertical sections of the hardened earth to be walls of mud-brick, so as to create some of his rooms, but in fact he failed to excavate them. It is from such errors that he established his monastery hypothesis.

I took an archaeologist with experience in Mesopotamia, an expert in mud-brick construction, to Qumran to see these walls. He looked at one wall and just laughed, declaring that they were not walls at all, just unexcavated earth.

This assessment proved to be correct: in mid-December 1991 a rare but heavy rain fell at Qumran. One of Father de Vaux's "mud-brick walls" was washed away in the torrent to reveal a clay pot sitting on a ledge. My informant, a worker for the Israeli Antiquities Authority, showed me a color photograph of it. He laughed too.

But we were finally able to disprove scientifically a cornerstone of Father de Vaux's theory that figured prominently in his historical reconstruction of the Dead Sea group: his assertion that the site was destroyed by the earthquake of 31 B.C. and a subsequent fire. He claimed to have found a crack through the ruins caused by this earthquake. This was the reason, he said, for the site's abandonment.[14] In 1992 we took ground radar equipment and two experts to operate it to Qumran. We found that his earthquake fault line did not exist and that the damage he claimed was caused by the earthquake was more likely – according to the two experts, both well experienced in such survey work – to have been caused by natural subsidence.[15]

The importance of all this in the context of our off-road journey of exploration is that the Dead Sea Scrolls issued from a real group of messianic Jews who lived in a real world – the same world that saw the rise of Jesus and the development of Christianity. Accordingly, these writings give us an unprecedented insight into the beliefs, the concerns, and, to a certain extent, the history of this group and their attitude toward their times. They reveal many themes in common with early Christianity, themes that parallel those expressed in the New Testament. But we should not forget that there are distinct differences as well. For Christianity broke away from Judaism and the law.

Importantly, the scrolls are original documents; they have never been altered by any later translation or revision, as have most of our other documents from the time. Nevertheless, it is difficult to approach and understand these documents without seeing them through the lens of our own modern belief structures.

The central problem with biblical scholarship is that most experts in the field have been trained as theologians or biblical historians. Pure historians in this field are rare. And those historians who have ventured into the field have very often found themselves subjected to fierce attacks by the theologians because such a dispassionate look at the data often leads to very different conclusions that are unwelcome to church teaching.[16]

The scrolls directly affect Christianity. They pose two problems for the hard-line exponents of Christian theology – those who support without question the theology of the Council of Nicaea, which is centered upon a unique and deified Christ.

First, the scrolls provide ample evidence that the New Testament and Jesus emerged from a preexisting messianic Jewish context. This reveals that Christianity is not based upon a unique event in history but was part of an existing movement that even used the term "son of God," formerly thought to be unknown in Judaism and so a particular marker of Christianity.

Second, the scrolls call into question the theological unity of the Gospels. They provide the key to exposing the deep theological clash between James – the brother of Christ and leader of the Jerusalem messianic community – and Paul, who never knew Jesus. This clash reveals a deep and irreconcilable split in the New Testament, particularly on the question of the law as maintained, for example, in the Pauline writings, where freedom from the law is expressed, and in the Letter of James, which stresses adherence to it.[17]

As a result, the scrolls provide additional data for the arguments that we have explored at length in our reconsideration of the divinity of Jesus.

But it is not just the scrolls that provide us with reasons for an alternative view: even the Gospels themselves fail to support the theology codified at Nicaea. Did Jesus really put forward a claim to be God? It seems not. In a remarkable admission, Joseph Fitzmyer avers, "The Gospels have not so presented that claim."[18]

This is all quite serious stuff: at the heart of Christianity is a belief in the uniqueness – and divinity – of Christ. But the Gospels do not make this claim, and the Dead Sea Scrolls prove that you cannot disentangle Christianity from messianic Judaism, which had no concept of a divine messiah. For these reasons at least, the Vatican had no choice but to keep any tendentious scrolls hidden for as long as possible. It had no choice but to take every opportunity to distance Christianity from the scroll community. And further, the Vatican had no choice but to try to control the interpretation of these texts once they emerged into the light; the potential downside was too destructive.

The basic problem, as Burton Mack, professor of the New Testament at the Claremont School of Theology in California, explains, is that the original Jesus movement was taken over by a Jesus mythology. This has produced an unstable situation for the Church in that "Christian myth claims to be history and asks its adherents to believe that it is true."[19] He explains the danger: if alternative explanations of this blend of history and mythology should be found, then "the Christian gospel will be in very deep trouble" and the Christian religion will need to make drastic revisions to its views, because the Gospels are the foundation of the "Christian's mythic world."[20] Mack is blunt in his criticism: "The Christ myth created a much more fantastic imaginary universe than anything encountered in the Jesus traditions."[21]

The Jesus tradition is Jewish; the Christ myth is not.

It must now be self-evident that there is a vast gulf between the Jesus of history and the Jesus of faith. The strict custodians of Christian theology insist that the two are identical, but any historian who looks honestly at the data can easily discover that they are not. We have already seen how the Vatican, for example, has long been forced to maintain its position through suppression and manipulated expression. But this hard-line position is becoming harder and harder to maintain – the strain is showing, and the levee is leaking. It would seem inevitable that at some stage the pressure will become too much, that the entire construction will collapse under the weight of its erroneous assumptions, blatant untruths, and deliberate misreadings.

It is helpful to note that details of the Dead Sea Scroll community can be matched, point for point, with the early Christian community in Jerusalem under the leadership of James as described in the Book of Acts.[22] So to this extent the Dead Sea Scrolls are early Christian documents and can help us bring some perspective to bear upon the extensive mythology that has grown over time. But the story we glean in this way is only a small part of the whole.

Nevertheless, we can say with some confidence that with Jesus gone, James adhered to the Zealot ideal of opposition to the Romans and to unbending support of the Jewish law. It was Paul who then carried part of the message away and created Christianity for the non-Jews. James cared only about Judaism and Judaea. Paul, for all his idiosyncrasies, gazed upon a more distant horizon. But he seems to have run amok.

Can we ever save Jesus from the dogma within which he has long been mired?

In this book, I have proposed that Jesus, with some help from his closest friends and the collusion of the Roman prefect, Pontius Pilate, survived the crucifixion. It was undoubtedly a very close-run maneuver. When Joseph of

Arimathea went to ask for Jesus's body, Pilate seems to have thought that the plan had not been a success and Jesus had in fact died, as indicated, according to Mark's Gospel, by his use of the Greek word *ptoma* (meaning "corpse") for Jesus's body.

Jesus had not died, but it appears that he was in urgent need of medical treatment. He was taken down from the cross and placed in an empty tomb. Then, once night had fallen, according to John's Gospel, Joseph of Arimathea and Nicodemus came with medicinal potions. Once Jesus was considered out of danger, I have suggested, they took him out of the tomb and away to safety, to a place where he could recuperate. It is this event – the removal of a living Jesus from his tomb – that is depicted in the painted relief of Station 14 of the Cross in the church at Rennes le Château.

And what happened then? We cannot know, but he did not – despite the mythology about him which has been created – vanish from the face of the earth. He went *somewhere*.

One of the tasks of any study of history is to try to account for the facts. Unfortunately, in this case, there are no facts, at least none that can be held up as being beyond criticism. We have no texts about Jesus, no Roman records, no family papers or inscriptions. All we have is the statement, reported secondhand by the Rev. Dr. Douglas William Guest Bartlett, that "Jesus was alive in the year A.D. 45" and that his survival was the result of help from "extreme zealots."

The Rev. Bartlett heard this from his mentor, Canon

Alfred Lilley, who had translated the original document and asserted this as a fact. Bartlett clearly considered the information to be accurate. Nevertheless, we are dealing with a manuscript that Lilley had read forty or more years earlier and was recalling late in his life. Bartlett was repeating the story another fifty or so years after that. We are right to wonder how accurate these recollections would be.

Mention of the "extreme zealots" sounds like an opinion rather than something within the document itself. To call any group "extreme" is to make a value judgement; who, in this case, is making that judgement? Canon Lilley perhaps? Furthermore, as we have seen, Jesus would have been hated by the Zealots after he refused to support their opposition to the Roman taxes. So this statement is difficult to support and is, as I suggest, more likely an opinion.

But what is significant is the date, A.D. 45, when Jesus is said to have been still alive. This is valuable data because a date is not open to reinterpretation: A.D. 45 is easy to remember, even after many years, and it is a fact that remains true whatever spin might swirl about it. This is the only part of Bartlett's letter that I can accept without dispute or suspicion that opinion has become confused with fact.

And what of Jesus afterwards? Where would he have gone to live? Where was he in A.D. 45, the date given in this document? Could he really have been in Rome and responsible for the later disturbances among the Jewish community there recorded by Suetonius?

At this point all I can do is speculate, but I can certainly do so within the bounds of what is known of the times. It would seem that there was really only one place Jesus would have gone to: back to Egypt. If he really had the clandestine support of the Romans – for the most cynical of reasons – then the easiest thing to do would have been to travel secretly to the port of Caesarea and sail from there. And it would make sense for him to be accompanied by his wife, who I have suggested would have been Mary Magdalene. She certainly disappears from view within a few days of the crucifixion. There is no mention of her whatsoever in the Acts of the Apostles.

But where in Egypt might Jesus have gone? It would seem unlikely that he would have gone to Alexandria, dominated as it was by the family of Philo and the Jewish Roman general Tiberius Alexander. They could not be expected to welcome a Jewish messiah, however mystical he might have been. In addition, although many Zealot sympathizers lived in Alexandria, several thousand were massacred by Tiberius Alexander when they began open agitation in A.D. 66, at the beginning of what became the ruinous war against the Romans in Judaea. Zealot sympathizers would certainly have noted and opposed Jesus's survival. No, it would have been wise for him and his family to stay well away from Alexandria.

Adding to the difficulties at the time Jesus and Mary might have arrived in Egypt was the increasing tension between the Greeks and the Jews in Alexandria and undoubtedly in the other large Jewish centers like Edfu in the South. These were fanned by the Roman prefect and erupted one day in August A.D. 38 when all the Jews in Alexandria were forced out of their homes, assaulted, and robbed; many lost their lives. This was just two years after the crucifixion, if Hugh Schonfield's redating of it to the Passover of A.D. 36 is correct.

My personal feeling is that Jesus and Mary would have found the safest refuge in or around the Temple of Onias, for it seems to have been mystical and Zadokite without being Zealot in the political sense. Those who adhered to this temple were ignored by Philo and the Alexandrian patricians; the Alexandrian Zealot sympathizers would have looked toward Judaea and the Temple in Jerusalem rather than to that of Onias, and of course the Judaean Zealots would have ignored this temple as a rival and one that did not adhere to their very worldly political plans.

It seems then that it would have been a place of safety – at least for a time. Long enough for the mystical traditions involving Jesus and Mary Magdalene to become known and taken up by the oral tradition.

Perhaps Jesus continued quietly teaching there. Perhaps he returned to the circles in which he had originally studied. Perhaps this is why the initiatory non-Pauline Christian groups – many of them allied to the Gnostic movement – appear in Egypt by the second century A.D. Were they carrying the residues of Jesus's teachings? Such questions beg us to take an even closer look at the texts that came out of Egypt and were rejected by the Pauline-influenced Church.

For it is in these texts that the authentic voice of Jesus is most likely to be heard.

And after it all fell to pieces? After the war in Judaea, after the Jewish Temple of Onias was closed down, where did Jesus go? Jesus and his family must have departed long before this time. Again, indulging in pure speculation, I would think it possible that Jesus and his family remained until the troubles of A.D. 38. At this point it would have been obvious that it was sensible to leave, to travel to a place of safety well away from Egypt and Judaea. Somewhere with a Jewish community that might be protected from Greek antipathy.

Narbonne, a major Roman trading port at the mouth of the Aude River in France, had perhaps the oldest Jewish population in the region. It was Roman, and unlike Marseilles, Lyon, and the Rhône Valley, the area took a long time to become Christian, evidence that the Pauline variety of Christian missionary efforts were absent or ineffective there. It is also the place where the earliest known documentary evidence of a Jewish community in France has been found, attesting to a vigorous Jewish population. Narbonne and Marseilles were the two major cities of the area where later legends told of Mary Magdalene arriving from the Middle East by boat.

It further seems plausible that this Jewish community in the south of France was the source of the document seen by Canon Lilley stating Jesus's existence in A.D. 45. Canon Lilley, as we have reported, believed that the manuscript had once been in the hands of the southern French Gnostic group, the Cathars. This line of speculation also suggests a southern French source for that document.

Could it have been some form of genealogy, a text carefully preserved by members of the families claiming descent from the Line of David who were known to be in Narbonne as late as medieval times? The famous Jewish traveler and writer Benjamin of Tudela visited Narbonne around 1166 and wrote of its Jewish community being ruled by "a descendant of the House of David as stated in his family tree."[23]

On the other hand, might we be dealing with a medieval French translation of an even earlier document, perhaps one from Jerusalem itself and dating from the first century A.D.? As we will see, this is very possible, for such documents have been found.

In the often strange world of Middle Eastern antiquities, there have always been rumors, always new findings of value, always deals to be made. And swirling around in hints and thirdhand rumors has always been talk of the existence of some documents that are dangerous to the Vatican, documents that, in touching upon Jesus in an unspecified manner, are, it is suggested, some sort of "smoking gun." No one quite knew the details. But the rumors persisted, and I was interested in tracking them down.

It was not until eight years after the publication of *Holy Blood, Holy Grail* that, with the help of contacts in the trade, I reached the source of the rumors and the owner of the documents that were the subject of the rumors.

He was an Israeli who had lived for many years in a large European city. He was a wealthy businessman, but his real love was ancient objects of religious symbolism, which he collected with no regard for price. He explained his reasoning to me: "All mankind is searching for a way to get direct communication with the Divine. We can use symbolism to help us to jump to the Divine."

He was very cultured, impeccably mannered, highly intelligent, and possessed of great cunning and intuition. Only a brave man would try to outsmart him on an antiquities deal. He welcomed me into his home and offered me coffee. Sitting on a sofa, I looked at the low table in front of me. It had a transparent glass top. Beneath was a large, gray ceramic tableau: it was a complete model of an entire Canaanite temple ritual frozen in time. The sacred stones stood at the end of the sacred space, and many small ceramic figures were depicted in the act of ritual worship, presumably at that moment. Each figure was unique, performing a different function in the ritual. I gazed at this, aware that it was utterly extraordinary. From it one could tell how the ritual worked. But so far as I knew, no scholars had ever seen this piece – not officially at any rate.

The house was filled with temperature- and humidity-controlled cabinets that contained many unique objects – the kind any museum in the world would have loved to get its hands on. He showed me around and pointed out a number of particular treasures before we returned to the sofas.

There his wife brought us some more coffee, and he told me something of his history.

In the past he had been a friend of Kando's, the dealer in Dead Sea Scrolls. He used to be the middleman between Kando and the Israelis, and he had been involved in the affair of the Temple Scroll, which had soured Kando against the Israelis. Kando was trying to sell the scroll. My friend went with a piece of it to Yigael Yadin, who told him to purchase it at any price. Negotiations were progressing when the Six-Day War broke out; after the seizure of the West Bank by the Israeli forces in June 1967, Yadin went to Kando's house in Bethlehem to seize the scroll himself. He knew that it was hidden there somewhere. Kando was taken away and interrogated for five days. The scroll was ultimately found stuffed up a chimney, which is why the ends had become damaged.

Kando, furious at this treatment, refused to deal with any more Israelis, but he did tell my friend that he had a big collection of scrolls and fragments and that he had transferred all of them to Damascus. He also said that there were other caves unknown to archaeologists in which the Bedouin had found even more scrolls. Regrettably, the practice of the Bedouin has been to cut the texts up and sell them fragment by fragment. This way they get a better price. My friend told me that over the last year he had received a twenty-centimeter piece of a larger scroll – specifically described as sectarian rather than biblical – but the price for the piece was $500,000; the entire scroll was offered at $10 million. Of course the price was negotiable.

My friend then told me a story about Yigael Yadin that I had also heard from other sources. When Yadin excavated Masada, he found many fragments of texts there. He certainly translated a number of them, but others he took to London, where he placed them in safe-deposit boxes in several banks under false names. My friend also said that he had sold Yadin a large scroll piece that he knew for certain Yadin took to London for safekeeping.

Unfortunately, Yadin died in 1984 and left no records of the banks in which he held boxes or the names under which they were registered. So, until the banks open the boxes and discover them, these texts will be lost to scholarship.

Then my contact brought up the subject of the "Jesus papers."

At this, his wife became almost hysterical, waving her hands in the air and yelling loudly and angrily as she stormed out of the room. I could not speak her language, so I did not know what she was saying, but it was very clear that she did not want these papers to be discussed.

He told me the story. In the early 1960s, in his search for antiquities, he had bought a house in the Old City in Jerusalem. He proceeded to excavate the cellar out to bedrock, digging down into what had been the environs of the temple area in early Christian times. In 1961 he found two papyrus documents bearing an Aramaic text, together with a number of objects that allowed him to date the finds at about A.D. 34.

The papyrus texts were two Aramaic letters written to the Jewish court, the Sanhedrin. The writer, my friend explained, called himself *bani meshiha* – the Messiah of the Children of Israel. I was stunned. Was I really hearing this? I listened intently to what my friend was saying. He continued to explain:

This figure, the Messiah of the Children of Israel, was defending himself against a charge made by the Sanhedrin – he had obviously been accused of calling himself "son of God" and had been challenged to defend himself against this charge. In the first letter, the messiah explained that what he meant was not that he was "God" but that the "Spirit of God" was in him – not that he was *physically* the son of God, but rather that he was spiritually an adopted son of God. And he added that everyone who felt similarly filled with the "spirit" was also a "son of God."

In other words, the messiah – who must be the teacher we know as Jesus – explicitly states in these letters that he is not divine – or at any rate, no more than anyone else. This, we can be sure, is something the Vatican would not like to be made public.

While listening to this story, I was struck by the similarity with a very curious incident described in the Gospel of John (10:33–35): in a short passage, it describes the "Jews" as being intent upon stoning Jesus for blasphemy. They hurl an accusation at him, saying, "You are only a man and you claim to be God." Jesus calmly answers their challenge, quoting from Psalm 82: "Is it not written in your Law: 'I said, you are gods?' So the Law uses the word gods of those to whom the word of God was addressed." Is this Gospel reporting some garbled residue of this investigation of the *meshíha* by the Sanhedrin?

Having discovered these two papyrus letters, my friend showed them to the archaeologists Yigael Yadin and Nahman Avigad and asked their opinion of them. They both confirmed that these letters were genuine and important.

Unfortunately, they also told some Catholic scholars – very likely one or another of the members of the École Biblique, consultants to the Pontifical Biblical Commission – for word reached Pope John XXIII. The pope sent word back to the Israeli experts asking for these documents to be destroyed.

My friend refused to do this, but he was prepared to make a promise that they would not be published for twenty-five years. This was done.

At the time I met him the twenty-five years were long expired, but my friend still refused to release the texts because he felt that releasing them would just cause problems between the Vatican and Israel and inflame anti-Semitism.

I could see why his wife had become upset.

Naturally I was desperate to see the Jesus papers for myself. I wanted to be certain that they truly existed, and I wanted to be able to say, "Yes. They exist. I have seen them." But my friend declined; he said that he was not prepared to show me at that time. But he had many other treasures that interested me greatly, and so, over the next few months, I traveled several times to his place to chat and to look at what he had recently purchased. Then one day, just as I arrived, he came out of his door putting on his coat.

"Come with me now," he said. "You have the time?"

Oh, I had the time all right.

We drove to another part of the city, where he led me to a large safe that was big enough to walk into and, like his cabinets, temperature- and humidity-controlled. I followed him in. There he presented me with two framed papyrus documents covered with glass. Each was about eighteen inches long and nine inches high. I held them. These were the Jesus papers, the letters from Jesus to the Sanhedrin. They existed. I had them in my hands. I was silent as I fully enjoyed the moment.

But it was also one of those moments of supreme frustration when I wished above all that I might have a familiarity with ancient languages, like some experts I know. It's like holding a treasure chest but not having the key to open it. There was, regrettably, nothing I could do. Despite my many years of experience with manuscript material, I was overcome with the significance of what I held in my hands. I was awestruck and speechless as I thought of the changes in our history that these letters might cause were they to be released publicly. But at least they were safe. I handed them back to him. He smiled. We went to lunch.

I have no idea what we ate that day because I was so utterly consumed by the implications of what I had just seen. I wanted everyone to know about the papers. I wanted to stand in the street and cry out to every passerby that the "smoking gun" exists, I have seen it and held it!

That day I resolved to make every effort to get these letters to an experienced scholar for checking and translating, and I knew just the person.

It was as I suspected when our informant, the Rev. Dr. Douglas Bartlett, told us of a manuscript containing incontrovertible evidence that Jesus was still alive in A.D. 45. I had long suspected that this evidence most assuredly would come in the form of secular rather than biblical documents. It is the dry, matter-of-fact nature of such documents that makes them so believable – as in the plain testimony of a man defending himself on a charge before a court. As I've asserted before, if we are ever to fully understand the Jesus of history, it is amid such mundane documents that we will get our greatest clues and insights.

In many cases the world's existing archives have hardly been touched; miles upon miles of original documents exist in the huge libraries and great archive collections of the Vatican, of Istanbul, Cairo, London, Paris, Berlin, and many other great cities. Discoveries of unknown or long-lost documents are regularly made in all these collections. Fragments or longer texts may yet lie undiscovered, in particular within the Islamic libraries, since many Muslim scholars in the early medieval period studied earlier texts and quoted large parts of them in criticism. Furthermore, many of these texts came from earlier work in Syriac – a version of

Aramaic, the language of Jesus – perhaps from Nestorian Christian communities and, later, monasteries, which, from the fifth century A.D. onwards, so often acted as a refuge for pockets of surviving Judeo-Christians and their manuscripts. Thus, it must be considered very likely indeed that some early texts relevant to the life and times of Jesus will be found within some poorly cataloged manuscript in one of these collections.

And then, of course, as we have noted, there are the private collectors, who, able to pay in cash, often get first choice of the material removed from ancient libraries or discovered in hidden rooms or in ruins found deep under the sand.

Inevitably, as we shall see, there will be further discoveries.

14

Trading Culture

It was early in the evening. The light in my study was beginning to fade. The English sky was preparing to slip across night's dim horizon. Professor Eisenman and I sat quietly talking, but both of us were distracted. Then the awaited time arrived: my fax machine suddenly chattered into action in its irritating, obtrusive way. We both fell silent thinking about what we might be about to see.

I was briefly caught by a bemused and weary wonder at the potential strangeness of the moment. We were anticipating the receipt of part of the text of a two-thousand-year-old Dead Sea Scroll from a hotel in Switzerland. And now, line by line, the fax was arriving.

When the first page appeared, Eisenman impatiently pulled it from the machine, glanced at it briefly, and then dropped it with disdain in my lap. I saw immediately that we had no cause for excitement. It was a copy of a text from a Jewish Torah scroll perhaps one hundred or two hundred years old – a good object to own, but hardly uncommon and certainly not part of any Dead Sea Scroll. It was evident to both of us that the Muslim owners of this text had no idea that there was any difference between the two. We were hardly surprised. Securing the kind of text we had hoped for had been a long shot. But we'd had to pursue it anyway since one never knows when something genuinely important might appear. And such opportunities often occur, as I was to find out shortly thereafter, in situations where they are least expected.

During the following spring my wife and I were at lunch at the home of an American friend who lived on the Mediterranean island of Mallorca. A number of other guests were present, including a businessman I had met once or twice before.

"I read your book on the Dead Sea Scrolls," he suddenly said, leaning toward me. I was surprised. I knew him as an entrepreneur operating within – but at the very edges of – the law, and reading about the Dead Sea Scrolls did not seem a likely interest of his. He lived in one of the Arab Gulf States with his latest wife, and he had made, and lost, several fortunes. Where he was in the cycle at that time I did not care to guess.

"I know where there are some more scrolls."

"More Dead Sea Scrolls?" I asked, still rather distracted by what seemed a slightly odd conversation to be coming from him.

"Yes," he replied. "In Kuwait. Are they worth much?" he added in a manner that would have sounded innocent enough coming from anyone else.

"Yes," I replied, maintaining a semblance of my distracted air but picking up the subtext, which had suddenly focused my attention. "If they are the right sort. The sectarian scrolls, that is, the ones specific to the Jewish community that produced them and detail their rules or their attitudes toward the Temple are valuable. So too are the ones called *peshers*, the commentaries on sections of biblical texts. The standard biblical texts are the least valuable."

He didn't reply for a minute. I waited. I think I was holding my breath. "You need to speak to a friend of mine," he finally said. "He is in intelligence." Then he mentioned the name of a Gulf State and added, "And he has very good contacts. But let me talk to him first."

"Fine," I said coolly. "Send me the details when you are ready."

Over the next few days I heard nothing, so I returned to my home in England. But soon afterwards I received a fax. "Ring Saad," it said, and gave his various numbers. But at the end it specified, "He does not want the scrolls to go to the Israelis." I noted that modern politics were, as ever, intruding.

I immediately phoned Saad and, suspicious of his claim

to have access to some scrolls, questioned him. He was forthcoming: his family had known Kando, the antique dealer in Bethlehem who had been the source of the original scrolls and who was suspected by many of holding even more. Saad repeated what I had already heard: the scrolls in discussion were in Kuwait, but in the hands of a family member.

"Can you get me a good description of them?" I asked, mindful of the confusion Eisenman and I had experienced earlier with the Torah scroll. Saad promised to get back to me.

A week or so later he contacted me with the information I had requested: there were two different scrolls, but both were inscribed on thin leather. I was now very excited: this sounded like the real thing. However, I needed one further bit of evidence before I could proceed.

"Saad," I said, "I can raise the money to purchase these texts, but in order to begin negotiations over the price, I need to know what sort of scrolls they are and how valuable they might be. Can you get me a photograph of a small section of the text on each scroll?"

Saad promised again to get back to me, but before hanging up he raised the same concern he had expressed earlier. He asked me to promise that these scrolls would not go to the Israelis.

I replied that this was an impossible promise since I had no idea what would happen to them after the sale, but I noted that the funds I was hoping to secure were coming from an American source. Saad seemed to be satisfied with this answer.

I immediately set about organizing the funds, assuming that the asking price would initially be in the range of $1–2 million. As it happened, some years earlier a group of American financiers had contacted me. They explained that they invested in ancient manuscripts rather than stocks and shares and asked me to let them know if I ran into any such items, especially Dead Sea Scrolls. Since this source of funding promised to be extremely useful in the future, I had agreed under one condition: that scholars be allowed access to such documents for study and translation once they were secured. If the investors abided by that one stipulation, they could then retain all publication rights. This seemed reasonable to them, so they assured me that this would indeed be the case.

I phoned the investors, and as I anticipated, they were interested. I promised to get back to them when I had seen the photographs of the scrolls and had been able to confirm exactly what type they were. I then waited for Saad to send me the images. Sadly, I am still waiting; I never heard from him again. The involvement of investors unknown to him without assurance as to where the scrolls might end up very likely scared him off.

In the end, though, whatever political posturing occurs, we know that such scrolls are being held in Kuwait by Saad, his family, and others like him as investments. Eventually money will change hands, and eventually scholars will get access to them, for an investment is only as good as the potential profit that can be realized from it, even if a generation passes before a sale can be made. The downside to conducting business in this way is that without expert care these scrolls may deteriorate badly and eventually disintegrate. One can only hope that even the most novice entrepreneur would consider this and take steps to protect his or her investment.

It is clear that these two scrolls were just one of a number known to be "out there." Magen Broschi, former director of the Shrine of the Book in Jerusalem, where the Dead Sea Scrolls are displayed, told me that other scrolls, not yet seen by scholars, certainly exist. I had once piqued his interest when talking to him about the Dead Sea Scroll offered to the CIA station chief in Damascus, Miles Copeland. It was then that Broschi proffered an interesting arrangement of sorts. He said, "If you get information on that, I'll exchange with you ..." and then he began to falter, searching for precision in his language, "I'll cross with you additional data concerning missing scrolls."[1]

More recently strong rumors from usually reliable sources began surfacing regarding another cache of Gnostic texts being offered for sale. The texts come from the Nag Hammadi area where the original find of Gnostic texts was made in 1945. If in fact they derive from the same ancient monastic library, then there is every chance that they are texts presently unknown to us. In other words, they will be a genuine treasure for scholars, and a source of data to be explored by a whole new generation of academics. I look forward with considerable excitement to these texts breaking cover.

It is true that the shadowy way in which this irregular market operates is frustrating to officials and scholars, yet all of them abide by its restrictions because it is, for a variety of reasons, the only way to gain access to the material quietly circulating within it.

Transactions are generally conducted very discreetly, even secretly. Hard information about what may, or may not, have changed hands, and at what price, is difficult to come by. Everything is done by word of mouth. Personal agreements, once entered into, are never broken. All the transactions are of high value but conducted lightly, almost on a whim. Yet behind the appearance of informality lies a keen eye for profit among the dealers and an equally keen eye for value among the collectors: none are fools.

All of those who participate hold on to the one and only certainty in this marketplace: that when money is made available, the antiquities will eventually emerge and make their contribution to the world's cultural heritage.

In my many years of involvement in this market, I have heard quite a few stories and I have met some of the men with whom those stories began. One story that excited me concerned the ancient Jewish city of Khaybar in Arabia, about ninety miles from Medina. At the time of Mohammed, it was a wealthy trading center, well fortified with walls and strong defensive castles, but when its army fought against Mohammed, he attacked and ultimately seized it. After Mohammed's death, most of the Jews were expelled, and many went to live in Jericho.

At some time during the 1980s, the Saudi Arabian government was building a road in the area. A bulldozer ripped up some ruins, exposing a house that had once belonged to a wealthy scholar as well as his personal library, which was filled with manuscripts and codices – several hundred of them. Among them, I was told, were plays by Greek and Roman authors, some of which hadn't otherwise survived in any other form. But the most important piece was a codex of an early edition of Josephus's Jewish histories. All our present copies of Josephus date from medieval times and have had Christian passages inserted and who knows what removed. This codex predated the political manipulation we have already addressed and was in the hands of a Jewish intellectual. We could assume it to be original. I was told that it contained all the original references to the *Zaddikim*, the "Righteous Ones" – evidently the same group that produced the Dead Sea Scrolls – all mention of whom had been removed from every other edition of Josephus that had survived.

Although most Jewish material found in Islamic countries is destroyed because of modern politics and the desire to suppress any evidence that might suggest a past Jewish presence in these countries, some material survives and is discreetly offered for sale. I met the owner of these texts, which filled six suitcases. He is storing them for now, perhaps for future profit. Unfortunately, he refused both my request to see them and my request to arrange for a scholar to catalog them.

In fact, this desire of mine once caused me quite a problem. I had mentioned the existence of these texts to a scholar I knew. I then introduced the two men in the hope that they would get on and perhaps then the scholar would be granted access to the collection for study and publication. The next week – without telling me anything about what he was planning – the scholar and the head of the university where he taught visited my contact and offered to construct a multimillion-dollar center and academic foundation to house these texts if indeed they were passed on to the university.

My contact phoned me later that day, in very considerable anger, to tell me that he had thrown the two academics out of his house and that if I ever put him in that position again, he would never speak to me. I was suitably chastised, as well as naturally disappointed that the scholar had approached my contact behind my back in that way. But I was hardly surprised. In fact, I had to admit that, from the scholar's perspective, it was certainly worth a try. In the end, though, the effort failed, and so far as I know the manuscripts remain in storage.

How long this type of tug-of-war will go on between scholars, dealers, and collectors no one knows.

Clearly a vast array of findings exist that I hope will become accessible to the world of scholars soon, but the mitigating circumstances keeping them under wraps are wide-ranging and complicated. In particular, there is the legal issue.

In 1970 UNESCO held a summit to investigate ways to stop the illegal trade in antiquities so as to ensure the preservation of a country's cultural heritage. The result was a proposal that member states of UNESCO repatriate any looted and exported antiquities discovered in other countries. Unfortunately, the impact of this accord was blunted when many states either declined to sign it or took many years to do so.

In 1995 a European convention involving UNIDROIT, an international legal institute based in Rome specializing in the coordination of laws between countries, was held to build upon the earlier 1970 UNESCO agreement. This convention focused specifically upon the return of looted cultural items. Whereas the earlier convention had dealt with objects stolen from museums, churches, or other institutions, the agreement reached in 1995 declared that all cultural objects illegally held by a collector – whether they had been originally excavated legally by an official excavation or looted – were to be considered stolen. Even if these objects were purchased innocently, they would still have to be returned to the country of origin. The law further stipulated that the purchaser – if innocent – was to be compensated for any financial loss. This mandate to compensate innocent purchasers put poorer countries at a disadvantage, and as a result, several member countries have failed to ratify this law too.

The introduction of these laws, whether ratified or not, has caused collectors of risky items to begin keeping them far more hidden or discreet. As already noted, some Middle Eastern countries wish to eliminate all historical evidence of a Jewish presence in their state. Any antiquities providing such evidence are supposed to be destroyed when found. Naturally, most are not destroyed and instead are smuggled out under diplomatic bag or with apparently sound export documentation and quietly sold to collectors. If the UNESCO or UNIDROIT principles were strictly applied, then these objects would be returned to countries where they would be destroyed for certain. So, to this extent at least, the collectors are preserving important heritage items. The problem is that they cannot show them officially to scholars or their academic or museum institutions, since such publicity would be sure to invoke the UNESCO and UNIDROIT provisions.

I was once shown a large, stone-carved Judeo-Christian symbol of the seven-branched candlestick – the menorah – sitting upon an equal-armed cross. The whole piece was about a yard square. The collector then showed me a photograph, reproduced in an old book, of an identical symbol high up on a wall in a synagogue in Syria. I was confused. "They look the same ..." I began. "Yes," he replied, "it's the same piece. The Syrians have destroyed the building and built a road over the site, but I managed to purchase the carving."

Would we truly want that piece returned to Syria?

But such examples cannot excuse much of this clandestine trade, for the preservation of the object – the written tablet or carving – is just a small part of its value to a country's culture. What is supremely important to scholars is the context in which these objects are discovered, for it is the context that allows them to glean information about the past. Unfortunately, the clandestine market operates in almost total secrecy, and furthermore, once an archaeological site has been dug up, it is finished – it cannot be put back together again. So when an item appears in the marketplace without any information about its provenance, its value to our cultural heritage is fatally diminished along with that of the site from which it was removed.

There is indeed a mass of inscribed texts, manuscripts, and secular documents of value out in the clandestine market – of this there is no doubt. And it is inevitable that much of this written material will, in due course, fall into the hands of scholars who can translate them. From this fact alone we can expect important discoveries to come. But as we have seen, translating a text is just the beginning of a more important process: the task of interpretation, of understanding what the text implies about the people who produced it. For this, the context is everything: it provides a measure of either the reality or the spin.

During the course of writing this book, I have sought out knowledge of a very special context – that of Egypt and Judaea in the first century of the modern era, a period about which there are few facts that we can be certain of. We have seen how the context can be controlled and forced to support a story that simply can't be true. The Jesus of history cannot have been as the theology of the Jesus of faith presents him.

During the course of our journey, we have discovered that Jesus rejected the political activity of his Zealot supporters. This is a crucially important piece of information that has been missed. We have seen too that there is no evidence that he died on the cross; in fact, what evidence survives suggests otherwise. And if he didn't die on the cross, where does that leave the resurrection? His divinity? His equality in the Holy Trinity? These claims all disintegrate once the spin stops.

We have discovered that all these assertions about Jesus came much later, the result of a glossy gift-wrapping of some historical events that were deliberately distorted in order to serve a strict theological agenda, one that maintains to the present day a number of extremely odd and eccentric notions. Foremost among these is the belief that only men were Christ's closest disciples and so women cannot serve as priests, bishops, or popes. With this discovery, the male domination of the apostolic succession crumbles away, along with the Rome-centered concept of the succession itself.

And crucially, we have also discovered that there is no evidence to suggest that Jesus intended to be worshiped as a god. On the contrary, his teachings indicate that he wanted each person to have the opportunity to travel to the Far-World to find the Divine for himself or herself – or as he put it, to travel to the kingdom of heaven and be filled with the "Spirit of God."

Where did Jesus learn all this? Not in Galilee, we have concluded, but much more likely in Egypt, where the Jewish community appears to have been more diverse than the Jewish community in Palestine and to have nurtured a more mystical approach to religion.

Furthermore, nothing in our findings suggests that Jesus ever planned to start a religion, let alone encourage others to write down his words and organize them into an official collection of sayings. In fact, quite the reverse is more likely. I suspect that he wouldn't have minded at all if people forgot him; what was more important to him was that people should not forget the way to the kingdom of heaven, a notion not restricted to Christianity and Judaism: "To be ignorant of the divine is the ultimate vice," proclaim the texts attributed to the Egyptian sage Hermes Trismegistus.[2]

It should be clear now that history is malleable: we have our facts, but we never have enough of them to be able to put our hands on our hearts and say, in all honesty, that we know for certain what happened. All history is a myth, a story created to make some sense out of the few events we can know. The past is a hypothesis erected to explain and justify the present.

In some ways this does not matter, for myths exist to communicate meaning, not history. But in this scientific age we want to know that the myths we live by are, if not true, at least based upon some approximation of the truth. We want to know that Jesus was really crucified, that Caesar was truly murdered by Brutus, that Paul did have a mystical experience on his way to Damascus. All these events are plausible, and there is no intrinsic reason why they might not be true.

But what do we do with beliefs such as Jesus walking on water? Jesus having been raised from the dead? Peter founding the Roman Church with infallible popes? None of these beliefs is plausible, and there is no intrinsic reason why any of them should be true. Yet there are many who equally believe both sets of assertions.

Our modern world is dominated by the "religions of the book" – Christianity, Judaism, and Islam. We can see that to base truth upon a written word makes it vulnerable to all the problems of interpretation and translation, to say nothing of religious distortion. The danger is that books foster a dependence upon belief rather than knowledge; if there has been one underlying theme of our journey, it has been that we need to travel the road for ourselves and experience its hardships, pleasures, and insights directly rather than secondhand or vicariously.

And with that plea I must bring our journey to an end, not because there is no further to travel, for of course there is, but because we have traveled much already and it is now time to pause and reflect on just how far we have come.

As we halt, it only remains to quote the great Persian Sufi Jelaluddin Rumi, who, cutting straight to the heart of the matter, as was always his way, cried out to all who would listen: "Jars of springwater are not enough anymore. Take us down to the river!"[3]

To drink from the river is our birthright. Let no one deny us that freedom!

Postscript

It is no secret that during February and March 2006, I and my colleague Richard Leigh were head to head in the High Court in London with the author of *The Da Vinci Code*. Our claim was that he had infringed our intellectual property in our book *The Holy Blood and the Holy Grail*.

Naturally, when the court date was announced, I was concerned that the trial might overshadow the publicity for *The Jesus Papers*, my new book with my new publishers, HarperCollins. I had finished the manuscript in the Summer of 2005 and was looking forward to the book's release in the United States on 28 March 2006 – a date that had been set by HarperCollins from the very start.

But worrying proved a waste of time: the court case began later than I expected and ran longer than I expected, with testimony ending only eight days before the book's publication. Meanwhile I had discovered on the Internet that Random House – by some weird coincidence – were going to release five million paperback copies of *The Da Vinci Code* on the same day as my new book was to go on sale!

Of course, every media interview I did began with some questions about the court case. That was inevitable and easily dealt with. However, one question which constantly came up was "Why is *The Da Vinci Code* so widely popular?" As if I would know! Dan Brown's earlier books had sold relatively few copies; what made his latest so successful? So far as anyone could tell, it wasn't as though he had changed his style.

It was clear from all the commentary in the press and from the Church's response, that it was the religious questions posed within the book which had caught the public's attention – both for and against – especially in the United States. What exactly was going on?

I had already been pondering this issue for quite some time, since the contention my co-author and I had argued in court was that these questions arose from material derived from our book *The Holy Blood and the Holy Grail*. But whatever the rights or wrongs of this intellectual property dispute – which, at the time of writing is still ongoing (after we lost the case in the High Court in London, we were given permission by the Court of Appeal to take it before three Court of Appeal Judges) –

the radical ideas about Jesus, Mary Magdalene and the rise of Christianity with which both books are concerned had struck a chord with the American public going far beyond the massive publicity campaign mounted by *The Da Vinci Code*'s publishers. The same interest subsequently appeared around the world.

It seemed to me the answer had something to do with the spiritual disenfranchisement of many people who saw themselves occupying the middle path of the three great religions: that is, the majority of the people within these faiths.

It is hardly surprising that most Christians, Jews, and Muslims stand upon the middle path; a moderate stance frames their beliefs, reflects the culture they feel part of, and it supplies a satisfying and comfortable faith, within which they can lead meaningful and moral lives without requiring of them the kind of special dedication expected of the clergy or monks. Equally as importantly, a middle path position ensures no great arguments: Christians, Jews and Muslims of the middle ground can be flexible, and generally tolerant of each other.

During the time this moderate stance prevailed complacency crept in. No one ever thought that the great religions would ever be subjected to the kind of disruptive forces which are now emerging. Few had ever felt the need to question their faith very firmly – or even at all. There was a quiet satisfaction with having a belief that allowed for the feeling of "each to his own."

But then, over the last decade or two, those operating at the very edges of these three great religions began to take over; they held rigid doctrinal positions; they claimed to speak for the whole of the religious body and they demanded in strident tones, which admitted no compromise, that those complacently but happily occupying the middle ground should move to join them in this rigid position.

And, worryingly, these hard-line religious teachers began getting their religious message tangled up with politics: the Christian fundamentalists claimed, on the basis of their chosen texts and eccentric interpretations, that the Middle Eastern wars of Bush and Blair were part of a divine plan which would see the return of Jesus at the head of a great army; the Jewish fundamentalists were claiming that their ancient texts gave them the right to territory in and about Israel and that the destruction of the Dome of the Rock and the rebuilding of the Temple would see the coming of the Messiah; the Islamic fundamentalists were finding justification in their sacred writings for blowing themselves up in buses and cafés, taking with them the lives of innocents including – all too often – other Muslims. They too saw the advent of a messianic spiritual figure – the Mahdi. Whether Jesus, the Messiah and the Mahdi were the same figure did not find any place in the discussion. To outsiders, it began to look as though three figures would be trying to occupy the same spiritual space; if successful, it would be a trinitarian miracle.

But could all this rigid doctrine be justified? In the face of this relentless attack upon their simple approach towards their religions, those who had never before thought to question the fundamentals of their faith began to worry. But never having been taught to question its fundamentals they did not know what questions to ask, let alone where to go to find answers. Too often it seemed simpler to accept the rigid doctrines which had, at least, an attractive certainty about them, doctrines which removed the need to ask any further questions.

But the questions did not disappear. With the *The Da Vinci Code* some sort of floodgate seems to have been opened, spilling forth variant ideas about Jesus and the rise of Christianity and exploring the differences between the historical Jesus and the theological Jesus which we raised in *The Holy Blood and the Holy Grail* and which has been explored in this book too. Many of these questions and the implications of them made sense. And why shouldn't they? For example, I am often asked whether I truly believe that Jesus was married to Mary Magdalene? I can only reply that there is no hard data for, or against, the notion so I can neither believe nor disbelieve. So my honest reply is one which recognises the plausibility of the matter: "Why not?"

And the question is also raised: is this assertion of a marriage not blasphemous for Christians? Perhaps, but this misses the point: such a charge is irrelevant to the historical Jesus who lived long before any theologians concocted a theory about him.

How often we forget the self-evident! Jesus was Jewish. We are saying no more than "a Jewish man gets married and has a child." How can any later theological position alter the overwhelming probability of that simple human action? An action, we should remember, in accordance with the teachings of the Hebrew scriptures – the Old Testament – as well as the social standards of the day. Blasphemy? I don't think so.

It is self-evident that the most severe reaction against exploring such ideas come from those with the most to lose – those whose religious beliefs depend more upon maintaining a difference between faiths rather than seeking harmony amongst them. We can, and should, continue to ask these critics: "Why do such ideas frighten you so much?"

As I state at the very beginning of this book, my position is that there are many paths to the top of the mountain and who can say which one is best? To claim that there is only one path is, in my opinion, to have departed from any understanding of spirituality and to have succumbed to the dangers of sectarian vanity, a vanity we can see all around us.

Of course, I have been concentrating upon Christianity because that is my tradition, but my call for further exploration also extends to those within the Jewish and the Islamic traditions. Nevertheless, within Christianity, the words of Jesus promoting love, forgiveness, and compassion reveal a good springboard from which to begin the process of reconciling the theological distinctions and seeking to bring people back together in harmony.

Naturally, this is ambitious, even foolhardy, given the abuse and enmity such attempts engender, but no one can say that it is not in accord with the very teachings which are found in the sacred texts, even those carefully selected out of the great number available by the theologians in the late second century.

The Jesus Papers has also pointed to the importance of what I term the clandestine antiquities market. It is to be regretted that much in this market remains inaccessible to scholars. Yet, contrary to what some commentators have argued, this secrecy does not invalidate its value. After all, without this market we should be very much the poorer.

When the Dead Sea Scrolls were found they might have all been discarded, even destroyed, were it not for the financial value which this market placed on them. Luckily the Bedouin who first found the Scrolls took them to a dealer in Bethlehem. And look at the great value which they have been to the world.

When the Nag Hammadi texts were first discovered by two poor farmers digging for nitrates to fertilize their land they were carried back to their home where some were burned as fuel for an oven; this was a practical use which made sense to them if to us it was a tragedy. It was only after the family was told of the possible value of these strange codices to purchasers from the clandestine antiquities market that they were taken to Cairo and sold to dealers. They too held tremendous value to the world of scholarship.

Despite the obvious relevance of this market I came under considerable criticism for taking it seriously and writing about texts which I had seen but which I was unable to produce – as if this was, in some way, a failure. My position was, and remains, that to have ignored them would have been the real failure.

In truth, all of the great discoveries emanating from the antiquities market over the past few decades—the Dead Sea Scrolls and the Nag Hammadi codices among them – have moved painfully and slowly out of the shadows of that market into the hands of scholars since private collectors are still in many ways free to do with their findings what they like; they can release or hide their purchases as they see fit. Their frequent reluctance to bring these documents out into the open stems not so much from a fear that their findings will be invalidated or devalued in some way, but comes more, in many instances, from concerns with the UNESCO laws and the ever-present possibility of the destruction of their findings, deliberate or accidental. It takes coaxing, trust and perseverance for such documents to surface. All someone like me can do is to keep encouraging disclosure and hope that this might prove successful. No one ever said it would be easy, but neither is it impossible.

The documents I have seen, in particular, the Jesus Papers, have not yet made this transition. And while I would have done a disservice had I not mentioned them and provided a context and a perspective in which they make sense, it is nonetheless, a genuine scandal that they remain locked away.

Naturally it was fascinating when during my publicity campaign in the United States *The Gospel of Judas* was released with much fanfare by the National Geographic Society. I was encouraged greatly by this for two main reasons. First, this text came straight out of the clandestine antiquities market which I had written about. Indeed, the story of this text and its companion pieces was more clandestine than most: they were stolen at one stage, spent many years in a bank vault and were mistreated to the point where it is lucky that they survived at all.

Secondly, these texts were being taken very seriously by scholars who, to their credit, were maintaining a very objective view of them. Some were taking interesting, even radical, positions with regard to *The Gospel of Judas*, its teachings, and the development of Christianity from the second century onwards, positions which support my arguments in *The Jesus Papers*.

Bart Ehrman, Professor of Religious Studies at the University of North Carolina, Chapel Hill, provides a commentary to the Gospel in which he explains that while there were many early Christian texts, the original sacred documents of Jesus and the early Christians were the Jewish scriptures. The different texts which later appeared revealed a very diverse expression of Christianity, each group claiming that its texts expressed the true message of Jesus. But, he explains,

> In brief, one of the competing groups in Christianity succeeded in overwhelming all the others. This group gained more converts than its opponents and managed to relegate all its competitors to the margins. This group decided what the Church's organizational structure would be. It decided which creeds Christians would recite. And it decided which books would be accepted as Scripture. This was the group to which Irenaeus belonged, as did other figures well known to scholars of second- and third-century Christianity, such as Justin Martyr and Tertullian.[1]

These early theologians will be recognized by readers, in particular Tertullian, whose rants against the inclusion of women in the running of the Church have caused so much damage over the last eighteen hundred years. Ehrman explains further,

> This group became "orthodox" and once it had sealed its victory over all of its opponents, it rewrote the history of the engagement – claiming that it had

always been the majority opinion of Christianity, that its views had always been the views of the apostolic churches and of the apostles, that its creeds were rooted directly in the teachings of Jesus.[2]

Readers will, by now, be familiar with this process. Reading Bart Ehrman's contribution, I was particularly struck by the difference in the modern approach from when our book *The Holy Blood and the Holy Grail* appeared. Then it seemed that every scholar was fixed on to a very conservative line. With *The Gospel of Judas* this seemed to have disappeared; scholars seem to have discovered the courage to speak out about the anomalies and the machinations abroad in Christianity particularly during the second century A.D.

The Gospel of Judas itself takes a distinctive theological position: like many of the Gnostic texts – especially those found at Nag Hammadi – it states that the creator god was not the One, and that the world was an evil place best left behind forever upon death. The thought of bodily resurrection was viewed with horror. Directly connected with this was the attitude that "salvation comes not through the death and resurrection of Jesus, but through the revelation of secret knowledge that he provides."[3]

For these Christians there was no reliance upon the Easter event for the validity of their faith. This also raises the question of how valid or widespread in the second century A.D. were the stories of the empty tomb and its apparent proof of the resurrection of Jesus; an argument still advanced today – even by otherwise competent academics – as if it were a given of history.

This raises too, questions of the importance of the Gospel of Mark for this discussion. It is well known and accepted that in Mark 16, verses 9–20 do not appear in the earliest manuscripts. Therefore they must have been added *after* the second century A.D. These verses deal with the post-crucifixion appearance of Jesus first to Mary Magdalene and then to the apostles. While, on the face of it, one could argue that this text reveals something of Jesus' actions after his survival of the crucifixion and prior to his fleeing into a place of safety, it could also be viewed as a statement directly opposing the assertions of those Christians now termed Gnostics for it depicts a "risen" Jesus returning to the earth prior to his final ascension to "heaven". It is implicitly stating that the Gnostic concept of an evil earth is not the one which is correct; it thus reclaims bodily resurrection as an article of faith thereby revealing to us that this was not an article of faith for the earlier Church. And it also, along the way, reveals how widespread this previous attitude must have been, otherwise there would have been no need to add such a passage to the Gospel to make the point.

These questions are relevant to the discussion provided at length in this book; the discussion concerning the meaning and understanding of Jesus' term "The

Kingdom of Heaven." In fact, the text of *The Gospel of Judas* states,

> Knowing that Judas was reflecting upon something that was exalted, Jesus said to him, "step away from the others and I shall tell you the mysteries of the kingdom. It is possible for you to reach it..."[4]

As with other texts we have already looked at we have the idea that this divine world – the Far-World – could be visited by means of a personal experience.

Given the seriousness with which this Gospel has been received it is hard to avoid the implication that there is an increasing pressure abroad causing all of us to take another look at the clash between the historical and the theological Jesus. And, of course, the historical events of the first century A.D. out of which all this appeared. *USA Today* quoted Ehrman as commenting,

> In the ancient world, Christianity was even more diverse than it was today. Not until later centuries did the standard devotional texts known as the New Testament become the bedrock of the Christian faith. Dozens of alternative gospels and creeds lost out in the process.[5]

Of course, we should expect that the Vatican would take a less ecumenical position and we are not disappointed:

in January 2006, prior to the publication of *The Gospel of Judas* but when the planned publication was well-known, Vatican theologian Monsignor Giovanni D'Ercole was quoted in the English newspaper *The Times*, as warning of the danger of seeking to, "re-evaluate Judas and muddy the Gospel accounts by reference to apocryphal writings. This can only create confusion in believers."[6]

The Vatican, as we know, does not like questions which might cause believers to re-evaluate their faith.

Which returns us to where *The Jesus Papers* began: with the very curious painted Station of the Cross on the wall of the little parish church in the French village of Rennes le Château in the foothills of the Pyrenees.

Prior to the publication of *The Jesus Papers*, NBC "Dateline" producer Stacy Reiss made a film exploring some of the issues raised in this book. We filmed in the church at Rennes le Château where, among other things, I explained the painted image of the fourteenth Station of the Cross on the wall of the church, the image which suggests that a living Jesus was taken out of the tomb by the light of the risen moon.

This part of the book and the film caused much discussion. It could be argued by those who have never been to Rennes le Château that the image of Station 14 did not depict the moon at all but rather a badly drawn sun; in this case the implication derived from this depiction – that Jesus survived the crucifixion – would not be correct. However Station 13 at Rennes le Château depicts

Jesus being taken down from the cross as the sun is setting gloriously behind him. It cannot, then, be disputed
that Station 14 depicts the risen moon. The only argument concerns what meaning we read from this enigmatic depiction.

Filming in Rennes le Château that day proved interesting on another level too. Late in the afternoon a
French writer, Jean-Luc Robin, arrived for an interview. His detailed knowledge of Rennes le Château is
unparalleled; he had lived in the village for several years
and had discovered the existence of papers belonging
to the priest, Béranger Saunière, in the hands of a local
family; personal papers which had never been studied
by any previous researchers.[7] M. Robin was interviewed
in the church about Station 14: "Was this the rising
moon?" interviewer Sara James asked. "Of course," he
replied without hesitation, explaining that the priest
had probably painted them himself.

I was amazed; I did not know this. It made the priest's
images all the more important and personal. There could
no longer be any doubt that the priest was deliberately
revealing a great secret that he had learned – a great
secret that he could not openly talk about: that Jesus
survived the crucifixion.

Running throughout *The Jesus Papers* is the attitude that
it would be to our advantage to focus upon what we
hold in common; that we should be aware of the power

of religious conviction; and that we can usefully distinguish between spirituality – which is eternal – and religion which has been created by very fallible humans. Religions exist to encompass and express, as best they can, spirituality, but like all human institutions they suffer from limitations.

That is one of the reasons why we need to avoid thinking that any one religion has a better grasp than another: all are attempting to express, in their very fallible ways, the eternal spiritual background to all existence. And when religion becomes entangled in politics we can end up with the worst of all possible worlds.

The figure of Jesus is a figure common to all three faiths which revere a descent from the Patriarch Abraham but the Jesus which theology later created is a potentially divisive factor which helps keep these three faiths apart. However, the spirituality available to each individual, summed up in the metaphor attributed to Jesus in the New Testament, that of "The Kingdom of Heaven" which we have explored in *The Jesus Papers*, can only add depth and meaning to our relationship with the Eternal – if we care to pursue such a thing of course – and this relationship is, after all, at least one of the aims of each of the three faiths.

Surely, it seems to me, it is better to focus upon the great flowing river rather than the different rocky trails and rivulets leading to it?

Bibliography

Abt, Theodor, and Erik Hornung. *Knowledge for the Afterlife: The Egyptian Amduat – A Quest for Immortality*. Zurich, 2003.

Apuleius, Lucius. *The Golden Ass*, trans. Robert Graves. Harmondsworth, 1976.

———. *Metamorphoses*, trans. J. Arthur Hanson, 2 vols. Cambridge, Mass., 1989.

Arberry, Arthur J., trans. *The Koran*. Oxford, 1998.

Aristophanes. *The Frogs*, trans. Kenneth McLeish. In *Plays: Two*. London, 1998.

Assmann, Jan. *The Search for God in Ancient Egypt*, trans. David Lorton. Ithaca, N.Y., and London, 2001.

———. *The Mind of Egypt*, trans. Andrew Jenkins. New York, 2002.

Baigent, Michael. *From the Omens of Babylon*. London, 1994.

Baigent, Michael, and Robert Eisenman. "A Ground-Penetrating Radar Survey Testing the Claim for Earthquake Damage of the Second Temple Ruins at Khirbet Qumran." *Qumran Chronicle* 9 (2000): pp. 131–37.

Baigent, Michael, and Richard Leigh. *The Dead Sea Scrolls Deception*. London, 1991.

———. *The Inquisition*. London, 2000.

Baigent, Michael, Richard Leigh, and Henry Lincoln. *Holy Blood, Holy Grail*. New York, 1982.

Bede. *A History of the English Church and People*, trans. Leo Sherley-Price. Harmondsworth, 1979.

Bleeker, C. J. "Initiation in Ancient Egypt." In *Initiation*, ed. Dr. C. J. Bleeker, pp. 49–58. Leiden, 1965.

———. *Egyptian Festivals*. Leiden, 1967.

———. *Hathor and Thoth*. Leiden, 1973.

Bowman, Alan K. *Egypt After the Pharaohs*. London, 1986.

Brandon, S. G. F. *Jesus and the Zealots*. Manchester, 1967.

———. *The Fall of Jerusalem and the Christian Church*, 2nd ed. London, 1974. (1st edition published 1951).

Bruce, F. F. *The New Testament Documents*, 5th ed., rev. London, 1974.

Burkert, Walter. *Lore and Science in Ancient Pythagoreanism*, trans. Edwin L. Minar Jr. Cambridge, Mass., 1972.

———. *Ancient Mystery Cults*. Cambridge, Mass., 1987.

Burrows, Millar. *The Dead Sea Scrolls*. London, 1956.

Caplice, Richard I. *The Akkadian Namburbu Texts: An Introduction*. Malibu, 1974.

Catholic University of America, ed. *New Catholic Encyclopedia*, 2nd ed. Detroit, 2002.

Cauville, S., and V-VI. Dendara. *Traduction: Les crypts du temple d'Hathor*. Leuven, Paris, and Dudley, Mass., 2004.

Charles, R. H. *The Apocrypha and Pseudepigrapha of the Old Testament in English*, 2 vols. Oxford, 1979.

Charlesworth, James H., ed. *Jesus and the Dead Sea Scrolls*. New York, 1995.

Chester, Greville J. "A Journey to the Biblical Sites in Lower Egypt." *Palestine Exploration Fund Quarterly Statement* (London) (1880): pp. 133–58.

Churton, Tobias. *Gnostic Philosophy*. Rochester, Vt., 2005.

Clark, R. J. "Vergil, *Aeneid*, 6, 40 ff., and the Cumaean Sibyl's Cave." *Latomus* 36 (1977): pp. 482–95.

Clement of Alexandria. *The Miscellanies*, trans. William Wilson, 2 vols. Edinburgh, 1867, 1869 (Ante-Nicene Christian Library, vols. IV and XII).

———. *Stromateis, Books One to Three*, trans. John Ferguson. Washington, 1991.

Cohn, Haim. *The Trial and Death of Jesus*. New York, 1971.

Copenhaver, Brian P., ed. *Hermetica*. 1992.

Cousin, Victor. *Fragments Philosophiques*. Paris, 1840.

Curnow, Trevor. *The Oracles of the Ancient World*. London, 2004.

Denton, Richard, producer. *Did Jesus Die?* Planet Wild Productions for the BBC, 2003 (transmitted on BBC Channel 4 in the United Kingdom, 2004).

De Vaux, Roland. "Observations sur le Commentaire d'Habacuc découvert près de la Mer Morte," *Revue biblique* 58 (1951): pp. 437–43.

———. *Archaeology and the Dead Sea Scrolls.* Oxford, 1977.

Dole, S. G. "New Evidence for the Mysteries of Dionysos." *Greek, Roman, and Byzantine Studies* 21 (1980): pp. 223–38.

Driver, G. R. *The Judaean Scrolls.* Oxford, 1965.

Dupont-Sommer, André. *The Dead Sea Scrolls: A Preliminary Survey,* trans. E. Margaret Rowley. Oxford, 1952.

———. *The Essene Writings from Qumran,* trans. Geza Vermes. Gloucester, Mass., 1973.

Ehrman, Bart D. *Lost Christianities.* Oxford, 2003.

Eisenman, Robert. *The Dead Sea Scrolls and the First Christians.* Rockport, Mass., 1996.

———. *James the Brother of Jesus.* London, 2002.

Eisenman, Robert H., and James M. Robinson, introduction and index. *A Facsimile Edition of the Dead Sea Scrolls,* 2 vols. Washington, 1991.

Eisenman, Robert, and Michael Wise. *The Dead Sea Scrolls Uncovered.* Shaftesbury, Rockport, Mass., and Brisbane, 1992.

Eisler, Robert. *The Messiah Jesus and John the Baptist,* trans. Alexander Haggerty Krappe. London, 1931.

Eliade, Mircea. *Rites and Symbols of Initiation.* New York, 1958.

Encyclopaedia Judaica, 16 vols. Jerusalem, 1974.

Enoch, The Book of. In *The Apocrypha and Pseudepigrapha of the Old Testament,* ed. R. H. Charles, vol. II. pp. 163–277.

Eusebius. *The History of the Church,* trans. G. A. Williamson. Harmondsworth, 1981.

Farnell, L. R. *The Cults of the Greek States*, 3 vols. Oxford, 1907.

Faulkner, R. O. *The Ancient Egyptian Pyramid Texts*. Oxford, 1969.

——. *The Ancient Egyptian Coffin Texts*, 3 vols. Warminster, 1994.

Fitzmyer, Joseph. *Atlantic Monthly* (December 1986).

Forman, Robert K. C. "Pure Consciousness Events and Mysticism." *Sophia* 25 (1986): pp. 49–58.

——. *The Problem of Pure Consciousness*. Oxford, 1990.

Fraser, P. M. *Ptolemaic Alexandria*. Oxford, 1972.

Fuller, Reginald C., ed. *A New Catholic Commentary on Holy Scripture*. London, 1969.

García Martínez, Florentino, trans. *The Dead Sea Scrolls Translated*, trans. Wilfred G. E. Watson. Leiden, 1994.

Gichon, Mordechai. "The Bar Kochba War – A Colonial Uprising Against Imperial Rome (131/2–135 C.E.)." *Revue international d'histoire militaire* (1979): pp. 82–97.

Gorman, Peter. *Pythagoras: A Life*. London, 1979.

Guthrie, W. K. C. *Orpheus and Greek Religion*. Princeton, N.J., 1993.

Halevi, Z'ev ben Shimon. *The Way of Kabbalah*. London, 1976.

Hardie, Colin. "The Crater of Avernus as a Cult-Site." Appendix to P. Vergili Maronis, *Aeneidos*, Liber Sextus, pp. 279–86. Oxford, 1977.

Hasler, August Bernhard. *How the Pope Became Infallible*, trans. Peter Heinegg. New York, 1981.

Hastings, James, ed. *Encyclopedia of Religion and Ethics*, 13 vols. Edinburgh, 1908–26.

Hayward, Robert. "The Jewish Temple at Leontopolis: A Reconsideration." *Journal of Jewish Studies* 33 (1982): pp. 429–43.

Heliodorus of Emesa. *An Aethiopian History*, written in Greek by Heliodorus, Englished by Thomas Underdowne Anno 1587. London, 1895.

Hippolytus. *Philosophumena, or, The Refutation of All Heresies*, trans. F. Legge, 2 vols. London, 1921.

Homer. *The Odyssey*, trans. E. V. Rieu. London, 1952.

Horbury, William. *Jewish Messianism and the Cult of Christ*. London, 1998.

Hornung, Erik. *Conceptions of God in Ancient Egypt*, trans. John Baines. Ithaca, N.Y., 1996.

Iamblichus of Apamea. *On the Mysteries of the Egyptians*, trans. Thomas Taylor, 1821. Frome (Prometheus Trust), 1999.

Irenaeus of Lyon. *Against Heresies*. In *The Writings of Irenaeus*, trans. Alexander Roberts and W. H. Rambaut, 2 vols. Edinburgh, 1868–69.

Iverson, Erik. *Egyptian and Hermetic Doctrine*. Copenhagen, 1984.

Jonas, Hans. *The Gnostic Religion*, 2nd ed. Boston, 1963.

Jones, Alexander, general editor. *The Jerusalem Bible*. London, 1966.

Josephus, Flavius. *The Jewish War*, trans. G. A. Williamson. Harmondsworth, 1978.

———. *The Antiquities of the Jews*, trans. William Whiston. London, n.d.

——. *The Life of Flavius Josephus*, trans. William Whiston. London, n.d.

——. *Wars of the Jews*, trans. William Whiston. London, n.d.

Justin Martyr. *Dialogue with Trypho*. In *The Writings of Justin Martyr and Athenagoras*, trans. Marcus Dods, George Reith, and B. P. Pratten. Edinburgh, 1867.

Kasser, Rodolphe, Meyer, Marvin and Wurst, Gregor. *The Gospel of Judas*. Hanover, PA, 2006.

Kerényi, C. *Eleusis: Archetypal Image of Mother and Daughter*, trans. Ralph Manheim. London, 1967.

King, Karen L. *The Gospel of Mary of Magdala*. Santa Rosa, Calif., 2003.

Kingsley, Peter. "Ezekiel by the Grand Canal: Between Jewish and Babylonian Tradition." *Journal of the Royal Asiatic Society* 3rd. ser., 2 (1992): pp. 339–46.

——. "Poimandres: The Etymology of the Name and the Origins of the Hermetica." *Journal of the Warburg and Courtauld Institutes* 56 (1993): pp. 1–24.

——. "From Pythagoras to the *Turba Philosophorum*: Egypt and Pythagorean Tradition." *Journal of the Warburg and Courtauld Institutes* 57 (1994): pp. 1–13.

——. *Ancient Philosophy, Mystery, and Magic*. Oxford, 1995.

——. *In the Dark Places of Wisdom*. Inverness, Calif., 1999.

——. *Reality*. Inverness, Calif., 2003.

Koester, Helmut. *Ancient Christian Gospels*. London, 1990.

Kramer, Heinrich, and James Sprenger. *Malleus Maleficarum*, trans. Montague Summers. London, 1996.

Layton, Bentley, trans. *The Gnostic Scriptures*. London, 1987.

Lea, Henry Charles. *A History of the Inquisition of the Middle Ages*, 3 vols. London, 1888.

Lichtheim, Miriam. *Ancient Egyptian Literature*, 3 vols. Berkeley, Los Angeles, and London, 1980.

Lilley, A. L. *Modernism: A Record and Review*. London, 1908.

Livius, Titus. *The History of Rome*, trans. Rev. Canon Roberts, 6 vols. London, 1905.

Lloyd, Seton. *The Archaeology of Mesopotamia*. London, 1978.

Mack, Burton L. *The Lost Gospel: The Book of Q and Christian Origins*. San Francisco, 1994.

Mazar, Amihai. *Archaeology of the Land of the Bible*. Cambridge, 1993.

Megarry, Tim. *Society in Prehistory*. Basingstoke, 1995.

Meinardus, Otto F. A. *The Holy Family in Egypt*. Cairo, 2000.

Mellaart, James. *Earliest Civilisations of the Near East*. London, 1965.

Messori, Vittorio. *The Ratzinger Report*, trans. Salvator Attanasio and Graham Harrison. San Francisco, 1985.

Modrzejewski, Joseph. *The Jews of Egypt*. Edinburgh, 1995.

Murphy, Richard Thomas Aquinas. *Lagrange and Biblical Renewal*. Chicago, 1966.

Naydler, Jeremy. *Temple of the Cosmos*. Rochester, Vt. 1996.

———. *Shamanic Wisdom in the Pyramid Texts*. Rochester, Vt. 2005.

Noonan, John T. *Contraception*. New York, 1967.

Ogden, Daniel. *Greek and Roman Necromancy*. Princeton and Oxford, 2001.

O'Shea, Stephen. *The Perfect Heresy*. London, 2000.

Oulton, John Ernest Leonard, and Henry Chadwick. *Alexandrian Christianity*. London, 1954.

Pagels, Elaine. *The Gnostic Gospels*. London, 1980.

———. *Beyond Belief: The Secret Gospel of Thomas*. New York, 2003.

Paget, Robert F. *In the Footsteps of Orpheus*. London, 1967.

Parpola, Simo. "The Assyrian Tree of Life: Tracing the Origins of Jewish Monotheism and Greek Philosophy." *Journal of Near Eastern Studies* 52 (1993): pp. 161–208.

Parrinder, Geoffrey. *Jesus in the Qur'an*. London, 1965.

Patrich, Joseph, and Benny Arubas. "A Juglet Containing Balsam Oil(?) from a Cave Near Qumran." *Israel Exploration Journal* 39 (1989): pp. 43–59.

Perry, Paul. *Jesus in Egypt*. New York, 2003.

Petrie, W. M. Flinders. *Hyksos and Israelite Cities*. London, 1906.

Philo. *On the Contemplative Life*, trans. F. H. Colson. Loeb Classical Library, vol. IX. Cambridge, Mass., and London, 1967.

Plato. *Phaedo*, trans. David Gallop. Oxford, 1999.

Pliny. *Natural History*, trans. H. Rackham and W. H. S. Jones, 10 vols. London, 1938–42.

Plutarch. *Isis and Osiris*, trans. Frank Cole Babbitt. Loeb Classical Library, *Moralia*, vol. V. Cambridge, Mass., and London, 1993.

Quirke, Stephen. *Ancient Egyptian Religion*. London, 1992.

———. *The Cult of Ra: Sun-Worship in Ancient Egypt*. London, 2001.

Ranke-Heinemann, Uta. *Eunuchs for the Kingdom of Heaven*, trans. Peter Heinigg. London, 1991.

Ratzinger, Joseph. *Church, Ecumenism, and Politics*. Slough, 1988.

Reiner, Erica. *Enuma Anu Enlíl, Tablets 50–51*. Malibu, 1981.

Robert, Louis. "Archaeological Reports for 1959–1960." *Journal of Hellenic Studies* 80–82: pp. 41–43.

Robinson, James M. *The Nag Hammadi Library in English*, trans. Coptic Gnostic Library project, Institute for Antiquity and Christianity. Leiden, 1977.

Rostovtzeff, M. *The Social and Economic History of the Hellenistic World*. Oxford, 1941.

Roux, Georges. *Ancient Iraq*. Harmondsworth, 1977.

Rumi, Jelaluddin. *The Glance*, trans. Coleman Barks. New York and London, 1999.

Runciman, Steven. *A History of the Crusades*, 3 vols. Harmondsworth, 1978.

Schmandt-Besserat, Denise. *Before Writing*, vol. 1, *From Counting to Cuneiform*. Austin, 1992.

Schonfield, Hugh J. *The Pentecost Revolution*. London, 1974.

———. *The Passover Plot*. London, 1977.

———. *The Essene Odyssey*. Shaftesbury, 1984.

Seneca, *Epistles*, xc. 29, trans. C. Densmore Curtis, in Hastings, *Encyclopedia of Religion and Ethics*, 7.

Shaw, Gregory. *Theurgy and the Soul: The Neoplatonism of Iamblichus*. University Park, Pa., 1995.

Shreeve, James. *The Neanderthal Enigma*. London, 1995.

Smith, Morton. *Jesus the Magician*. London, 1978.

———. *The Secret Gospel*. Clearlake, Calif., 1982.

———. "Clement of Alexandria and Secret Mark: The Score at the End of the First Decade." *Harvard Theological Review* 75 (1982): pp. 449–61.

Stanley, Arthur Penrhyn. *Lectures on the History of the Eastern Church*, 4th ed. London, 1869.

Starbird, Margaret. *The Woman with the Alabaster Jar*. Rochester, Vt., 1993.

Steckoll, S. H. "The Qumran Sect in Relation to the Temple of Leontopolis." *Revue de Qumran* 6 (1967): pp. 55–69.

Strabo. *Geography*, ed. H. C. Hamilton and W. Falconer, 3 vols. London, 1854–57.

Stroumsa, Guy G. *Hidden Wisdom: Esoteric Traditions and the Roots of Christian Mysticism*. Leiden, 1996.

Suetonius. *The Twelve Caesars*, trans. Robert Graves. Harmondsworth, 1979.

Szpakowska, Kasia. *Behind Closed Eyes: Dreams and Nightmares in Ancient Egypt*. Swansea, 2003.

Tacitus. *The Annals of Imperial Rome*, trans. Michael Grant. Harmondsworth, 1979.

———. *The Histories*, trans. Kenneth Wellesley. Harmondsworth, 1988.

Tarn, W. W. *Hellenistic Civilisation*, 3rd ed. London, 1952.

Taylor, Joan E. "A Second Temple in Egypt: The Evidence for the Zadokite Temple of Onias." *Journal for the Study of Judaism* 29, no. 3 (1998): pp. 297–321.

Taylor, Joan E., and Philip R. Davies. "The So-called Therapeutae of *De Vita Contemplativa*: Identity and Character." *Harvard Theological Review* 91 (1998): pp. 3–24.

Temple, Robert. *Conversations with Eternity*. London, 1984.
———. *Netherworld*. London, 2002.

Saint Teresa of Ávila. *The Life of Saint Teresa of Ávila by Herself*, trans. J. M. Cohen. London, 1957.

Tertullian. *The Writings of Tertullian*, 3 vols., ed. Rev. Alexander Roberts and James Donaldson. Ante-Nicene Christian Library, vols. XI, XV, XVIII. Edinburgh, 1869.

Thompson, Thomas L. *The Bible in History: How Writers Create a Past*. London, 1999.

Vermes, Geza. *The Dead Sea Scrolls: Qumran in Perspective*. London, 1977.

———. *The Complete Dead Sea Scrolls in English*. London and New York, 1997.

Virgil. *The Georgics*, trans. L. P. Wilkinson. Harmondsworth, 1982.

———. *The Aeneid*, trans. Robert Fitzgerald. London, 1985.

Wakefield, Walter L. *Heresy, Crusade, and Inquisition in Southern France, 1100–1250*. London, 1974.

Wente, Edward F. "Mysticism in Pharaonic Egypt?" *Journal of Near Eastern Studies* 41 (1982): pp. 161–79.

Williams, Margaret H., ed. *The Jews Among the Greeks and Romans*. Baltimore, 1998.

Zias, Joseph, and Eliezer Sekeles. "The Crucified Man from Giv'at ha-Mivtar: A Reappraisal." *Israel Exploration Journal* 35 (1985): pp. 22–27.

Zuckerman, Arthur J. *A Jewish Princedom in Feudal France 768–900*. New York, 1972.

Notes

INTRODUCTION

1. Zuckerman, *A Jewish Princedom in Feudal France*, pp. 372–74.
2. Baigent, Leigh, and Lincoln, *Holy Blood, Holy Grail*, pp. 349–55.
3. Zuckerman, *A Jewish Princedom in Feudal France*, p. 58.
4. *Encyclopedia Judaica*, vol. 12, p. 827.
5. Baigent, Leigh, and Lincoln, *Holy Blood, Holy Grail*, pp. 224–33.
6. Runciman, *A History of the Crusades*, vol. 1, p. 292. Runciman comments, "Who constituted the electors is unknown."
7. Baigent, Leigh, and Lincoln, *Holy Blood, Holy Grail*, pp. 290–98.

CHAPTER TWO: THE PRIEST'S TREASURE

1. The story of Béranger Saunière and his mysterious wealth is told in Baigent, Leigh, and Lincoln, *Holy Blood, Holy Grail*, pp. 3–18. We now know that there were two sources of his funds: the first was the Hapsburg wife of Henri de Chambord, the pretender to the French throne during the nineteenth century. This was passed over to

Saunière for a specific task that he carried out. Having tasted wealth, Saunière then embarked upon a more venal moneymaking exercise: trafficking in masses – simony – a crime in the Catholic Church. During the 1980s several members of the French internal security organization, the DGSE, gave us access to a wooden chest once owned by Saunière that contained the daily financial records of his business. The papers we saw proved that he was trafficking in masses from at least the late 1890s into the early 1900s.

2. Lilley, *Modernism*, p. 35.
3. Quoted in Hasler, *How the Pope Became Infallible*, p. 246.
4. *How the Pope Became Infallible*, p. 247.
5. *How the Pope Became Infallible*, p. 247.
6. Suetonius, *The Twelve Caesars*, p. 202.

CHAPTER THREE: JESUS THE KING

1. Arberry, ed., *The Koran*, IV, 155ff, p. 95. See also Parrinder, *Jesus in the Qur'an*, p. 108.
2. Brandon, *The Fall of Jerusalem*, p. 102.
3. *The Fall of Jerusalem*, p. 102.
4. Brandon, *Jesus and the Zealots*, p. 328.
5. All scriptural quotations are taken from either the Jerusalem Bible or the Authorized King James Version.
6. Eisenman, "Maccabees, Zadokites, Christians, and Qumran," in *The Dead Sea Scrolls and the First Christians*, p. 29.
7. There is no evidence in extant Roman or Jewish records of the existence of such an amnesty.
8. Josephus, *The Jewish War*, pp. 113 – 14.
9. *The Jewish War*, p. 128.
10. Josephus, *The Antiquities of the Jews*, XVIII, I, p. 375.
11. Josephus, *The Jewish War*, p. 380.
12. Josephus, *Wars of the Jews*, IV, III, p. 109.
13. Interviews with Miles Copeland, 10 April 1990 and 1 May 1990.

14. See De Vaux, *Archaeology and the Dead Sea Scrolls*, pp. 33 – 41, for a description of the coin finds on which he based much of his dating. For a critical analysis of De Vaux's interpretation of these coin finds, see Eisenman, "Maccabees, Zadokites, Christians, and Qumran," in *The Dead Sea Scrolls and the First Christians*, pp. 44 – 47; p. 44, n. 88. For a summary, see Baigent and Leigh, *The Dead Sea Scrolls Deception*, pp. 156 – 59.

15. García Martínez, *The War Scroll*, XVI, 3 – 8, p. III.

16. García Martínez, *The Rule of the Community*, IX, II, pp. 13 – 14.

17. García Martínez, *The Damascus Document*, XX, I, p. 46.

18. García Martínez, *The Temple Scroll*, LVI, 14 – 15, p. 173.

19. Horbury, *Jewish Messianism and the Cult of Christ*, p. 11.

20. *Jewish Messianism and the Cult of Christ*, p. 37.

21. Eisenman, "Maccabees, Zadokites, Christians, and Qumran," p. 107. "What is new in 4 B.C.," writes Eisenman, "is the appearance of the 'Messianic' variation of this 'Zealot Movement.'"

22. The Gospels of Mark, Luke, and John differ slightly in the wording.

23. Schonfield, *The Passover Plot*, pp. 118 – 24.

CHAPTER FOUR: THE SON OF THE STAR

1. Josephus, *The Jewish War*, p. 154.

2. *The Jewish War*, p. 208.

3. Eisler, *The Messiah Jesus and John the Baptist*, p. 557. The other friend present was probably Mucianus, military governor of Syria.

4. Josephus, *The Jewish War*, p. 212.

5. *The Jewish War*, p. 350.

6. Suetonius, *The Twelve Caesars*, Vespasian, IV, p. 281.

7. Tacitus, *The Histories*, V, XIII, p. 279.

8. Josephus, *The Jewish War*, p. 272.

9. Dio Cassius, *Roman History*, Xiphilini, LXVI, 8; cited in Eisler, *The Messiah Jesus and John the Baptist*, p. 556.

10. Eisler, *The Messiah Jesus and John the Baptist*, pp. 556 – 57.

11. Josephus, *The Jewish War*, p. 350.

12. Eusebius, *The History of the Church*, III, XII, p. 124, quoting Hegesippus.

13. Jones, ed., *The Jerusalem Bible, The New Testament*, p. 467.

14. With the Passover at hand, Jesus visits Jerusalem. He is told that the building of the Temple took forty-six years. The Temple was commenced in the period 20 – 19 B.C.; hence, forty-six years later would be A.D. 27 – 28.

15. Tacitus, *Annals*, p. 365.

16. García Martínez, *The Temple Scroll*, col. 66, p. 179.

17. Schonfield, *The Pentecost Revolution*, pp. 46 – 47.

18. Justin Martyr, *Dialogue with Trypho*, CVI, p. 233.

19. Eusebius, *The History of the Church*, III, V, p. 111.

20. *The History of the Church*, I, I, p. 73. Eusebius places this conversion during the lifetime of Jesus, which is more likely a confusion with the family member who converted to messianic Judaism.

21. Josephus, *The Antiquities of the Jews*, XX, II, p. 416.

22. Eisenman, *James the Brother of Jesus*, pp. 892 – 95, 902.

23. Josephus, *The Jewish War*, p. 166.

24. A copy of chapter 37 of Ezekiel was discovered by archaeologists beneath the floor of the synagogue at the fortress of Masada.

25. For a full discussion of the ideology behind the Zealot suicides as explained by Eisenman, see Baigent and Leigh, *The Dead Sea Scrolls Deception*, pp. 211 – 17. See also Eisenman, "Maccabees, Zadokites, Christians and Qumran," in *The Dead Sea Scrolls and the First Christians,* p. 62, where he points out the crucial importance to the Zealots of "making a pious end."

26. Eisenman, "Maccabees, Zadokites, Christians and Qumran," in *The Dead Sea Scrolls and the First Christians,* p. 31, n. 54, quoting the source as *Abot de Rabbi Nathan*, 4.5.

27. Eusebius, *The History of the Church*, IV, II, pp. 154 – 55.

28. Modrzejewski, *The Jews of Egypt*, pp. 204 – 5.

29. *The Jews of Egypt*, p. 199.

30. Gichon, "The Bar Kochba War," p. 88.

31. Eisenman, "Maccabees, Zadokites, Christians and Qumran," in *The Dead Sea Scrolls and the First Christians*, p. 108; see also p. 108, n. 180.

32. Gichon, "The Bar Kochba War," p. 92.

33. Dio Cassius, *Roman History*, LXIX, 12, 2 – 3.

34. Gichon, "The Bar Kochba War," p. 94.

35. "The Bar Kochba War," p. 97, n. 41, quoting one of the laws from the reign of Roman Emperor Septimus Severus, 193 – 211.

36. Justin Martyr, *Dialogue with Trypho*, XLIX, p. 149.

37. *Dialogue with Trypho*, L, p. 151.

38. *Dialogue with Trypho*, XXVI, p. 119.

CHAPTER FIVE: CREATING THE JESUS OF FAITH

1. Koester, *Ancient Christian Gospels*, p. 31.

2. *Ancient Christian Gospels*, p. 41.

3. Horbury, *Jewish Messianism and the Cult of Christ*, p. 11.

4. *Jewish Messianism and the Cult of Christ*, pp. 8, 12.

5. *Jewish Messianism and the Cult of Christ*, pp. 121 – 22.

6. *Jewish Messianism and the Cult of Christ*, pp. 110 – 11.

7. *Jewish Messianism and the Cult of Christ*, p. 124.

8. *Jewish Messianism and the Cult of Christ*, p. 126.

9. It has been argued that Paul wrote his Letter to the Galatians before the council in Jerusalem mentioned in Acts 15; by this view, it would have been written A.D. 48. See Bruce, *The New Testament Documents*, p. 14, n. 1.

10. Chester Beatty Biblical Papyrus No. 9 contains 86 leaves of Paul's letters from the early third century, which were discovered in Egypt.

11. Tertullian, *Apologeticus*, 21, 1, p. 95: "All these things Pilate did to

Christ ... he sent word of Him to the reigning Caesar, who was at that time Tiberius."

12. Tacitus, *The Annals of Imperial Rome*, XV, 44, p. 365.

13. Pliny, *Epistles*, XCVI.

14. Eisler, *The Messiah Jesus and John the Baptist*, pp. 9–10.

15. Suetonius, *The Twelve Caesars, Claudius*, XXV, p. 202.

16. Gospel of Thomas, II, 32:25–33:5, in Robinson, *The Nag Hammadi Library in English*, p. 118.

17. Koester, *Ancient Christian Gospels*, p. xxx.

18. *Ancient Christian Gospels*, p. xxx.

19. *Ancient Christian Gospels*, p. 36.

20. Irenaeus, *Against Heresies*, I, I, 1, vol. 1, p. 1.

21. *Against Heresies*, II, XL, 2, vol. 1, p. 147.

22. *Against Heresies*, I, I, 2, vol. 1, p. 2.

23. *Against Heresies*, I, XXV, 5, vol. 1, p. 96.

24. *Against Heresies*, I, VIII, 2–3, vol. 1, pp. 32–35.

25. *Against Heresies*, II, XXXI, 2, vol. 1, p. 241.

26. *Against Heresies*, II, XXXI, 2, and XXXII, 4, vol. 1, pp. 241, 246.

27. Pagels, *Beyond Belief*, pp. 150–53.

28. Authority for this claim derives from I Peter 5:13.

29. Pagels, *Beyond Belief*, p. 173.

30. Stanley, *Lectures on the History of the Eastern Church*, p. 86, quoting Gregory of Nyassa.

31. Bede, *A History of the English Church and People*, I, 30, pp. 86–87.

32. The term "theurgy" was coined by the late classical philosopher Iamblichus, the major exponent of this divine ritual. For a modern review of the subject, see Shaw, *Theurgy and the Soul*.

33. Cousin, *Fragments philosophiques*, pp. 186–87.

CHAPTER SIX: ROME'S GREATEST FEAR

1. O'Shea, *The Perfect Heresy*, p. 25.

2. *The Chronicle of William Pelhisson*, p. 216, cited in Wakefield, *Heresy*,

Crusade, and Inquisition in Southern France, pp. 207–36.

3. *The Chronicle of William Pelhisson*, p. 216.

4. *The Chronicle of William Pelhisson*, p. 216.

5. Wakefield, *Heresy, Crusade, and Inquisition in Southern France*, pp. 65–66.

6. O'Shea, *The Perfect Heresy*, p. 77.

7. *The Perfect Heresy*, p. 23.

8. Lea, *A History of the Inquisition of the Middle Ages*, I, p. 541.

9. Messori, *The Ratzinger Report*, p. 111.

10. *The Ratzinger Report*, p. 45.

11. *The Ratzinger Report*, p. 61.

12. Ratzinger, *Church, Ecumenism, and Politics*, p. 58.

13. Messori, *The Ratzinger Report*, p. 52.

14. Baigent and Leigh, *The Inquisition*, pp. 64–67.

15. *The Inquisition*, pp. 104–6. The text of the bull is given in Kramer and Sprenger, *Malleus Maleficarum*, xix–xxi.

16. Kramer and Sprenger, *Malleus Maleficarum*, pt. I, question 6, pp. 41–48.

17. *Malleus Maleficarum*, pt. I, question 6, p. 47.

18. Ranke-Heinemann, *Eunuchs for the Kingdom of Heaven*, p. 141, quoting *Responsum Gregorii*.

19. *Eunuchs for the Kingdom of Heaven*, p. 121, quoting John Chrysostom, *On Priesthood*, VI, 8.

20. *Eunuchs for the Kingdom of Heaven*, p. 135.

21. *Eunuchs for the Kingdom of Heaven*, p. 32.

22. *Eunuchs for the Kingdom of Heaven*, p. 347.

23. For a discussion on these points, see *Eunuchs for the Kingdom of Heaven*, pp. 29–30.

24. Cephas, mentioned in this letter, is, of course, a surname given to Peter; see John 1:42.

25. Clement of Alexandria, *Stromateis*, III, 53, p. 289.

26. For a review of the arguments, see Baigent, Leigh, and Lincoln, *Holy Blood, Holy Grail*, pp. 290–97.

27. Ranke-Heinemann, *Eunuchs for the Kingdom of Heaven*, p. 40.

28. *Eunuchs for the Kingdom of Heaven*, p. 40.

29. *Eunuchs for the Kingdom of Heaven*, pp. 45–46.

30. Elaine Pagels interviewed in *Secrets Behind "The Da Vinci Code,"* *Dateline NBC*, 2005.

31. Quoted in *Eunuchs for the Kingdom of Heaven*, p. 9.

32. Quoted in *Eunuchs for the Kingdom of Heaven*, p. 46.

33. *Eunuchs for the Kingdom of Heaven*, p. 126.

34. Tertullian, *The Writings of Tertullian*, vol. 1, *On Female Dress*, I, i, p. 304.

35. *The Writings of Tertullian*, vol. 1, *On Baptism*, xvi, p. 252.

36. Neither Mark, Luke, nor John mentions this statement, even though both Mark and Luke describe the same conversation with Peter.

37. Gospel of Philip 63, in Robinson, *The Nag Hammadi Library in English*, p. 138 (translated by Wesley W. Isenberg).

38. Gospel of Philip 64, *The Nag Hammadi Library in English*, p. 138.

39. King, *The Gospel of Mary of Magdala*, 6, p. 15.

40. *The Gospel of Mary of Magdala*, 10, p. 17.

CHAPTER SEVEN: SURVIVING THE CRUCIFIXION

1. The Jerusalem Bible notes the two sources of Jesus's quote, which conflates both.

2. The Gospel of Luke (7:37–38) has the woman anointing Jesus's feet.

3. Patrich and Arubas, "A Juglet Containing Balsam Oil(?) from a Cave Near Qumran."

4. García Martínez, *The Temple Scroll*, pp. 154f.

5. John's Gospel describes the woman as anointing Jesus's feet rather than his head. I take this to be a garbled example of the same ceremony described by Matthew and Mark.

6. Starbird, *The Woman with the Alabaster Jar*, pp. 50–51.

7. The Jerusalem Bible, p. 1503, note f.

8. Starbird, *The Woman with the Alabaster Jar*, p. 51.

9. Burkert, *Ancient Mystery Cults*, p. 102.

10. Hastings, *Encyclopedia of Religion and Ethics*, vol. I, p. 557.

11. See Acts 15:13, 21:18. See also Eisenman, *The Dead Sea Scrolls and the First Christians*, pp. 118 – 19.

12. The original Greek text has *lesten*, which is translated in the Jerusalem Bible as "brigand" and in the King James Bible as "thief." But *lesten* (singular) relates to *lestai* (plural), the name used for the Zealots.

13. Zias and Sekeles, "The Crucified Man from Giv'at ha-Mivtar," pp. 26 – 27.

14. Cohn, *The Trial and Death of Jesus*, p. 230.

15. Josephus, *The Life of Flavius Josephus*, pp. xxiii – xxiv.

16. Parrinder, *Jesus in the Qur'an*, p. 108.

17. Schonfield, *The Passover Plot*, pp. 166 – 67.

18. Denton, *Did Jesus Die?*

CHAPTER EIGHT: JESUS IN EGYPT

1. See *Encyclopaedia Judaica*, 12, col. 900, and Baigent, Leigh, and Lincoln, *Holy Blood, Holy Grail*, pp. 363 – 64.

2. In fact, these "Christians of St. Thomas" were founded by Nestorian missionaries who roamed far to the east from Palestine; see Schonfield, *The Essene Odyssey*, p. 126.

3. *The Essene Odyssey*, p. 88.

4. Modrzejewski, *The Jews of Egypt*, pp. 73 – 74.

5. Fraser, *Ptolemaic Alexandria*, I, p. 83.

6. Modrzejewski, *The Jews of Egypt*, pp. 26ff.

7. *The Jews of Egypt*, pp. 41 – 43.

8. *The Damascus Document*, col. IV, 3 – 4, in García Martínez, *The Dead Sea Scrolls Translated*, p. 35.

9. Taylor, "A Second Temple in Egypt," p. 310.

10. *Encyclopaedia Judaica*, 12, p. 1403.

11. Vermes, *The Dead Sea Scrolls*, p. 140.

12. Taylor, "A Second Temple in Egypt," pp. 308–9.

13. Chester, "A Journey to the Biblical Sites in Lower Egypt," p. 137.

14. Petrie, *Hyksos and Israelite Cities*, p. 20, plate XXVII.

15. Josephus, *The Jewish War*, pp. 27, 393.

16. Vermes, *The Dead Sea Scrolls*, p. 140.

17. Taylor, "A Second Temple in Egypt," p. 309.

18. Driver, *The Judaean Scrolls*, pp. 326–27.

19. Hayward, "The Jewish Temple at Leontopolis," pp. 434–36.

20. Taylor, "A Second Temple in Egypt," p. 312.

21. Josephus, *The Jewish War*, p. 392.

22. *The Jewish War*, p. 292.

23. Philo, *On the Contemplative Life*, pp. 125–27. See also Taylor and Davies, "The So-called Therapeutae of *De Vita Contemplativa*," pp. 10–12.

24. Philo, *On the Contemplative Life*, p. 115.

25. Taylor and Davies, "The So-called Therapeutae of *De Vita Contemplativa*," p. 14, quoting Philo, *Hypothetica*, 11.14–18; Josephus, *The Antiquities of the Jews*, XVIII, I; Pliny, *Natural History*, V, XV.

26. Taylor and Davies, "The So-called Therapeutae of *De Vita Contemplativa*," pp. 18–19.

27. Philo, *On the Contemplative Life*, p. 125.

28. *On the Contemplative Life*, p. 119.

29. *On the Contemplative Life*, p. 129.

30. *On the Contemplative Life*, pp. 167–69.

31. Naydler, *Shamanic Wisdom in the Pyramid Texts*, p. 319.

CHAPTER NINE: THE MYSTERIES OF EGYPT

1. Quirke, *Ancient Egyptian Religion*, p. 70.

2. Assmann, *The Mind of Egypt*, p. 58.

3. *The Mind of Egypt*, p. 58.

4. Also called by various translators the "Netherworld" or the "Underworld."

5. Assmann, *The Mind of Egypt*, p. 66.

6. Szpakowska, *Behind Closed Eyes*, p. 191.

7. Assmann, *The Mind of Egypt*, pp. 18–19.

8. *The Mind of Egypt*, p. 61, quoting the Berlin Leather Roll (Berlin Papyrus 3029), dating from the Middle Kingdom.

9. Saint Teresa, *The Life of Saint Teresa of Ávila, by Herself*, p. 127.

10. Bleeker, *Hathor and Thoth*, p. 147.

11. Bleeker, "Initiation in Ancient Egypt," p. 56.

12. The story of the development from tokens to writing is given in Schmandt-Besserat, *Before Writing*, vol. 1, *From Counting to Cuneiform*.

13. Lloyd, *The Archaeology of Mesopotamia*, p. 39. Georges Roux claims in *Ancient Iraq* (p. 68) that an "inescapable conclusion was that the same religious tradition had been handed down from century to century." His confidence cannot be supported by the evidence.

14. Mellaart, *Earliest Civilisations of the Near East*, pp. 89–101.

15. Shreeve, *The Neanderthal Enigma*, p. 53.

16. Faulkner, *The Ancient Egyptian Pyramid Texts*, Utterance 305, p. 94.

17. *The Ancient Egyptian Pyramid Texts*, Utterance 213, p. 40.

18. *The Ancient Egyptian Pyramid Texts*, Utterance 260, p. 69.

19. Naydler, *Temple of the Cosmos*, pp. 202, 203.

20. Szpakowska, *Behind Closed Eyes*, pp. 150–51; for translations of text from the tombs of Rekhmire and Seti I, see p. 190.

21. Iamblichus, *On the Mysteries of the Egyptians*, 1:12, pp. 37–38.

22. *On the Mysteries of the Egyptians*, 8:4, p. 139.

23. Quirke, *Ancient Egyptian Religion*, p. 159.

24. Bleeker, *Egyptian Festivals*, p. 136.

25. Quirke, *Ancient Egyptian Religion*, p. 159.

26. *Ancient Egyptian Religion*, p. 159.

27. Plutarch, *Isis and Osiris*, cap. xx, p. 51.

28. See, for example, Cauville, *Les Crypts du temple d'Hathor*, for detailed plans of the ten crypts at Denderah.

29. Heliodorus, *An Aethiopian History*, p. 241. I have modernized the sixteenth-century language.

30. For a detailed discussion of this academic attitude, see Naydler, *Shamanic Wisdom in the Pyramid Texts*, ch. 5, especially pp. 140–45.

31. Bleeker, "Initiation in Ancient Egypt," p. 55.

32. Federn, reported by Wente, "Mysticism in Pharaonic Egypt?" p. 161.

33. Abt and Hornung, *Knowledge for the Afterlife*, p. 9.

34. *Knowledge for the Afterlife*, p. 144.

35. Wente, "Mysticism in Pharaonic Egypt?" p. 174.

36. "Mysticism in Pharaonic Egypt?" p. 175.

37. "Mysticism in Pharaonic Egypt?" pp. 175–76.

38. "Mysticism in Pharaonic Egypt?" pp. 177–78.

39. Quirke, *The Cult of Ra*, p. 122.

40. *The Cult of Ra*, p. 118.

41. Naydler, *Shamanic Wisdom in the Pyramid Texts*, p. 85.

42. *Shamanic Wisdom in the Pyramid Texts*, p. 202.

43. *Shamanic Wisdom in the Pyramid Texts*, p. 21.

CHAPTER TEN: INITIATION

1. Vergil, *The Aeneid*, VI, 855–56, p. 182.

2. Suetonius, *The Twelve Caesars*, *Augustus*, 16, p. 61; Temple, *Netherworld* (p. 28), referring to Strabo, *Geography*, V, 4, 5, who states that Agrippa had cut down all the original woodland. Robert Paget, in *In the Footsteps of Orpheus* (p. 57), remarks that the woodland destroyed included groves sacred to Apollo and that the timber was used for Agrippa's ships. This construction took place before the battle of 36 B.C. At the same time, Paget assumes, the underground complex at Baiae was sealed.

Raymond Clark of Memorial University of Newfoundland, in a personal communication (July 2002), is more cautious about the sealing of the site, noting that Strabo's account of Agrippa changing the area around Lake Avernus "need not include Baiae, since he was concerned with naval works at the lakeside. Agrippa was not anti-religious, as his building of the Pantheon at Rome proves. Without further evidence I am keeping an open mind on the date of closure."

3. Paget, *In the Footsteps of Orpheus*, p. 136; Temple, in *Netherworld* (p. 31), extrapolating from Paget's figures, suggests that this filling took around two years.

4. Paget, *In the Footsteps of Orpheus*, p. 19.

5. Vergil, *The Aeneid*, VI, 149 – 87, pp. 163 – 64; see also Clark, "Vergil, Aeneid, 6, 40 ff., and the Cumaean Sibyl's Cave," p. 485.

6. Vergil, *The Aeneid*, VI, 187, p. 164.

7. Vergil, *The Georgics*, 4, 563 – 65, p. 143. "Parthenope" is a poetic term to denote Naples (see p. 160).

8. Livius, *The History of Rome*, 24, 12 – 13.

9. Strabo, *Geography*, V, 4, 5.

10. Paget, *In the Footsteps of Orpheus*, p. 106.

11. Strabo, *Geography*, V, 4, 5.

12. Paget, *In the Footsteps of Orpheus*, p. 102.

13. *In the Footsteps of Orpheus*, p. 111.

14. *In the Footsteps of Orpheus*, p. 111.

15. *In the Footsteps of Orpheus*, p. 113.

16. *In the Footsteps of Orpheus*, pp. 127 – 30.

17. Temple, *Conversations with Eternity*, pp. 12 – 13, quoting from Paget, *In the Footsteps of Orpheus*, p. 137.

18. Temple, *Conversations with Eternity*, p. 17.

19. Paget, *In the Footsteps of Orpheus*, p. 135.

20. Temple, *Netherworld*, p. 10.

21. *Netherworld*, p. 10.

22. "The Cults of Magna Graecia," symposium held by the Vergilian Society at the Villa Vergiliana, Cuma, 19–22 June 2002.

23. Vergil, The Aeneid, VI, 850–53, p. 182.

24. Homer, The Odyssey, book XI, p. 171.

25. Strabo, Geography, V, 4, 6.

26. Geography, V, 4, 5.

27. See, for example, Ogden, Greek and Roman Necromancy (p. 22), who claims that because the literary tradition seems to locate the oracle on the shores of Lake Avernus, that is where it must be. There is no need to come to this conclusion, however, given the imprecision of the traditions he cites. Others, such as Burkert, Lore and Science in Ancient Pythagoreanism (p. 155), are open but cautious. Both approaches simply reinforce the need for systematic excavation of the site at Baia.

28. See, for example, Hardie, "The Crater of Avernus as a Cult-Site," p. 284.

29. Ogden, Greek and Roman Necromancy, pp. 19–21.

30. Kingsley, Ancient Philosophy, Mystery, and Magic, p. 252, n. 6.

31. Apuleius, Metamorphoses, XI, 23, p. 340. The translation cited here is from Burkert, Ancient Mystery Cults, p. 97. A popular translation by Robert Graves is entitled The Golden Ass.

32. Burkert, Lore and Science in Ancient Pythagoreanism, p. 155; Robert, Archaeological Reports for 1959–1960, pp. 42–43.

33. Peter Kingsley, personal communication (March 2002).

34. Burkert, Ancient Mystery Cults, p. 174.

35. Plato, Phaedo, 64a, p. 9.

36. Phaedo, 67e, p. 14.

37. Burkert (Ancient Mystery Cults, p. 162, n. 11) considers that this extract is from Plutarch, not Themistius, as stated by Stobaeus.

38. Quoted in Farnell, The Cults of the Greek States, III, p. 179.

39. Seneca, Epistles, p. 327.

40. Quoted by Eliade, Rites and Symbols of Initiation, p. 111.

41. *Rites and Symbols of Initiation*, pp. 112–13.

42. Gorman, *Pythagoras*, pp. 48–49.

43. Kingsley, *In the Dark Places of Wisdom*, p. 198. See also Kingsley, *Ancient Philosophy, Mystery, and Magic*, pp. 340–41.

44. Kingsley, *Ancient Philosophy, Mystery, and Magic*, p. 341.

45. Interview with Peter Kingsley, "Piloting the Ship of Life," *Freemasonry Today* 28 (Spring 2004), p. 24.

46. Parmenides' poem is translated by Kingsley in *Reality*, p. 26.

47. Zuntz, *Persephone*, pp. 370–76; Kingsley, "From Pythagoras to the *Turba Philosophorum*," pp. 3–4.

48. Cole, "New Evidence for the Mysteries of Dionysos," pp. 233–34.

49. Guthrie, *Orpheus and Greek Religion*, p. 173.

50. Prof. Dr. Walter Burkert, personal communication (May 2005). Burkert explains that this is a difficult text and that two variant readings are possible. The alternative reading is: "And for you are waiting beneath the earth the celebrations, which also other blessed ones [are performing]."

51. Aristophanes, *The Frogs*, p. 308.

52. Kingsley, *In the Dark Places of Wisdom*, pp. 78–79.

53. *In the Dark Places of Wisdom*, p. 284.

54. *In the Dark Places of Wisdom*, p. 83.

55. *In the Dark Places of Wisdom*, p. 141.

56. *Asclepius*, 24, in Copenhaver, *Hermetica*, p. 81.

57. Iamblichus, *On the Mysteries of the Egyptians*, VIII, IV, pp. 138–39.

58. Iverson, *Egyptian and Hermetic Doctrine*, p. 43. Iverson also explains: "Thus considered, as reflections of corresponding divergencies in Egyptian cosmology, the seeming inconsistencies in the Hermetic conception of creator and demiurge find a natural explanation, which at the same time will be seen to throw unexpected light on the problem of the mutual relations of the two traditions, and the dependence of the corpus [that is, the Hermetic texts] on Egyptian sources" (p. 40).

59. Kingsley, "Poimandres," p. 5.

60. Iverson, *Egyptian and Hermetic Doctrine*, p. 30.

61. *Egyptian and Hermetic Doctrine*, pp. 37–38, referring in particular to the Hermetic *Asclepius*, 38, in Copenhaver, *Hermetica*, p. 90.

62. Iverson, *Egyptian and Hermetic Doctrine*, p. 41.

63. See note 49.

64. Iverson, in *Egyptian and Hermetic Doctrine* (pp. 35–36), discusses how the explanation of the Egyptian concept of "the breath of life" can be augmented by means of the Hermetic texts.

65. Clement of Alexandria, *The Miscellanies*, VI, VI, p. 324.

66. Iamblichus, *On the Mysteries of the Egyptians*, I, I, p. 21.

CHAPTER ELEVEN: EXPERIENCING THE SOURCE

1. The Jerusalem Bible, The New Testament, p. 19, note d.

2. Philo, *On the Contemplative Life*, 28, p. 129.

3. Caplice, *The Akkadian Namburbu Texts*, p. 10.

4. Parpola, "The Assyrian Tree of Life," p. 174, n. 64.

5. "The Assyrian Tree of Life," pp. 185, 206. Parpola writes: "There is nothing unique in Jewish monotheism to differentiate it from its Assyrian predecessor"... The same applies to Christianity with its doctrines of the Trinity ... all of which are derived from Assyrian religion and philosophy" (p. 190, n. 107).

6. Kingsley, "Ezekiel by the Grand Canal," p. 339.

7. "Ezekiel by the Grand Canal," p. 342.

8. "Ezekiel by the Grand Canal," p. 341, quoting from VAT 8917 (Vorderasiatisches Museum), Berlin.

9. "Ezekiel by the Grand Canal," p. 345.

10. "Ezekiel by the Grand Canal," p. 345.

11. Parpola, "The Assyrian Tree of Life," p. 169.

12. "The Assyrian Tree of Life," p. 190, n. 106.

13. "The Assyrian Tree of Life," p. 168.

14. "The Assyrian Tree of Life," pp. 174, 189.

15. Halevi, *The Way of Kabbalah*, p. 98, fig. 16.
16. Tertullian, *On Female Dress*, III, vol. I, p. 307.
17. Charles, *The Book of Enoch*, pp. 196, 204, 208, and 212; on the eastern portals, see also Baigent, *From the Omens of Babylon*, pp. 74–75, and Reiner, *Enuma Anu Enlil Tablets 50–51*, pp. 2–3.
18. Charles, *The Book of Enoch*, p. 235.
19. *The Book of Enoch*, p. 235.
20. *The Book of Enoch*, p. 236.
21. *The Book of Enoch*, p. 236.
22. Faulkner, *The Ancient Egyptian Pyramid Texts*, Utterance 213, p. 40.
23. Cave 4 texts: 4Q201, 4Q202, 4Q204, 4Q205, 4Q206, 4Q207, 4Q212. See García Martínez, *The Dead Sea Scrolls Translated*, pp. 246–59.
24. Charles, *The Book of Enoch*, pp. 168–69.
25. *The Book of Enoch*, p. 267.

CHAPTER TWELVE: THE KINGDOM OF HEAVEN

1. Smith's story is given in his autobiographical account in *The Secret Gospel*, pp. 1f.
2. *The Secret Gospel*, p. 5.
3. *The Secret Gospel*, p. 5.
4. *The Secret Gospel*, p. 6.
5. *The Secret Gospel*, p. 15.
6. See Clement of Alexandria, *Miscellanies*, V.vi and viii. Was Clement in contact with some residual Therapeutae group? No one knows.
7. Stroumsa, *Hidden Wisdom*, p. 5.
8. Hippolytus, *Philosophumena*, V, 10.
9. Clement of Alexandria, *The Miscellanies*, I, I.
10. Smith, *The Secret Gospel*, p. 148.
11. *The Secret Gospel*, p. 144.
12. *The Secret Gospel*, pp. 27–30.

13. Ehrman, *Lost Christianities*, pp. 83–84.

14. Saint Teresa, *The Life of Saint Teresa of Ávila*, p. 139.

15. *The Life of Saint Teresa of Ávila*, p. 146.

16. *The Life of Saint Teresa of Ávila*, p. 285.

17. Fuller, *A New Catholic Commentary on Holy Scripture*, p. 1009. The last sentence is attributed to J. Schmid in Wikenhauser and Kuss, *Regensberger New Testament*, p. 209.

18. James B. Robinson, personal communication (November 1989).

19. Gospel of Thomas, in Robinson, *The Nag Hammadi Library in English*, p. 51.

20. *The Nag Hammadi Library in English*, p. 3.

21. *The Nag Hammadi Library in English*, p. 113.

22. *The Nag Hammadi Library in English*, p. 106.

23. *The Nag Hammadi Library in English*, p. 22.

24. *The Nag Hammadi Library in English*, p. 39.

25. Baigent and Leigh, *The Dead Sea Scrolls Deception*, pp. 180–87.

26. Stroumsa, in *Hidden Wisdom* (pp. 34–38), gives a summary of Patristic sources.

27. *Hidden Wisdom*, p. 6.

28. King, *The Gospel of Mary of Magdala*, p. 3.

29. *The Gospel of Mary of Magdala*, 4:3–8.

30. *The Gospel of Mary of Magdala*, 6:1–2.

31. *The Gospel of Mary of Magdala*, 6:3.

32. *The Gospel of Mary of Magdala*, 10:3–4.

33. *The Gospel of Mary of Magdala*, 10:10.

34. Gospel of Philip, 63, p. 138. It is interesting that the first edition of Robinson, *The Nag Hammadi Library in English* (1977), renders the text (with reconstructions) as "[But Christ loved] her more than [all] the disciples [and used to] kiss her [often] on her [mouth]." The third edition of 1988 and the paperback edition of 1990, published after considerable controversy over the potential marriage of Jesus, changed this line. It rendered the same text as

"[... loved] her more than [all] the disciples [and used to] kiss her [often] on her [...]" (p. 148).

CHAPTER THIRTEEN: THE JESUS PAPERS

1. Specifically, to the reign of Alexander Jannaeus, 103–76 B.C.; see de Vaux, "Observations sur le Commentaire d'Habacuc découvert près de la Mer Morte," *Revue Biblique*, LVIII, 1951, pp. 438 and 443.

2. Habakkuk Pesher, 1QpHab, II 3, in García Martínez, *The Dead Sea Scrolls Translated*, p. 198.

3. Dupont-Sommer, *The Dead Sea Scrolls*, pp. 95–96. This is an English translation of his 1950 publication *Aperçus préliminaires sur les manuscrits de la mer Morte*. His term for the Teacher of Righteousness is translated as "Master of Justice" in the English edition.

4. *The Dead Sea Scrolls*, p. 373.

5. Catholic University of America, *New Catholic Encyclopedia*, vol. XI, p. 551.

6. Burrows, *The Dead Sea Scrolls*, p. 51.

7. *The Dead Sea Scrolls*, p. 52.

8. De Vaux, "Observations sur le Commentaire d'Habacuc découvert près de la Mer Morte," *Revue Biblique*, LVIII, 1951, p. 438.

9. "Observations sur le Commentaire d'Habacuc découvert près de la Mer Morte," p. 93.

10. "Observations sur le Commentaire d'Habacuc découvert près de la Mer Morte," p. 94.

11. Murphy, *Lagrange and Biblical Renewal*, p. 60.

12. John Allegro, letter to Father Roland de Vaux, 7 March 1956. For an account of the disputes between John Allegro and the other members of the international team, see Baigent and Leigh, *The Dead Sea Scrolls Deception*, pp. 45–60.

13. Baigent and Leigh, *The Inquisition*, p. 230, translation from García Martínez, *The Dead Sea Scrolls Translated*, p. 138; see also Eisenman and Wise, *The Dead Sea Scrolls Uncovered*, pp. 68–71.

14. De Vaux, *Archaeology and the Dead Sea Scrolls*, p. 20.

15. Baigent and Eisenman, "A Ground-Penetrating Radar Survey Testing the Claim for Earthquake Damage of the Second Temple Ruins at Khirbet Qumran," pp. 136–37 and maps on pp. 134–35.

16. For the attacks on Oxford's Professor Godfrey Driver and Reader in Jewish Studies Cecil Roth, see Baigent and Leigh, *The Dead Sea Scrolls Deception*, pp. 152, 163–64; see also Mack, *The Lost Gospel* (pp. 248–49), on the problem of theologians trying to investigate Christian origins; for similar problems with the events of the Old Testament, see Thompson, *The Bible in History* (p. xv), in which Thompson describes how his removal of the history of Israel from the mythology of the Old Testament lost him tenure at his American university. Happily, he was appointed professor of the Old Testament at the University of Copenhagen.

17. For example, compare James 2:10 with Romans 3:28.

18. *The Atlantic Monthly*, December 1986, p. 39.

19. Mack, *The Lost Gospel*, p. 237.

20. *The Lost Gospel*, p. 238.

21. *The Lost Gospel*, p. 219.

22. Baigent and Leigh, *The Dead Sea Scrolls Deception*, pp. 132–36. Eisenman and Wise, in *The Dead Sea Scrolls Uncovered* (p. 69), write: "It is impossible to distinguish ideas and terminology associated with the Jerusalem Community of James the Just from materials found in this corpus" – the "corpus" being the Dead Sea Scrolls.

23. Zuckerman, *A Jewish Princedom in Feudal France 768–900*, p. 58.

CHAPTER FOURTEEN: TRADING CULTURE

1. Interview with Magen Broschi, 21 May 1990.

2. Copenhaver, *Hermetica*, tractate XI, 21, p. 42.

3. Rumi, "Jars of Springwater," in *The Glance*, p. 1.

POSTSCRIPT

1. Ehrman, in Kasser, Meyer and Wurst, *The Gospel of Judas*, p. 118.

2. *Ibid.*

3. *Ibid.*, p.102.

4. *The Gospel of Judas*, 35 (Kasser, Meyer and Wurst, p.23).

5. Vergano, Dan, and Grossman, Cathy Lynn, "Long-lost gospel of Judas casts 'traitor' in new light," *USA Today*, April 7-9, 2006, p.2A.

6. Owen, Richard, "Judas the Misunderstood," *The Times*, 12 January 2006, p.3.

7. His research, which is particularly valuable on the subject of the funds which this priest had access to and their ultimate source, is given in his book *Rennes le Château. Le secret de Saunière.*

It has been well-known for some time that after discovering a small treasure Saunière, by the late 1890s, was saying masses for money; the crime of trafficking in masses. A curiosity of his personal financial records which detail his income from this is that many of the masses were being said for Catholic institutions which had their own priests. Why did they need the help of Saunière? The answer is that this was a large-scale money-laundering operation with the funds originating with the Habsburgs (Robin, J-L., personal communication, 14 January 2006).

Index